Praise for Phil Keith and Tom Clavin's *All Blood Runs Red*

"An incredible, meticulously researched, star-studded tale. *All Blood Runs Red* is a true 'moveable feast' that will forever change the way you see 20th century history."

—**Kristin Harmel, internationally bestselling author of** *The Winemaker's Wife* and *The Room on Rue Amélie*

"An exultant trumpet song to the human spirit. My God, how I admire this man."

—**Robert Coram, author of** *Boyd: The Fighter Pilot Who Changed the Art of War*

"Keith and Clavin bring us a well-crafted book about a truly admirable American."

—**Gregory A. Freeman, author of** *The Forgotten 500: The Untold Story of the Men Who Risked All for the Greatest Rescue Mission of World War II*

"A whale of a tale, told clearly and quickly. I read the entire book in almost one sitting."

—**Thomas E. Ricks,** *New York Times* **Book Review**

"An engaging portrait of a true free spirit."

—*Christian Science Monitor*

"A dazzling biography."

—*Publishers Weekly*, **starred review**

"An excellent and significant portrait of a long forgotten, now rightfully reclaimed hero."

—*Booklist*, **starred review**

"Two intrepid authors and researchers...team up in this dogged effort to excavate the facts of the amazing life of Eugene Bullard."

—*Kirkus Reviews*

"Recommended for readers who enjoy compelling biography and fast-paced narrative."

—*Library Journ*

Also by Phil Keith

Settling Up

America and the Great War

Stay the Rising Sun: The True Story of USS Lexington, Her Valiant Crew, and Changing the Course of WWII

Fire Base Illingworth: An Epic True Story of Remarkable Courage Against Staggering Odds

Missed Signals

Blackhorse Riders: A Desperate Last Stand, an Extraordinary Rescue Mission, and the Vietnam Battle America Forgot

Crimson Valor

Belladonna

Animus

Also by Tom Clavin

Wild Bill: The True Story of the American Frontier's First Gunfighter

Valley Forge (with Bob Drury)

Dodge City: Wyatt Earp, Bat Masterson, and the Wickedest Town in the American West

Being Ted Williams: Growing Up with a Baseball Idol (with Dick Enberg)

Lucky 666: The Impossible Mission (with Bob Drury)

Reckless: The Racehorse Who Became a Marine Corps Hero

The Heart of Everything That Is: The Untold Story of Red Cloud, An American Legend (with Bob Drury)

The DiMaggios: Three Brothers, Their Passion for Baseball, Their Pursuit of the American Dream

Gil Hodges: The Brooklyn Bums, the Miracle Mets, and the Extraordinary Life of a Baseball Legend (with Danny Peary)

Last Men Out: The True Story of America's Heroic Final Hours in Vietnam (with Bob Drury)

One for the Ages: Jack Nicklaus and the 1986 Masters

Roger Maris: Baseball's Reluctant Hero (with Danny Peary)

ALL BLOOD RUNS RED

THE LEGENDARY LIFE OF EUGENE BULLARD— BOXER, PILOT, SOLDIER, SPY

PHIL KEITH with **TOM CLAVIN**

HANOVER
SQUARE
PRESS

HANOVER
SQUARE
PRESS™

Recycling programs
for this product may
not exist in your area.

ISBN-13: 978-1-335-01666-9

All Blood Runs Red: The Legendary Life of Eugene Bullard—Boxer, Pilot, Soldier, Spy

First published in 2019. This edition published in 2020.

This edition published by arrangement with Harlequin Books S.A.

Library of Congress Cataloging-in-Publication Data has been applied for.

Hanover Square Press
22 Adelaide St. West, 40th Floor
Toronto, Ontario M5H 4E3, Canada
HanoverSqPress.com
BookClubbish.com

Printed in U.S.A.

To Lolly, "the Muse," who has always believed; so, therefore, I write.
And to Pierce, for whom I write, for his legacy and mine.

—P.K.

To Bob and AnnEllen Rosen.

—T.C.

CONTENTS

ACT IV: THE IMPRESARIO

ACT V: THE SPY

ACT VI: THE PIONEER

PROLOGUE

On November 17, 1917, history's first African American fighter pilot, Corporal Eugene Bullard of the 85th Pursuit Squadron, Lafayette Flying Corps, scored, in all likelihood, his first aerial victory. In so doing, however, he had a terrifying clash with a Grim Reaper, painted all in black, equally determined to rip his fragile craft from the skies above the Western Front and fling it, engulfed in fire, to the mud-churned earth below.

Here's how that fateful flight began: flying opportunities had been few and far between during the previous two weeks. On the cusp of winter, the days were often cold with wind-swept skies and pelting rain. It was virtually impossible to conduct combat sorties in anything but clear skies considering the exposed cockpits and severe airframe limitations of the early flying machines. The seventeenth, however, had dawned bright and clear—although it remained decidedly chilly.

At dawn, the barracks steward raced through the rooms

shaking pilots out of their deep slumbers—or, in some cases, hangovers. The commandant had deemed it a day fit for missions. Bullard had been sound asleep but jumped up quickly, already fully dressed. This was not unusual, since many of the pilots slept in their flying gear when they were on duty. It saved precious minutes toward getting aloft.

As Bullard remembered, "There was no breakfast in those days. No meals were served until after eleven. If a pilot had a morning mission, it was hot coffee, then off to the field."

Bullard raced to the flight line where Sergeant Viel, his mechanic, had his SPAD VII warmed up, prop spinning, ready to fly. He quickly scanned the cockpit and the big Vickers guns with which his aircraft was armed. All seemed to be in order.

A group of fourteen planes was soon in the air, headed for the German lines, which that day would be the contested turf around Metz. Jimmy, Bullard's usual "copilot," a feisty and fearless capuchin monkey, was not along for this ride. The "little bugger" was aggravated by a sniffling cold, so Bullard had left him in the care of fellow aviators back at the base. It was Jimmy's lucky day.

At a little more than 3,000 feet, it was desperately frigid. Even Bullard's fur-lined boots were insufficient to keep his feet from becoming numb. This was a significant danger for the pilots in that frozen extremities could be a hindrance to working the rudder pedals in a dogfight. Many early aviators suffered from frostbite and blackened or even lost toes were not uncommon.

As Bullard shivered in the prop blast, several dark shapes poked in and out of the low, scudding clouds a few miles ahead. Captain Pinsard (the flight leader for that mission) made the hand signal to "pursue." As the French flew closer, the identity of the ships in the other group became clear: the

"Boche."[1] It was a mixed group of ten Fokkers, including four all-black triplanes. The French had a height and sun advantage, so they sped up and dove eagerly on their foes.

The sky was instantly transformed into a mass of swirling machines, each trying to blast the other apart. Bullets and black smoke filled the air. Bullard was soon engulfed in a maze of enemies, one of whom swooped in and made a lateral pass. He felt his plane shudder as rounds ripped through the fabric and tore into the fuselage immediately behind his cockpit. He desperately spun away with a deft barrel roll left, followed by a nose-up climb at full power.

His "crate" was holding together, Bullard felt, so the damage was not fatal. After climbing several hundred feet he kicked the rudder pedal hard left and made a port-leaning full-on dive, down, down. The German who had attacked him was nowhere in sight. Bullard had ended up about a half mile from the circle of snarling aircraft.

At that moment, one of the black triplanes punched out of the melee. For whatever reason, the German pilot did not see Bullard. The Fokker completed a wide, sweeping turn, away from Bullard, apparently intent on getting enough space to come about and plunge back into the dogfight. Bullard was on him like fleas on a hound dog.

He couldn't believe his luck. He fell in behind the big plane and as soon as he was wings level, he steadied the aircraft with his right hand on the control stick, and with his left he squeezed his firing button. Two dozen rounds hammered into the black shape. Bullard could see bits of material flake off the plane and a wisp of black smoke began to trail from the engine. Was this it? Would this be his first successful score? And such a big one, to boot?

---

1 French slang for "a German soldier." Term originated in the phrase *"tête de caboche,"* or *"cabbage head."*

Before he had time to fully contemplate his mates toasting him with champagne, the Fokker, in a series of lightning moves, pulled up, over and away. Bullard had lost him. Where could he have gone so quickly? The answer was soon obvious: the more experienced German and his big three-winged machine was squarely on Bullard's tail. Bullets began tearing into his fuselage again.

He ducked the other way this time, to the right and down. The Fokker stayed with him, hammering away. The earth began to race toward him at a frightening clip. How was he going to shake his tormentor? Providence intervened.

Bullard's initial attack had apparently done some serious damage. The black cloud from the German's triplane thickened. His motor coughed and sputtered. Before the German pilot could finish his attack, his engine started seizing. Bullard's last sight of the black-lacquered bird, from over his shoulder, revealed his opponent turning away, trailing smoke and corkscrewing toward the earth.

Meanwhile, Bullard had plunged perilously close to the ground. He was, in fact, flying between two steep hills bracketing a small valley. He was at an altitude of less than three hundred feet. As fate would have it, atop one of the hills, and very close by, was a German machine-gun nest. As Bullard flew past, level with the gun's lofty perch, the German crew opened fire. Several well-aimed slugs slammed into Bullard's engine, causing it to fail instantly. Thick black castor oil splattered all over his windscreen as well as his face and goggles. He was effectively blind. The prop stopped spinning and the dreaded whooshing of the wind told Bullard he was going down.

Quickly wiping his goggles with a gloved hand, he gently eased up on the stick and looked for a place to set down. He didn't have but a few seconds of time and airspace. At about thirty miles an hour, he pancaked into a muddy bog, which quickly grabbed the crippled plane in its gooey grip. Immediately, Bullard unstrapped and leaped from the aircraft seeking shelter behind the fuselage. He had no idea if he was in friendly or enemy territory, and knowing that he had been downed by ground fire, he had to wonder *Is that gun still nearby?*

Shots smacking into the mud all around the downed plane gave Bullard his answer. He was in somebody's sights, and they were not friendly. Covered in muck, he decided to wait things out. When darkness fell, he'd make a break for where he thought his lines might be—presumably, in the opposite direction of where he was receiving fire. After another few minutes the gunners either lost interest or became distracted, and the firing ceased.

Right after dusk, Bullard heard voices, and they were coming toward his position. He unholstered his revolver and hunkered down closer to the skin of the plane. Much to his relief he soon discerned the voices were speaking French. One of his fellow pilots had, apparently, pinpointed the position where Bullard had gone down. It was just inside friendly lines, so the base commander sent several mechanics to try to recover the aircraft—and maybe find the pilot while they were at it.

Bullard was delighted to see friends instead of foes. With a lot of tugging and straining, they managed to extricate the plane from the mud. It was rolled to a nearby road, hooked up to a truck and, tail first, towed back to the field. One of the mechanics counted the bullet holes in Bullard's plane: ninety-six.

Safely back at base and reasonably cleaned up, Bullard repaired to the bar, where his fellow pilots received him enthusiastically. He was then asked by Major Minard, the squadron commander, if he had wanted to commit suicide. Somewhat puzzled by the question, Bullard replied that he did not. Minard informed him that he had tangled with a member of the Red Baron's (Manfred von Richthofen's) famed Flying Circus, the best of the best of the German aviators. Bullard was lucky to be alive, he was told.

He was absolutely certain he had shot down his foe, Flying Circus expert aviator or not. His last glimpse of the plane told him it was certainly smoking heavily, if not on fire, and spiraling toward the ground. Maybe the pilot had been able to control the landing—or maybe he had crashed uncontrollably, but in either case, he had been going down hard, and not at any aerodrome.

Perhaps so, but Minard told him that whoever the opponent might have been, he had at least made it back behind his own lines and, therefore, the victory could only be rated as "possible" and not "certain." C'est la vie.

The champagne continued to flow freely and the pilots spent the night in boozy reverie. No one was concerned about the following morning. It had already started to rain with some sleet mixed in. Flying was unlikely.

Corporal-Pilot Bullard had been, as his commander pronounced, extremely lucky, both to have had some success in the air, and to make it back alive. This would have been in line with his father's predictions for his "seventh child," his "lucky child." There had been some mystical attachment to the number seven in his father's Haitian tradition, along with ever-present hope that at least one of his ten children would escape the desperate poverty and prejudice of his own post-slavery experiences in the rural South of his day.

Bullard had, indeed, been fortunate to break free of the bleak future that faced him as a black youngster in a racist Georgia early in the twentieth century. Lucky, also, to have survived five years of wandering, living from hand to mouth, until stowing aboard a freighter bound for Europe in 1912. Lucky to have found success in the boxing rings of England and France; the company of good friends and benefactors; and, finally, the racial freedom he had craved for so long.

He even found favor with the gods of war, whom he had tempted mightily when he volunteered for the French Foreign Legion after the Great War exploded across the landscape of Europe. While thousands died around him, the bombs and bullets did not kill him; wound him, yes, and grievously so, but even these afflictions led him to greater opportunity—in the skies above the trenches he had so recently occupied.

Improbably, fortuitously and upon a bet, Lady Luck had literally lifted him up, until, there he was, the very first black man to grasp the control stick and trigger pulls of a fighter plane. Yes, Bullard was certain he had made history that November day, for himself and for his race, and no one would be able to convince him otherwise. It brought a smile to his face and yet another offer of champagne.

What he did not know then—what he couldn't possibly know—was that Lady Luck was not done with him—not by a long shot. Destiny had Eugene Bullard in its tightfisted grip and it was going to take him for one hell of a ride.

ACT I
THE RUNAWAY

1

THE SEVENTH CHILD

Eugene Bullard, the future nightclub-owning spy, boxer, fighter pilot, musician, and decorated soldier, was born to William Octave Bullard and Josephine Yokalee Thomas Bullard on October 9, 1895, in the sleepy town of Columbus, Georgia, just east of the Georgia-Alabama border, right on the banks of the Chattahoochee River. William was jovially dubbed "Big Ox" by an employer because he was six foot five and at least two hundred fifty pounds. The nickname stuck. William was the son of a slave of Haitian ancestry and Josephine was a full-blooded Creek Indian.

The Bullards had ten children in all, but three died in infancy. The entire family lived crammed in a three-room house at 2601 Talbotton Avenue, which was then part of the African American community on the west side of town. Big Ox, from the moment Gene was born, felt this seventh of his children would be the "lucky one" with seven being somehow mysterious and considered charmed. History ultimately might say he was correct, but Gene's actual beginnings were far from auspicious.

The records do not contain any physical description of Gene's mother, so we do not know if she was short or tall, small or large. We do know that Gene did not achieve the same height and physical stature of his impressively built father. Ultimately, he stood just under six feet and never weighed much more than one hundred sixty pounds. Then again, with the family always on the thin edge of poverty and many hungry mouths to feed, it is entirely possible that Gene's height and weight suffered early on from a diminished availability of nutrition.

William eked out a living as a general laborer, mostly among the warehouses and docks strung along the Chattahoochee River, separating Columbus from Phenix City, Alabama. By the early 1890s, William Bullard was working full-time for cotton broker William C. Bradley. Born at the height of the Civil War in 1863, Bradley was an ambitious and clever merchant who eventually owned several textile mills, a bank and a robust share of the early Coca-Cola Company. Coke, in fact, owes its ultimate corporate survival to Bradley and his partners who saved the firm from collapse during the sugar crisis that occurred in America after World War I; but that, as they say, is another story.

What matters for the Bullards is that Bradley proved to be a benevolent employer, especially for a white man in the racially charged postbellum south. Blacks, like Bullard, were not always welcome in the workplace alongside white workers. Bradley was reported to have been fond of his "black giant" and his willingness to work hard. That, too, did not sit well with some of the white Georgians toiling along the river, men who were not similarly inclined, and less appreciated. Any hardworking black man with a good work ethic and positive attitude was a magnet for trouble in the Jim Crow Era, and so it would be for William Bullard.

At the age of six, Gene was enrolled in the 28th Street School in Columbus. The school was rough-hewn, the supplies minimal and the education standards were low, but during Gene's time there—until 1906—he learned to factor, read and write. He later calculated that he had accumulated the equivalent of a second-grade education before he left, which was still more than many poor black children ever received in the segregated South of the early twentieth century.

On a sweltering Sunday in August 1902, when Gene was two months shy of his seventh birthday, his mother died unexpectedly. It was a horrendous blow to the family. The cause was not known, beyond a general malaise that weakened Josephine until she simply expired. The hard work and stresses of poverty along with bearing and raising ten children—and burying three of them—undoubtedly had something to do with her death at only thirty-seven years old.

Gene's older siblings were pressed into service to take care of the younger children and complete all the household chores. They were required to take any opportunity that might come along to pick up spare income by doing odd jobs or tasks for others. It was a hardscrabble existence on the very cusp of survival, but there was usually food on the table and plenty of self-reliance.

The best records available, combined with Eugene Bullard's own oral history, indicate that his father's side of the family had its origins in the sugarcane plantations of Haiti. During the mid-1800s Haiti went through a series of upheavals and revolutions that rocked the island and roiled its French white aristocracy. As the island encouraged immigration, thousands of freed and escaped slaves from the United States poured in,

especially in the 1840s. Many white families began an opposite migration, most taking their slaves with them, which
is apparently what occurred with William Octave Bullard's
forebears.

William had been born into slavery on the Georgia plantation of Wiley Bullard, of Stewart County, Georgia. Wiley's property bordered the Chattahoochee River (in the next
county south of Columbus) and was considered good bottom
land for the production of cotton. Wiley had come to Georgia from the Carolinas, migrating with his parents, who first
settled on the Georgia land Wiley eventually inherited. As was
the custom in those days, William took the surname of the
family headed by the man he called "old Massa"—which was
both a signal of ownership as well as important census data.

It should be noted that Gene often told a different story of
his father's birth saga, one that does not square with the actual records. He stated in his autobiography—and in his oral
history, which he recited to many over the years—that his
grandparents' owners were a certain "Strawmaker" family,
who had come to Georgia from Mississippi and before that
from Haiti. Eugene even invented a Moses-like "creation
myth" for his father: as the Strawmaker family was torn apart
by the Civil War, they were forced to disband and flee the
marauding Union forces. Gene offers up that his infant father
was placed in a straw basket (they were, after all, straw makers)
and set adrift in the meandering Chattahoochee. Somewhere
farther down the river, the Bullards pulled up the basket, and
took in the black baby "for good luck." Gene also believed
that the Bullard family spoke French, but there is no solid
evidence for that.

William Bullard was also likely to have been part Creek Indian himself. The Creek Nation was strongly rooted in Georgia before their lands were taken from them by the belligerent

Andrew Jackson administration in the late 1820s and early 1830s. Some Creek families even owned African American slaves, and the races intermarried with some frequency during those times. William Bullard would likely have grown up in proximity to, and even possibly among, Creeks and it would not have been anything unusual for him to take a Creek bride, which he did in 1882, when he was nineteen and Josephine was seventeen.

The Strawmaker family was a myth with vague French underpinnings. The Bullard family and their holdings were the true foundations of Gene's ancestry; but, they, too, had a strong streak of French history somewhere in their background, pre-Georgia and pre-Carolinas. The "French connection" was so persistent that it led William to imbue his children with an ideal that centered on the French culture being one where the color of a man's skin made no difference. France was, in William's belief system, a land where racial prejudice did not exist. This conviction had the strongest of all possible influences on Gene. It shaped his whole frame of reference and, ultimately, his entire life.

As Gene told it, he had no real understanding of the divide between whites and "coloreds" until he was five or six years old. He played with children of both races as a young boy; but, as children grow, they often assimilate their parents' views. Gene's childhood friends soon became aware that there were real differences between blacks and whites. One day a playmate explained that "you was borned brown and that what makes white folks despise you."

The racial taunts began, which Gene admits he did not understand, at first. His mother, just before her death, and Gene's father began to school him on life's harsh realities. His parents finally forbade him the freedom to play with his former white chums. The dual tragedy of Josephine's death and William's fear of white retribution made the divide clear and absolute.

The white foreman in Bradley's company, a man named Billy Stevens, took a strong personal dislike to Gene's father. Day after day, Stevens taunted Bullard, foisting the worst, the most difficult, the most demeaning jobs upon him. Nothing, apparently, got to "Big Ox," which infuriated Stevens even further. Bradley was aware of the harassment, but did nothing, ignoring behavior that was often par for the course in these racially biased times. He was unaware of what William had told his children, a statement Gene remembered the rest of his life: "If I have to hit Stevens, I want you all to be good children. Always show respect to each and every one, white and black, and make them respect you. Go to school as long as you can. Never look for a fight. I mean never. But if you are attacked, or your honor is attacked unjustly, fight, fight, keep on fighting even if you die for your rights. It will be a glorious death."

One day, most likely in 1904, the situation finally escalated to a point where a single verbal spark set off a spectacular interpersonal conflagration. Stevens suspected that Bullard had talked to Bradley about Stevens's behavior once again. Bradley, it was rumored, had promised to do something about it, but of course, he never did. Stevens confronted Bullard, wanting to know what he had complained of to Bradley. Bullard shrugged and turned his back, walking away without responding. Incensed at this disrespect, Stevens snagged a large iron hook, the type used to grab and carry the big bales of cotton, and swung it as hard as he could against the side of Big Ox's head. The blow opened a deep, blood-bubbling wound and staggered the big black man, but he did not go down.

Bullard had finally taken all he could. He turned, lurched toward Stevens, who stumbled back in fear, dropping the hook. Bullard grabbed the man with his powerful hands, lifted him, screaming, over his head, and threw him down into the cargo hold of a large barge tied up to the loading dock. Stevens hit the steel hold at the bottom of the boat with a sickening thud. The shocked workers nearby figured Stevens was surely dead.

Clutching his bleeding head, Bullard managed to walk to Bradley's office and told him the story. Shocked, and flummoxed, Bradley told Bullard to go home and lie low, promising to "take care of things." The injured man staggered off.

Bradley told one of his men to fetch the doctor, who, ironically, was a Dr. William L. Bullard, a nephew of Wiley Bullard. The young doctor had received his medical degree from Emory University and set up practice in Columbus. Dr. Bullard found Stevens severely injured, but still alive. As treatment was being administered, Bradley told Stevens that if he ever wanted to work again, he'd shut up and keep this incident quiet.

Too late. Some of the other white workers had begun to spread the story across the docks. It wound its way into a nearby saloon and soon enough, a group of liquored-up hooligans determined they would ride out to Bullard's house and lynch him.

William, in the meantime, made it home. Gene recalled being very frightened by his father's ugly-looking head wound and even more frightened when his father loaded up the family shotgun and sat down with it behind the front door. William told his quivering brood what had happened and directed them all to go into the back room and hide under the beds or anywhere they could, out of sight. The single kerosene lamp was extinguished.

Soon after dark, a group of thoroughly drunken white men came riding and shouting right up to the Bullard front door.

Everyone inside stayed deathly quiet as the men pounded on the barricaded entrance. William cocked the shotgun. The men outside could not gain entrance and the lack of any lights or sounds finally convinced them that Bullard must have already fled the area. The men remounted and went off to drink some more. It was a close call for William and his children.

The near-lynching was a seminal event in young Gene's life. It was at this time that he formulated the idea to leave, to escape the awful Southern prejudice and flee to that magical, mystical nirvana his father had called "France." He had no idea, yet, how he was going to make it happen, but his resolve was firm.

Bullard did not go back to Mr. Bradley's warehouse for a month. Bradley apparently arranged for William to work elsewhere until the furor over a black laborer assaulting a white supervisor died down. Bradley himself came out to the Bullard house several times bringing food, small gifts and treats for the children. He also had several of his own servants look after the frightened youngsters.

Gene loved his father, but as time passed and Columbus's racism chafed even more, his resolve to escape only deepened. According to cousins who were close to the Bullard children, Gene made several attempts to run away from home when he was ten and eleven years old. William always tracked down and found his seventh child. One time, William even put Gene in the Columbus pillory and whipped him for his "crime." The extent of the whipping was not recorded, but since it left no permanent scars it was probably more of a stern deterrent than a true thrashing.

Gene finally did make it out of Columbus. By his account, he was eight years old, but a more reliable timeline has him on the cusp of twelve. He was leaving his native city and its blatant racism, or so he hoped. He may well have felt sorry for leaving his family and the adoration of his father behind, but as would be true throughout Eugene Bullard's life, he always looked forward, never back.

2

THE WANDERER

Gene's final, successful escape from Columbus—in early 1907—was financed by the sale of his beloved goat and cart, a rig that he had traveled in all over town. He sold it to another local boy and it put $1.50 in his pocket, enough to inspire the confidence to make the break he desired. With that money and a small sack of food and clothes, he started walking down the railroad tracks leading out of Columbus.

It did not take his father long to notice that Gene was gone—again. Like every time before, William took off after his errant son, determined to haul him back, infuriated by the boy's persistent disobedience and his lack of desire to stay put and help take care of his siblings. This time, however, Gene got farther, faster than he ever had before, and he outpaced his father's ability to pursue him. This was due to a fortuitous meeting Gene had with a black sharecropping family he came across several miles up the tracks. The family was staying in a camp alongside the railroad and gathering in the cotton from the adjoining fields.

Gene spent his first night away from the Bullard brood with Tom and Emma, as they introduced themselves, and their large menagerie of children. He impressed the itinerant cotton pickers with his story and his ambitions. When they all arose the next morning, Gene was given a single dollar to help him pursue those dreams. It was enough to get him on the next train to Atlanta. With this kind of head start, he was soon too far away from his father's hard-charging but on-foot pursuit.

Exactly what Gene did when and where and with whom from mid-1907 until March 1912 is not neatly chronicled. Almost all of what we know about this period in his life comes from his own recollections, written down decades later, and a few scraps of letters, journals, local newspapers, and official documents, like the 1910 Census. During these five years, Gene spent most of his time among the poorly educated, subsisting on the ragged edge of poverty. Fellow blacks, purposely kept down by harsh restrictions on education and upward mobility, didn't have much time or energy to concern themselves with posterity. We have to take Gene at his word wherever it is backed up by someone else's recollections or that elusive piece of evidence, like a notice in a local paper of a horse race with Gene listed as one of the jockeys. Gene did a lot of wandering during this time but we know for certain that the journey was still focused on finding his way to France.

He was helped greatly by being a bright young man who smiled readily, made friends easily and worked hard and well. He endeared himself to nearly everyone he met. That he achieved his goals gives the most credence to what he remembered about his adventures along the way.

Gene rode the train all the way to the last stop on the line: Atlanta. For a poor kid from a rural riverfront village, Atlanta must have seemed like Dorothy arriving at the Great City of Oz. One can only imagine the bewildered, barefoot, thread-bare, rural black youth transported to the bustling, populous, noisy, big-city environment of downtown Atlanta, long recovered from its post–Civil War devastation. Gene was a quick study, however, and he immediately fell in with a group of Gypsies he happened to come across who were encamped near the stockyards close to the Atlanta railroad station.

Perhaps Gene gravitated to the Gypsies because they were a culture with which he had some familiarity: a small band had taken up residence in Phenix City, Alabama, across the river from Columbus, and he had actually tried to hide out with this group during one of his unsuccessful attempts at running away. The Gypsies outside Atlanta belonged to the Stanley Tribe, originally from England, and they were on an extended foray in America. The Stanleys were expert horse traders (some said thieves) and trafficked mostly in racehorses and thoroughbreds. They held periodic competitions and participated in local horse racing events whenever they were held, mostly at county fairs.

Being outcasts nearly everywhere they went, Gypsies had no trouble at all welcoming another wanderer into their midst, especially if he was willing to work hard, learn the horse business and help around the stables and wagons. It made no difference to anyone in the Gypsy camp that Gene was black. The Stanleys also told him that England was very close to France, and when the tribe went back to England he would be more than welcome to go with them. He decided to stay awhile.

Over the course of the next several months, Gene learned

a great deal about horseflesh, and he worked his way up from mucking out the stables to racing as a jockey. He was light, agile and an excellent rider. He went by "Jamesy," which was a bastardization of his middle name (James). This was also an attempt to avoid detection by his father, who may not have given up the search for his son.

His stay with the Stanleys soured when he was told that the tribe was going to continue its sojourn in America for a few more years instead of returning to England. Gene had more or less counted on his new friends getting him closer to France. Determined to continue his quest, he made up his mind to head on down the road. At that point, the Gypsy campground was near Bronwood, Georgia. Although Gene had made it as far north as Atlanta, initially, the Gypsies had gone south from there and, ironically, in Bronwood he was only about sixty miles from Columbus. His father did not know this, however, and likely Gene did not either.

He struck out going farther south. Just five miles later, toward Leesburg, he was offered a wagon ride by a white gentleman named Travis Moreland. Scaring the teenager with tales of bears and snakes overtaking the local roadways at night, he induced Gene to ride home with him to the Moreland farm a mile east of Leesburg. In exchange for the ride and a place to sleep, Gene offered to rub down the horses, feed them, stow the gear and get the animals in the Moreland barn.

It didn't take long for Moreland to figure out that Gene was pretty good with horses. That led to an offer of work, which he accepted, at least until he could figure out what his next move should be. The stay at the Morelands' lasted several weeks until the urge to move on grabbed him again, which it would—constantly—until Gene finally made it to his ultimate destination.

His next stop was with the Matthews family of Sasser,

Georgia. Mr. Matthews was a barber and Gene soon found himself sweeping out the barber shop and performing chores around the Matthews's home. While staying in Sasser, Gene fell seriously ill with a mysterious "fever." It was troubling enough that Matthews paid for both a doctor and a private room for Gene until he was able to recover. Gene insisted on working off the cost of his treatment and recovery, but the good-hearted Mr. and Mrs. Matthews demurred, sending him off on his continuing journey with the admonition to be patient, for "true democracy" would someday come to the South. Gene was not sure that would ever happen, nor was he willing to stick around and wait.

The 1910 US Census records "Eugene Bullard, laborer," in Thomasville, in southern Georgia. He was listed as a resident in a local boardinghouse, and his occupation was working at the local sawmill. Gene would have been fifteen at this point, and still circling within an area that encompassed most of the lower third of Georgia—and far enough away from Columbus that his father could not seem to find him.

Dawson, Georgia, was his next stop, where he was taken in by the John Z. Turner family. "Zack" Turner was in the livery business, hiring out wagons and horses. He also served as sheriff of Dawson (and would eventually be elected sheriff of Terrell County). The Turner home was full of children, three boys and six girls, plus assorted hired hands and help, most of them black. The Turners were reasonably progressive but still called their black male workers "boys" and "niggers." This included the new addition.

One day early in Gene's employ with the Turners he simply failed to show up for work. Zack Turner went looking for Gene, who was found sitting in the barracks, apparently healthy, but refusing to go to work. When Zack, somewhat miffed, asked why Gene was refusing to do his job, he looked

Zack right in the eye and told him, in no uncertain terms, he was not going to be called "nigger" or "boy." He insisted that he be called "Gene" or, at the very least, by his nickname, "Gypsy."

After a few uncomfortable moments of staring each other down, Zack turned on his heel, saying to Gene, "Follow me," and the two marched outside. Turner called out all the workers and the family, telling them to gather round.

Turner then announced to the assembled crowd, "This here is Gene. He wants to be called 'Gene' by everybody, not 'nigger,' and that's what we're going to do—even the rest of you niggers." We can only wonder if the irony in Zack's statement registered.

Capitalizing on his previous experiences with the Stanleys, Gene soon fell into working with Zack Turner's considerable stable of horses. Turner, an astute observer, saw great possibilities for Gene's abilities as a rider, too. Not long after, with a series of greatly anticipated county races pending, Gene was decked out in Turner's livery and set up as a jockey.

Terrell County had a long tradition of horse racing, which had been suspended during the Civil War and not revived until many years later. By 1910, however, the races were back, with thundering hooves pounding down Dawson's main street at breakneck speeds, cheered on by large crowds. When Zack Turner put up a $500 bet on each of two races at the 1911 fair, he guaranteed a tremendous turnout, large betting pools and a circus-like atmosphere. The attendees became even more curious when they learned that a "black boy" would be riding Turner's racehorses.

Dressed in Turner's silks, Gene beat every other horse and rider in the two featured events, earning a great deal of money for his patron, and $25 for himself, for each race. It was more money than Gene had ever possessed at one time. Although it was only a small fraction of what his boss raked in, he felt as if he had earned a fortune.

With the Turners, Gene entered into a peaceful time of acceptance and harmony, but he was not getting closer to his ultimate dream. There were also periodic reminders of what life could be like in a less salubrious environment.

During the autumn of 1911, Gene requested permission to visit his uncle and cousins in nearby Richland, about twenty miles from Dawson. Zack Turner gave him some time off, and he made his way to the family's home. The successful young man, wearing a new suit purchased with his winnings, sauntered into town one afternoon, casually strolling down the main street. Suddenly, a white man jumped up from the porch on which he had been rocking the afternoon away with his favorite beverage and accosted Gene, demanding to know where he had "stolen" such fine clothes.

The angry white man chased Gene into a nearby store where he trapped him behind a counter and proceeded to beat him with a whip. After scooting under a table, Gene managed to escape and run back to his uncle's house, stinging welts, torn suit and all. When his uncle asked him what had happened, Gene decided it was better to lie than blame a local white man, so he told his uncle that his cousins had attacked him. His uncle, suspecting the lie, took another switch to Gene, and rendered a few more licks on the hapless lad.

Needless to say, the familial visit was cut short. Gene returned to the Turners' home, saddened, and reminded once again, with crystal clarity, that life in America was still a challenge.

Not many weeks later, Zack Turner gave Gene an assignment to deliver a prize horse to a gentleman who lived in the Florida panhandle, near Pensacola. Turner told Gene that after he handed over the horse and collected the money he could use whatever he needed from the funds to obtain transportation back to Dawson.

Gene did exactly as he was told and brought the horse to its new owner and collected the monies owed, after which he had some sort of transformational revelation. While standing on the shore of the first ocean he had ever seen (the Gulf of Mexico) he made up his mind to renew his quest, then and there, to get to France.

From the proceeds he had obtained from delivering and selling Zack Turner's horse, he extracted what he was owed as his fee. He then made arrangements to send the rest of the money back to Turner. Gene bought a train ticket and hopped aboard—sitting in the rear car where blacks were allowed to ride. He never returned to Dawson or saw any of the Turners ever again. It was early in 1912, and the next long phase of Gene's eventful life was about to begin.

The next leg of Gene's odyssey began with a train to Montgomery, Alabama, and a short stay at Mrs. Palmer's Boarding House. Within a few days he was on another train, this time back to Atlanta. On Decatur Street, he found a room for rent with the family of Charles Butler, a black man who worked for the railroad. It was with the Butlers that he saw his first motion picture, at the Bijou Theater, twenty-five cents a ticket. It was likely an "oater," as the popular Western genre was then known. From Mr. Butler he also gleaned a great deal about train schedules and the destinations of the various lines.

Gene and the Butlers formed an instant friendship—enough so that he felt comfortable confiding that he intended to find a ship to take him to France. The Butlers were surprised by Gene's ambitions but admired his pluck. Mr. Butler, knowing a bit about southeastern geography, thanks to his work on the railroad, was able to steer Gene in the direction of getting to one of the Carolina or Virginia coastal cities where he could most likely find a ship bound for Europe.

Gene felt a new suit was in order, in preparation for his next adventure, since his only good one had been cut up by the beatings he had endured from the drunken redneck and his uncle in Richland. Since then he had been wearing what was then known as a "Buster Brown" suit, in honor of the popular cartoon character of the same name. Knee britches and a short waistcoat were a bit too juvenile for Gene's expanding worldly tastes as well as his physique, so he set out to acquire an outfit with the even more current "peg pants" (high-waist trousers that tapered to tight cuffs).

He wandered the downtown Atlanta streets until he came across a men's clothing shop that caught his eye. The owner was a Jewish tailor, aided by his son, who was about Gene's age. Gene picked out some fabric and brought it to the tailor, who promptly asked, "Say little nigger, where are you from?"

Once again, Gene heard the N-word. Gene dropped the fabric, turned on his heel and left the shop. The tailor, not wanting to lose a customer, sent his son running after him. The young man, apologizing for the slight, managed to convince Gene to return to his father's establishment. The tailor, himself many times a victim of prejudice against Jews, apologized and agreed to make Gene's new suit at cost.

A few days later Gene, in his new duds, strode with obvious pride down the streets of Atlanta. On a busy street, headed back to the Butlers', he was brushed by a tall white youth who bumped into Gene then quickly moved on. Seconds later, Gene noticed a slight pain in his left leg. He looked down to see a large slash, probably done by a razor, in his new pants and a shallow cut across his leg that stung and bled onto his new trousers.

Mrs. Butler was able to mend the trousers, but not Gene's pride. Venting his frustration aloud, he swore that as soon as he could, he was going to learn to box, so that "when anybody is mean, I can show them it don't pay." Gene didn't know it but at that moment, he was accurately forecasting his first significant occupation.

That night, he could not sleep. He was too angry. He resolved to leave the next day. With Mr. Butler at work, Gene donated his repaired new suit to Mrs. Butler's only child, Sonny, and said a tearful goodbye. He went to the station and found a train he had previously scouted: it was a Seaboard Line passenger and freight hauler. The name "Seaboard" had convinced Gene the line must have something to do with the ocean. Rather than pay the fare, he snuck under the dining car and nestled his lithe body into the latticework of frames and rods.

The train sped through the night, heading northeast, whistling through a myriad of towns and hamlets, nonstop. When it finally slowed to cross a trestle bridge over a large river, Gene wriggled out of his hiding spot and dismounted. He was outside of Richmond, Virginia.

After daybreak, Gene walked down the tracks with his meager satchel until he hit the outskirts of the city. He found lodging with a black family named Hughes. Mr. Hughes was a brick maker and Eugene agreed to go to work for Mr. Hughes to replenish his dwindling stash of cash.

After two weeks, Gene confided in Mr. Hughes, as he had others before, that he was bound for France. Would Hughes, he asked, point him in the direction of Norfolk, where he had heard he could catch a ship? Hughes advised that there was a port much closer by: Newport News. Gene decided that was where he would go.

The Hughes family threw a small party for their affable young guest, then off he went, to the Richmond train depot. On Hughes's advice, Gene hopped on a line of the Chesapeake & Ohio that headed due east. Instead of paying for a ticket, however, he once again decided to "ride the rails" under a bouncing passenger car. Gene stayed with the train until the end of its line, which happened to be right next to the "beautiful wide water," as Gene remembered, "of Hampton Roads."

Exhausted and unfamiliar with the area, he elected to spend the night sleeping in a coal bin near the docks. He woke up the next morning covered in coal dust, which occasioned a passing sailor to comment, "Son, ain't you already black enough?" Since the man had meant it as a joke, and not in a mean-spirited way, they both laughed. Gene asked the sailor which one of the nearby vessels might be headed to France. "Can't say for sure," the sailor replied, "but they all get there eventually. Pick any one you like."

Gene wandered down closer to the line of ships busily being loaded and off-loaded. He ended up near a long line of men hauling crates of vegetables up the gangway of a mid-size steamer.

A deep, booming voice shouted from behind his left ear, "Hey! Boy! I ain't payin' you to stand around! Now pick up that crate and move it!" Mistaking Gene for one of the local longshoremen, the stevedore in charge of loading the ship pointed to a crate of cabbages near Gene's feet and angrily gestured to the ramp.

Seizing the opportunity, Gene hefted the burden onto his back and joined the procession loading the ship. After several trips, he slipped between two large bales of cotton on the main deck and hid. Two hours later, toward late afternoon, the ship unmoored and sailed away; but, only three hours later, it docked again. Sensing that France had to be much farther away than just a few hours, Gene snuck off the ship.

On the pier he ran into another black lad about his age. He asked him, "Where is this?"

The other young man looked at Gene like he was crazy and replied, "Norfolk, Virginia, dumbhead!"

It was, as he suspected, not France, but as he looked around, the ships were bigger than the one he had just sailed aboard. Surely one of these larger vessels would be headed to where he wanted to go. He picked the biggest one he saw and went to the slip where she was moored. Several men who looked to be sailors were standing near the ship's gangway, chatting and casually smoking. They spoke a language that Gene had never heard before and did not understand.

One of the men finally noticed Gene and motioned him to come forward. The sailor spoke passable English and explained that the men were crewmen from the ship, which was named the *Marta Russ*. They were all from some country called "Germany" and they were soon shipping out to their homeport, a city called "Hamburg." They would, however, stop at a couple of ports along the way.

The English-speaking sailor then said to Gene that he might be able to make a little money by running personal errands for the crew. They would be sailing in two days and most of the men were too busy with their duties to get extra bread, beer, and cigarettes from the local shops. The man told Gene to come back the next morning and he might find employment. Gene eagerly accepted—although he had another plan in mind that involved much more than running errands.

He found a shabby, cheap room for the night, cleaned up his clothes and got some rest. The next morning, bright and early, he was back at the dock where the *Marta Russ* was moored.

The ship was sailing on Monday, so that Saturday and the next day Gene stayed busy, meeting many of the crewmen and taking their orders for various needs. He ran all across the area picking up laundry, liquor, food items and newspapers. Every trip put a few cents in his pocket.

Sunday, Gene went shopping for himself, buying bread, cheese, and filling a bottle with water. After the crew had bedded down for the night he slipped aboard the *Marta Russ*. He loosened the canvas on one of the lifeboats, slipped underneath, and hid.

At dawn the next morning, amid a flurry of bells and whistles, the *Marta Russ* threw over her lines and sailed away. Gene had heard the crew talking about some place called "Aberdeen," which he hoped was in France, and that they would arrive before his food and water were exhausted. It was March 4, 1912, and the sixteen-year-old Eugene Bullard would not return to the shores of his native land for another twenty-eight years.

ACT II
THE FIGHTER

3

UPON NEW SHORES

The *Marta Russ* was a sturdy, single-screw steamship, slightly under three hundred feet long and two thousand gross tons. She was built in 1899 by Ernst Russ, of Hamburg, Germany, and named for his wife. One of hundreds of similar transoceanic general freight vessels built during the pre–World War I period, she gamely plied her trade across the North Sea and the Atlantic for a remarkable sixty-four years before she was finally broken up in Helsinki, Finland, in 1963. During her long career she hauled a little bit of everything, including cabbages, coal, lumber, and steel, and somehow managed to avoid the bombs and torpedoes of two world wars. Certainly one of her most interesting "consignments" was a young stowaway by the name of Eugene Bullard.

After three days at sea in the lifeboat, his food and water ran out, and he was no doubt desperate for some clean air as well as nourishment. Though he had no clear idea how long the voyage would last, he at least felt the ship had sailed on long enough that it was not about to return to port and throw him off. He crawled out of his hiding spot and surrendered himself to the first startled crewman who strode by.

The sailor immediately took the teenager to Captain Ernst Westphal, the skipper of the ship, who was none too pleased. He threatened to toss the young Bullard overboard, but when the stowaway pointed out "The fish have plenty to eat without me," the captain laughed. Westphal was a decent sort and told his crewman to let the boy get cleaned up and feed him a meal in the crew's mess. As soon as Bullard was seated in front of a steaming bowl of soup and slices of fresh-baked bread, several of the men recognized him as the boy who had been running errands for them in Norfolk.

After a promise to the captain that he would work hard and obey the orders of the men, Bullard was put to work in the galley, cleaning up, toting and tossing the garbage, and helping the cook. He also did a few shifts down in the engine room shoveling coal into the ship's hungry boiler.

During the next two weeks, the crew came to enjoy the lad's cheerful company as the *Marta Russ* toiled across the choppy Atlantic, headed toward her first port of call. Bullard, always a quick learner, soaked up a passable acquaintance with the German language which was the native tongue of most of the men aboard. His facility with German would be an important aspect of his life in the coming years, and this was where he began to learn the language.

After a slow but uneventful crossing, the plodding steamer chugged into Aberdeen Harbor. Captain Westphal told Gene he would have to leave, as the "law of the sea" required stowaways to be deposited at the next port of call. The crew, who had come to like their guest, took up a collection of clothes and toiletries for Bullard and a small valise to carry the items.

Captain Westphal generously paid him about $25 in earned wages, and Bullard and his new friends said their goodbyes.

He was not in France, but a new and confusing place called "Scotland." The people spoke English, which was helpful, but they employed a lot of long, rolling Rs with a strange accent that Bullard found difficult to grasp: "Their talk made me feel hard of hearing," he later wrote in his autobiography. He was, however, able to recognize that by reading signs like "England" and "Europe," he was getting closer to his goal. He eagerly looked for ways to take the next steps, the first one being to survive in a strange, new land.

Very few Scots, in 1912, had ever seen a black person in the flesh. They invariably referred to Bullard as "Darky" or "Jack Johnson," the heavyweight boxer who was, without question, the most famous African American on earth at that time. Bullard was not a boxer and certainly no heavyweight, but he seemed to enjoy the association with the well-known Johnson. Perhaps the comparison influenced his thinking because a boxer is exactly what Bullard would become during the next important phase of his life.

He was treated well by the Scots, much as he had hoped he would be treated in France. He stayed in Aberdeen for only a few days, then bought a train ticket for Glasgow where he had heard work was more readily available. Despite the cordiality of the Scottish people, Bullard was still yearning for France, which he finally learned was hundreds of miles away and across one more stretch of water.

By the time he reached Glasgow, he had just enough money to get himself a cheap but clean room in a downtown boardinghouse. His uniqueness as a black-skinned man was of immense curiosity to the Glaswegians and that, combined with his usual upbeat disposition, made it easy for him to make friends and acquaintances who could be beneficial to him. Being somewhat in the public eye also availed him of the opportunity to take on a few gigs singing and dancing with the street entertainers common to downtown Glasgow.

Part of the vibrant street scene were the card sharks who plied their three-card monte scam and the universal shell gamers of find-the-pea fame. These itinerant gamblers would set up a card table on a street corner at a moment's notice. Their schemes were decidedly less than legal, however, and Gene quickly discovered he could make some pretty good money acting as a lookout for these manipulators. Whenever the bobbies were about to turn the corner, or come down the street, it was Bullard's sharp whistle and running feet that would alert the con men to hurriedly shut down and scurry away.

He stayed in Glasgow, happily making money, for about five months. Toward the end of August 1912, he was ready to take the next step toward France. Stuffing his earnings in his socks, he bought yet another train ticket, this one to Liverpool, England, one more country closer to his goal.

Liverpool was then and still is one of the world's great seaports. Bullard, seeking something a little more profitable than working scams on the streets, decided to try his hand at becoming a longshoreman. It was, after all, a task with which he had some familiarity, having loaded crates of cabbages in Newport News and sailed across the broad Atlantic. Although treated with respect, and not the racial discrimination he had been used to in America, he spent too many days at the hiring hall without landing a single assignment. Finally, a new friend told him he'd have better luck if he joined the union, which Bullard promptly did.

He was picked up by a job foreman immediately after returning with his new union card and assigned to a crew unloading huge sides of frozen mutton. It was back-breaking work for a youth as slender as Bullard, but after a few weeks he noticed that his muscles were filling out, his shoulders broadening and his legs getting stronger. That was a plus, but the work was not to his liking, so he switched to becoming a helper on a fish wagon.

During the Christmas holiday in 1912, Bullard, with a little time off, wandered down to Birkenhead. At the time, this was the site of Liverpool's primary amusement park. He came across an attraction that both tickled him and ignited possibilities in his brain. One of the popular games allowed patrons to pitch soft rubber balls at someone poking their head through a large canvas sheet—a type of dodge ball, for a penny a throw. Three hits won you a prize. Bullard went straight to the game's owner and offered his services, suggesting that the man could make a lot more money if the targeted head was uniquely black instead of white. The tactic worked like a charm. The game's popularity soared with Bullard's noggin and bright smile protruding through the sheet. He made enough money to quit his aromatic job on the fish wagon and he only had to work weekends, to boot, to triple his income.

With a great deal of time on his hands, and real money in his pocket, Gene had the luxury of being able to explore Liverpool and further expand his options. What he found most appealing was Baldwin's Gym, the nexus for boxer training and the scheduling of local matches in Liverpool.

The owner, Chris Baldwin, was a burly man of booming voice who was widely respected as a trainer. One day in late December, a thin but wiry black youth showed up and stared at the boxers and other gym rats working out. In this particular location, dark faces and skin were not novelties: a number of black boxers trained at Baldwin's, many of them expatriate Americans.

It took a while, but Baldwin finally noticed the unfamiliar, wide-eyed face. He was not happy to see a freeloader hanging around his gym and growled at the boy that he was not welcome and that he should leave immediately. Undeterred, Bullard immediately offered to help out, to work at whatever the cantankerous owner might need. No job was too small, too menial. Impressed by the teenager's spunk, Baldwin grinned and put him to task.

For the next several weeks, while still working his weekend job at the fair, Bullard cleaned out slop buckets, lugged pails of water, wiped down the canvas rings, swept the floors, fetched towels, and ran any errand Baldwin needed done.

His persistence and work ethic paid off. One day, in February 1913, Baldwin called Bullard into his office.

"Listen, Bullard. You seem like a bright lad. I wasn't sure at first, but you've been working hard. I have an idea for you."

"Sure thing, Mister Baldwin. I'm game for anything."

"How would you like to start sparring with the lads? A few rounds at a time?"

Gene could hardly believe what he was hearing. It was exactly what he had decided he wanted to do.

"Yes, sir, Mister Baldwin! I'd be very delighted!"

"You're likely to get your crown knocked about, you know," Baldwin chuckled.

"Don't make no never mind, sir. I can duck!"

Baldwin burst out laughing, "Well, now, that black noggin of yours is going to be an easy target to spot!"

"Maybe so, but I can fly like a bird, too."

"We'll see there, 'Mister Bird.' We'll just see."

His smallish stature put him in the welterweight class, but he was totally unafraid to take on anyone who wanted to go a few rounds, even the heavyweights. He was also a very quick learner. Before long, Baldwin realized he had much more than a live punching bag: he had a young boxer with some impressive natural talent.

Early in March 1913, and after much pestering by his eager pupil, Baldwin arranged a real match for Bullard: a ten-round fight with an Irish boxer from Wales, Bill Welsh. The fight was on the undercard headed by the welterweight Aaron Lister Brown, more famously known as the "Dixie Kid," one of the more popular fighters in Europe.

Bullard boxed, at first, under the nickname of "The Sparrow." Like the bird he had joked about, he was on the small side, but could flit gracefully around the ring, picking and choosing the most advantageous moments to "peck" away at his opponents. "Sparrow" was also a nickname he had picked up in Georgia from one of his boardinghouse landladies who told him, "Like the sparrow, you were born to fly!"

Like Jack Johnson, Bob Scanlon, and other black boxers, Aaron Brown was an American who had come to Europe to make a living and, as they all hoped, to get the type of title shots that had been denied to them in America because of their race. Brown had been born in 1883 in Missouri and while still a teenager had fought professionally in California, where he became a real contender. His big opportunity came in April 1904, when he challenged "Barbados Joe" Walcott for the World Welterweight Championship. Walcott had the upper hand for much of the fight, and by the twentieth round the Dixie Kid was tiring. Suddenly, the referee, "Duck" Sullivan, disqualified Walcott, giving the title to the challenger. Soon after, the title was taken away when it was discovered that Sullivan had bet on the Dixie Kid to win. The "Kid's" name was nonetheless secured, and he went on to much bigger and better bouts.

Brown continued to fight black boxers, winning more than he lost, but opportunities grew scarce. He sailed to Europe in 1910 and scored an impressive victory the following year, in Paris, against George Carpentier, a major sports hero in France who would become a fighter pilot in World War I.[2] By the time Brown retired in 1920, he had fought over one hundred fifty bouts, and his new occupation was as a jazz drummer for an orchestra in Berlin. Musical fame would elude the Dixie Kid but he would be inducted into the International Boxing Hall of Fame in 2002. At the time that Eugene Bullard met the Dixie Kid, the latter had just lost to Harry Lewis, the World Welterweight Champion.

A scrappy and determined Gene Bullard went the full ten rounds with Welsh and was awarded the fight on points. Looking on, awaiting his turn, was the Dixie Kid, who came away impressed with Bullard's form and raw skill. The Kid won his scheduled twenty-round bout with a second-round knockout, and afterward he invited Bullard to dine with him. They talked about "possibilities."

The net result was that Brown offered Bullard a position in his company of fighters, a group of about a dozen pugilists in various weight classes who toured as a group. Baldwin, who was Bullard's unofficial manager, agreed to the deal after extracting from Brown a promise to "take care" of the young man—and, no doubt, some immediate compensation or a small percentage of future purses. That being settled, the troupe prepared to leave for London in two days. Bullard was eager to go, but he had some very important unfinished business to attend to first.

It was during his Liverpool days that Bullard became involved in his first serious, intimate relationship. In his auto-

---

2   He would be awarded the Croix de Guerre and the Medaille Militaire for his aerial heroics, and his bravery only enhanced his boxing career, which lasted until 1927. Like Gene Bullard, he would become a very successful club owner, and even a part-time movie actor. He died of a heart attack at age eighty-one in 1975.

biography, he refers to her as "Cherie." She was, as the naive young man discovered only after some weeks with her, a local prostitute.

In 1913, there were approximately five thousand expatriate African Americans living in England. Nearly all, like Bullard, had fled America in the hopes of a better life, which meant one free of racial prejudice. Many were among the most skilled in their professions: musicians, vaudeville performers, craftsmen, boxers, athletes and, yes, even "ladies of the night." Attractive African American girls were considered intriguing and many Englishmen were willing to pay a high price for their company.

Cherie was, according to Bullard, one such intoxicating distraction. The following paragraphs, about Cherie, are taken from *All Blood Runs Red*, Bullard's own account of their love affair:

Promoters came [to Baldwin's Gym] to judge boxers for possible matches. But there were others, more interesting: the women and girls who came to watch. They seemed to be attracted to men in good physical condition, wearing shorts, sweating and breathing hard. *Mon dieu,* the women were pretty and friendly. One group came almost every day, and this one time there was a new girl. Wow! She was slim, her skin almost teak, her deep dark eyes reminded me of my mother. From the minute she arrived, she stared at me. I was in the ring, and turned to take a good look and our eyes met.

She nodded her head. I was entranced and didn't notice my sparring partner's left cross to my head. Bam! Down I went. Went down but got up with a smile.

"Damn Sparrow, you weren't concentrating!" yelled Mr. Baldwin. At the end of the evening session, she

winked, waved, walked over and said, "*S'il vous plait*
(please) meet me when you are done." I showered
quickly, my hair was still wet, rushed to dress and headed
out wondering, "Will she be there?" Miracle! She was
waiting. We reached out and took each other's hand,
walked, chatted. "I hear you are called Sparrow and you
are an American. Why are you here?"

"Because this is the way to Paris," I told her. She listened as I explained my dream of France.

She took me to a small pub, where we had dinner.
I looked into those eyes and this Sparrow listened to
a nightingale's voice. The sweet smell of her perfume
was captivating. When her palm caressed my face, fires
burned inside of me. "You are so young, so strong and
untouched. Why do they call you Sparrow? Were you
a slave?"

"No, never a slave and never will be. My name was
given to me a long time ago by a wonderful woman who
was sure I would fly," I answered. Didn't know what she
meant about being young and strong, but untouched.
Being with her was breathtaking. I knew I was in love.

Cherie was a little older than I. She told me she did
special hairdressing and cosmetics for wealthy customers.
She knew so much about everything. Dinner ended. It
was after midnight. Don't remember what I ate. At her
boarding house I started to say goodnight. She put her
fingers to my lips, whispered, "Hush, hush. The night
is not over, little bird." With her leading the way, we
walked quietly up the stairs and Cherie unlocked the
door to her room. "*S'il vous plait,* come in." I was never
in a woman's room before and was shy. She started to
hum and slowly undressed. Her naked body was like a

goddess, soft, maple-teak color, smooth and gleaming clean...

"My Sparrow, now let me show you love." It was my first time. I became a man and it was wonderful![3]

Within days, the two of them moved in together and Bullard spent several blissful yet exhausting weeks working the gym by day and enjoying his partner's ministrations by night. Sometimes he would rush home only to find Cherie absent. She would, however, always leave a note, usually indicating she was with a client.

"I never suspected or realized why her 'special assignments' were at odd hours, afternoons and some nights," Bullard wrote. "Alas, it is true that love is blind, especially for a first time love."

As he tells it, when he came back to the flat he shared with Cherie to pack his bag for London, he found all of his belongings neatly stowed in his valise, sitting outside the door— which was locked. Bullard thought he heard Cherie softly crying behind the door, but no amount of coaxing or knocking would get her to open up. With the time for his departure at hand, he picked up his belongings and sadly trudged away. The two star-crossed lovers would never see each other again.

In London, Bullard moved into Mrs. Carter's Boarding House at Number 2 Coram Street, Holborn, not far from Soho. Holborn was the epicenter of expatriate African American London. The borough was chockablock with entertainers, musicians, singers, actors, aspiring athletes, and boxers. The Dixie Kid lived close by, with his wife and infant daughter. The Kid, as he had promised Chris Baldwin, took Bullard

---

3 *All Blood Runs Red*, Eugene Bullard's unpublished autobiography, 1960.

under his wing and made sure he was trained properly and scheduled for any fights for which he was qualified.

In this large and close-knit community Bullard found opportunities to do more than box. With his natural talent and winning personality, he soon found himself employed as a slapstick performer in the wildly popular Belle Davis's Freedman's Pickaninnies.[4] "Belle's Picks" toured around Europe and presented, in vaudeville format, a complete revue of Southern black culture in song, dance, and comedy routines. Over the course of the next year, in addition to his boxing matches, Bullard toured with the troupe from St. Petersburg to Moscow, Berlin to Paris. The group offered him his first views of France, and these teasing trips only sharpened his desire to end up there.

Bullard's career as a fighter provided him with a very good income. The work was also steady. During the years before the Great War, the average Englishman was doing quite well financially. The long decades of Queen Victoria's reign had been mostly peaceful and economic possibilities had exploded, giving rise to incomes that offered money for discretionary spending. The economic boom had continued during the reign of her son, Edward VII, who had ruled 1901-1910, and under the then-reigning king, George V, Victoria's grandson, who would rule until 1936.

Football (soccer, as we know it in America) had not then risen to the heights of frenzied fandom it enjoys today among the British general public. Boxing was all the rage. Gentlemen's clubs and major boxing venues, like the fabled Blackfriar's, were packed nearly every night of the week, tightly

---

4   Pickaninny (also picaninny, piccaninny or pickinniny) is a racist American slang term referring to dark-skinned children of African descent. Its origin may be derived from the Portuguese *pequenino*, a diminutive version of the word *pequeno*, "little."

scheduled with bouts offering the spectacle of men pummeling each other with abandon.

From early 1913 until mid-1914, Bullard could always find a spot on someone's fight card or get an invite to box privately at a gentleman's club. He was popular and had a good record. He was clearly tenacious and always entertaining. In an era when fights went twenty rounds or more, lasting several hours, he was seldom knocked out of a bout. He most often fought in the middle or welterweight classes which routinely set him below the "premier" heavyweight level. His limitations were that he was a good fighter, but not a great one, and his size, which always tended toward the lower weight of his class. He had the stamina and courage needed, but he never developed the finesse and technical expertise necessary to make it to the top level. He was not going to be the next Jack Johnson of his weight class—although while in London he did get to meet that legendary boxer and participated in several fights on a card where Johnson was the main attraction.

John Arthur "Jack" Johnson was born in 1878 and grew up around Galveston, Texas. One of nine children of hard-working former slaves, he was a scrawny and rather skinny child. He had two older sisters who did any fighting necessary to protect their little brother. Totally opposite of Bullard's experiences as a child, Johnson recalled that everyone around his family in Galveston was so poor it didn't matter if they were black or white. He ran, in fact, with a gang of "white boys" until he was a teenager and recalled being in the homes of many of his white friends, dining with them, playing with them, going to church and school with them.

By the time Johnson was sixteen he had had enough of working low-paying laborer jobs in Galveston. He struck out for, of all places, New York City, just to see what the "big city" was all about. Having done some sparring and a little recreational boxing, he gravitated to working in a Manhattan gym, and roomed for a time with Joe Walcott, a welterweight from the West Indies, who introduced him around. This was not the more famous, and later, "Jersey Joe" Walcott but was the same fighter that had once gone twenty rounds with the Dixie Kid.

At the age of twenty, Johnson entered the ring for the first time as a professional, back in Galveston, and beat a fellow named Charley Brooks, in fifteen rounds, for the "Texas State Middleweight" title—even though prizefighting was illegal in the state at that time. A second bout, in 1901, resulted in both fighters being arrested. A bail of $5,000 was set, which neither man could fork over. As a compromise, the sheriff would let the men out at night if they would spar, in jail, during the day, and allow crowds to watch. After three weeks of this, the local grand jury threw out the case. Johnson later credited his "jail time" with the success of his career.

In 1903, Johnson won his first official title, defeating "Denver Ed" Martin for the World Colored Heavyweight Championship. Over the next few years he won several more fights, and successfully defended his title, but he could not claim the "real" world title until he beat the white man who actually held the belt at that time, a Canadian by the name of Tommy Burns.

Burns finally agreed to the fight, in 1908, after getting a guarantee of $30,000. The contest took place in Sydney, Australia, in front of twenty thousand screaming fans. The fight lasted fourteen rounds but was stopped by the police who feared the nearly all-white crowd was getting too agitated about watching a black man pummel their favored white champion. The referees settled the contest—to the amazement of the world—in Johnson's favor.

Almost overnight, Johnson became the most famous black

man on the planet. He kept beating white challengers, one after another. Racial animosity demanded a "Great White Hope" to bring this black upstart down. That "hope" arose in the return of the former undefeated world champion James J. Jeffries. He had retired in 1904 and was happy farming his alfalfa fields. He had also gained one hundred pounds since his retirement. White promoters were so anxious to bring Johnson down, that they finally got Jeffries to agree to a fight with an offer of $120,000 (about $3.2 million in today's currency). It was a staggering and unheard-of amount for a fight. What did Jeffries have to lose? Well, one hundred pounds, to start, which he did, and then he entered the ring on July 4, 1910, in Reno, Nevada, in front of a huge crowd.

The odds on Jeffries were reported to be 10-7. Tension was so high that the entire arena was ringed with police who did not allow any alcohol, fans who had consumed too much alcohol, or guns. Enormous amounts of money had been wagered on the fight. Using his trademark style of dodging his opponent until he had tired him out, Johnson knocked Jeffries down for the first time in his professional career, then knocked him down again. The fight went fifteen rounds and then Jeffries's corner threw in the towel. This "Fight of the Century," as it had been billed, earned Johnson $65,000, or well over a million in today's dollars. It was a stunning blow to racism. Alas, it also resulted in race riots erupting all over the country. Cities like New York, Pittsburgh, Philadelphia, Houston, New Orleans and more saw riots that injured hundreds of people. Twenty people actually died in the clashes.

What racism couldn't do in the ring to bring Johnson down it finally did outside the arena. In 1912, Johnson was tried and convicted on trumped-up charges of violating the notorious Mann Act. It was alleged that he had crossed state lines, with a white woman, "for immoral purposes." An all-white jury in the courtroom of Judge "Kennesaw Mountain" Landis (the future commissioner of Major League Baseball) convicted Johnson and sentenced him to a year and a day in jail. Johnson's response was to skip his bail, flee to Canada disguised as a member of a Negro league baseball team, and sail to France. Johnson would live the next seven years of his life in European exile, boxing, and that's where he met and befriended Eugene Bullard.

Unlike the larger-than-life Jack Johnson, Bullard knew his limitations, and accepted them. He knew how fortunate he had been to get as far as he had. His heart was not set on becoming a world champion. His only overriding goal, using boxing as a means to an end, was to settle in France, and that was, by early 1914, at long last, finally going to happen.

4

"*BON POUR LE SERVICE*"

Bullard's few days here and there performing in Paris with Miss Belle's "Picks" gave the young expatriate his first, tantalizing tastes of the fabled France he had so long sought. As soon as he returned to London, he began haranguing the Dixie Kid about arranging fights in Paris. The Kid was game to give it a try, so in November 1913, the Dixie Kid and the Sparrow gave their first exhibitions there. Actual bouts followed, also featuring Sam Langford, Bob Scanlon, Blink Mc-Closkey, and Jack Johnson.

These initial fights brought the Dixie Kid and Bullard into the orbits of Sam McVey and Joe Jeanette. These two pros, both heavyweights, had been leaders in popularizing the sport of boxing in France during the previous decade. Like Johnson, McVey (sometimes listed as "McVea") and Jeanette had done very well in the United States but saw their possibilities blocked by the color barrier. Both men, at different times, would win the World Colored Heavyweight Championship, but after Johnson beat Jim Jeffries, neither boxer could get a shot at another white fighter. The possibility that white "favorites" could be beaten by more than one black man made bouts impossible to even think of, much less promote.

Jeanette and McVey brought English-style boxing into the French arenas in contrast to "*La boxe Française*," which was little more than street fighting where kicking was legal and gloves were not worn (much like today's mixed martial arts fights). The two men, who were actually good friends, had fought several times, including twice in Paris in 1909. On February 20, McVey beat Jeanette on points. The April 17 rematch, at the Cirque de Paris, in front of a sold-out crowd of twenty-five thousand, became the longest fight in boxing history, going an incredible fifty rounds. After three and a half hours of pummelings and knockdowns, McVey's trainer finally realized that his man's left wrist was broken, and he threw in the towel.

After memorable bouts like these, French-style boxing was finished. The much more entertaining English style took over, and a flood of very good English, American, Australian, and Canadian fighters flocked to the Continent.

Bob Scanlon, a member of McVey's entourage, hailed originally from Mobile, Alabama. Scanlon's main claim to boxing fame was a powerful right hand. Many of his opponents felt it at one time or another, and Blink McCloskey was once hit so hard by Scanlon that he went out cold for thirty minutes. Scanlon would reappear in Gene Bullard's life on several occasions, especially in both world wars.

Sam Langford, although born in Canada, grew up in and around Boston; thus, the colorful nickname of the "Boston Tar Baby." Over a very long career, more than 250 professional fights, he scored an impressive 180 wins, 128 of them knockouts. He has been called the "Greatest Fighter Nobody Knows," and a number of boxing historians place him in the top five fighters in boxing history. He beat, at one time or another, McVey, Jeanette, and the Dixie Kid. He narrowly lost, on points, the World Colored Heavyweight title to Jack Johnson in 1906.

McCloskey's real name was Louis Silverman, and he was a Jewish kid from Philadelphia. His journeyman boxing career lasted from 1906 until 1921. Winning about as much as he lost, he was respected for his persistence and powerful punches. He got his nickname of "Blink" because he actually had a glass right eye, the result of damage in the ring. The injuries were so severe that the eye had to be surgically removed. To the amusement—or sometimes the horror—of each opponent, before a fight, he'd carefully remove his glass eye, hand it to the referee for safekeeping and proceed to box. That he won any fights at all with his degraded depth perception was something of a miracle. McCloskey would come to play an important role in Bullard's life in Paris, after World War I, and in a different occupation.

These men, all boxers of great renown in their time, formed the core of a new wave of French boxing promotion and exhibition in the days immediately before the Great War. The press in France called it *"Toujours l'invasion Americaine."* Bullard became part of that "invasion" in early November 1913, when he won a twenty-round contest at the Élysée Montmartre against the French boxer Georges Forrestal.

From that moment forward, he was determined to find a way to live, work, and stay forever in Paris. When the Dixie Kid and a few members of his boxing clan returned to London, Bullard was told that a series of fights had been arranged for him in England over the next few months. For him, that was dismal news. He told the Dixie Kid, "I could never be happy for the rest of my life unless I could live in France."

Reluctantly, the Kid let Bullard go. Without any arranged fights in France, he returned to Miss Belle and toured with the Picks again from that December until the spring of 1914. When the troupe left Paris, Bullard stayed behind. He finally picked up a few bouts, sparred with other boxers and took jobs interpreting for other fighters. He hung out with Mc-Closkey, Langford, Scanlon, and Jack Johnson, all of whom looked out for and tried to help the "Sparrow." Bullard had finally found a home, and a refuge: Paris was, indeed, all that he had hoped for, and more. He vowed to live in the City of Light for the rest of his days.

Parisian weather in the spring and early summer of 1914 was spectacular. Warm sunshine and comfortable temperatures prevailed. The citizens of "Gay Paree" strolled down the boulevards sporting new fashions from the noted houses of couture and a decent economy ensured that all but the poorest would have a few spare francs to plunk down at the cafés and cabarets scattered about the capital.

For Bullard, it was Paradise. His haphazard travels and many months of careening from one city to the next, one means of employment to another, had finally landed him in the city of his dreams. His abilities as a boxer and his occasional singing and dancing gigs made him enough money to afford a small flat of his own near Montmartre. He was only eighteen years old that summer, in very fine shape physically, and had every prospect for continued success and enjoyment in his adopted land. Then, as August headed toward September, the roof he had so carefully built over his hopes and dreams unceremoniously fell in.

On June 28, in Serbia, the Archduke Franz Ferdinand and his wife, the Grand Duchess Sophie, were gunned down by a penniless student anarchist. By August, the haphazardly constructed patchwork of intercontinental alliances between the European nations had been lit off, like a string of firecrackers, and the world, or at least a large piece of it, was at war.

It must have seemed a cruel irony to Bullard that his hard-won nirvana was instantly under the threat of being crushed by the Central Powers.[5] The military leaders of France were guilty of jingoism, too, as war loomed, and perhaps even more than the Germans. The honor of France was still stained by the crushing blow dealt to it by the legions of Otto von Bismarck in 1871. During lightning-quick strikes, the Iron Chancellor and his troops had quickly defeated an overconfident France and Napoleon III. The monarchy fell (again) and French pride was utterly crushed.

As what would become World War I took hold, the French, in their bright red-and-blue uniforms, heads topped with jaunty kepis, felt they could march to Berlin in a month. Many believed the war would be over by Christmas. French lancers polished the tips of their spears and saddled their horses. The tank had not yet been invented, but rapid-fire artillery and the heavy machine gun had been. By the end of 1914, the gaudy uniforms would be discarded, tens of thousands of young Frenchmen would be dead, and both sides would begin frantically digging long muddy trenches from Dunkirk to the Pyrenees.

Friends that Bullard had made in Paris disappeared—swallowed up by the massive call to arms. Many of them were already wounded or dead. He concluded he had to pitch in on behalf of his new country, so he determined to sign up, too. There were challenges, however, the first being that

---

5   The Central Powers in WWI were Germany, Austria-Hungary, the Ottoman Empire, and Bulgaria.

he was too young. The soonest he could enlist would be his nineteenth birthday, October 9. Secondly, he was a foreigner.

Most young Frenchmen of military age were preregistered to fight for their country, much like the Selective Service System that would be activated in the United States in three years. Each recruit was preliminarily assigned to a regiment, so that when the calls went out, as they did in August and September, millions of men dropped whatever they were doing and reported to their units or to the training centers associated with their ultimate assignments. There were many foreign nationals living or working in France who wanted to fight, like Bullard, for their adopted nation.

The only service open to non-French nationals was the Foreign Legion. Even so, the minimum enlistment was for five years. Since most potential recruits believed that the war would be over in a matter of weeks or months, the five-year minimum was daunting. Not wishing to turn away thousands of much-needed volunteers, the minister of war came up with a clever compromise: he would allow foreigners to enlist in the Legion for "the duration of the war," and the wartime volunteers would be assigned to special marching regiments that were, essentially, troops signed on for temporary service.

On his nineteenth birthday, Bullard walked into the local Foreign Legion recruiting office. He had no official papers, either French or American, but he was taken at his word. The fluent French he was already able to speak—and the good German he knew—were, no doubt, assets. His excellent physical condition was a benefit to his acceptance; although, as Bullard wrote later in his memoirs, the exam given by the French Army doctor was cursory, at best:

[The doctor] listened momentarily with a stethoscope for some sound of heartbeat. The volunteer opened his mouth. Queries about his height and weight. The officer prodded his body in a few obvious places. He nodded to the clerk, *"Bon pour le service"* (good to serve).

With a tacit nod to the staggering casualties already being endured, and the willingness to take on anyone who volunteered, he was signed up: Eugene Bullard of Georgia was instantly a member of the French Foreign Legion, committed to serve "for the duration."

Bullard was in the second wave of Americans to enlist in the Foreign Legion. Almost as soon as the first "guns of August" began booming, young men from the United States gravitated to France, anxious to get in on the action, or as they often said, "to do my bit." Most of these early volunteers were idealists, fixated on "battling the Hun," and defending democracy and freedom. Many were disappointed that the pacifist President Woodrow Wilson was not interested in getting America into the war, so they would take up the cudgel themselves. A great many of these men were the sons of wealth and privilege. A disproportionate number were from Harvard, Yale, and Princeton, referred to as the "Ivy League crowd."

There were others, too, from less privileged or dramatic backgrounds: men who operated on the fringes of society and were simply looking for the next adventure or something to do to fill their needs or their wanderlust. Bob Scanlon, Gene's boxing pal, was among these men. There were roustabouts, salt-encrusted sailors, cooks, race car drivers, stevedores, even one medical doctor, an advertising executive, and men with shadowy backgrounds of unknown pedigree. The Foreign

Legion had always been a refuge for men running from something, and in 1914 it was no different.

Among the Americans in that first wave was Alan Seeger, one of the Harvard graduates who gravitated to France immediately after the war commenced. Already a poet of some note, he had been living the Bohemian life in New York's Greenwich Village for a time. (Seeger's Class of 1910 also included T.S. Eliot and Walter Lippmann.) Alan's brother, Charles, would become the father of famed folk singer Pete Seeger who would play a peripheral role in Eugene Bullard's later life.

Alan Seeger had originally come from a family of means, but his father's import-export business stumbled in the 1890s and the family moved from a palatial home on Staten Island to a smaller house in New York City. Then an opportunity to improve their fortunes took the family to Mexico City for two years before Seeger went to Harvard. By temperament and conscience, he was a poet and a dreamer, but he also matured into a large man, with powerful energy and confidence. He was daring and had no great fears about the possibilities of perishing in combat. His most famous poem would, in fact, become "I Have a Rendezvous With Death," written just before the Battle of the Somme in 1916.

Brothers Paul and Kiffin Rockwell, North Carolinians then living in Atlanta, Georgia, were in the advertising business and doing fairly well when the war began. Both men immediately felt the pull to France—and looked forward to what they hoped would be a great adventure. They quit their jobs, took a train to New York and then a liner bound for Le Havre. Kiffin had done short stints at the Virginia Military Institute and the US Naval Academy, but neither had stuck with him, and he then joined his brother at Washington and Lee University. The brothers had sent a letter requesting to join the Foreign Legion, but they did not wait for a reply before boarding the ship to Europe. Kiffin Rockwell was, quite possibly, the first American to fight with the French in the war.

Forty-five-year-old Jack Bowe was a veteran of the Spanish-American War and comfortably situated with a wife and four children in Minnesota. He had served as the mayor of the town of Canby. Bowe had very strong feelings about the contest: "[He] saw the coming struggle as one between France, 'a people with an army,' and Germany, 'an army with a people.'"[6]

Victor Chapman was nicknamed the "Gentle Giant." He was, indeed, a big man, and known throughout his all-too-short life as someone who cared deeply and was always willing to help others. He was extraordinarily wealthy, thanks to his father's Wall Street millions, and although born in New York City was also a citizen of France. After graduating from Harvard in 1913 he moved to Paris to study architecture and to paint. As soon as the war broke out, he went to his father, who advised against enlisting, but Chapman did anyway.

Yale dropout William Thaw was also fabulously wealthy. His father, in fact, bought him his own airplane, to race with, in 1913. One of his first stunts was to take his new "flying boat" (a Curtiss Hydro) and fly under all four of the suspension bridges on the East River. A mustachioed ladies' man and inveterate partygoer, he donated his plane to France as soon as the war started, and then enlisted in the Foreign Legion.

Bob Scanlon seems most like a tale out of the Eugene Bullard mold. Like Gene, Scanlon escaped as a young man from poverty and racism in the American South. Like Bullard, he wanted a place free from prejudice and the constant fear of violence and lynching. Like Bullard, he found his way across the Atlantic, fell easily into boxing, and worked his way onto

---

6   David Hanna, *Rendezvous with Death* (Washington, DC: Regnery History, 2016), 42.

cards in England and France. He felt a strong personal bond with his adopted country and, also like Bullard, when the signal for volunteers went out, he heeded the call to arms.

There were more: René Phelizot, originally from Chicago, was an internationally acclaimed African big game hunter; professional race car driver Bob Soubiron; Philippine-American War veteran Edward Morlae; Dennis Dowd, a Columbia grad, enlisted after being jilted by his girlfriend; taxi driver Bert Hall; jeweler Charles Trinkard; Ferdinand Capdevielle, fencing master; and Harvard grad Edward Mandell Stone, Class of 1908, who would attain a particular distinction among all his fellow Americans.

Organizing this ragtag contingent of Americans was Charles Sweeny, West Point Class of '04, who held daily drills for these citizen-soldiers in the courtyard of the Palais Royale. Sweeny, who would go on to fight under five different flags in his lifetime, was said to have been the inspiration for Ernest Hemingway's hero Jake Barnes in *The Sun Also Rises*.

The Americans were forced to wait until August 21, 1914, before being accepted into the French Foreign Legion. Some of them would go on to greater glories and several would share the trials and tribulations of the war with Gene Bullard. Most would not come out of the conflict unscathed—or alive.

On February 15, 1915, in trenches near the Aisne River, Private Edward Mandell Stone dutifully stood by his machine gun as the Germans bombarded the Legion positions. A general attack, Stone feared, would follow, and if so, he wanted to be ready. Suddenly, a shell splinter pierced his right lung and lodged inside his chest. He was evacuated and treated swiftly, but the doctors could not remove the lethal splinter. After twelve days of agony and tortured breathing, Stone finally expired. He was, by most accounts, the first American to die in the Great War.

On July 4, 1916, at Belloy-en-Santerre, Private Alan Seeger charged across the battlefield, shouting at the top of his lungs, urging his mates onward. The German machine guns erupted, spitting death. Forty of the forty-five men in Seeger's unit were cut down, including Seeger, who crumpled to the earth stitched across his midsection by six bullets. He died at the bottom of a shell hole crying for both water and his mother. It was not a poet's demise.

Paul Rockwell was severely wounded in 1916 and invalided out of the Foreign Legion. He became a correspondent for the *Chicago Daily News*, and enjoyed writing stories about all his former comrades, especially his brother.

Kiffin Rockwell was also wounded, at Verdun, in 1916, by a bullet through the leg. As he convalesced he formed the idea to go into aviation and did so, becoming one of the first Americans to qualify as a pilot flying for the French. On May 18, 1916, Kiffin became the first American pilot to score an aerial victory, shooting down a two-man observation plane over Alsace. He was immediately awarded the Medaille Militaire and the Croix de Guerre. On September 23, 1916, above the Vosges River, Kiffin was flying a brand-new Nieuport 17 on its first mission, and he dove on a German Aviatik two-man observation plane. A French artillery captain, watching from the ground below, saw Rockwell fire a burst at the German, and saw the rear gunner in the Aviatik fire back. An explosive bullet tore through Rockwell's chest, killing him instantly. The left wing of the Nieuport tore off during its spiral earthward. Rockwell became the second American pilot killed in the war.

The first American pilot to die had been Sergeant Victor Chapman on June 24, 1916, near Fort Duaumont, Verdun. Typical of Chapman, he was not even on an official patrol, but bringing a basket of oranges to a wounded comrade. He spotted an American patrol, grossly outnumbered by German Fokkers, below. He dove on the enemy to distract them. The Americans safely flew away, but Chapman, immediately surrounded, was shot to pieces. His plane plunged straight into the ground from ten thousand feet.

Jack Bowe would survive the war, but only after being wounded and gassed. He was lucky enough to be able to go back to his family in Minnesota, but he was broken in both health and spirit.

William Thaw climbed out of the trenches, too, and became a pilot, and probably the first American to fly a combat mission against the enemy. He eventually joined the US Army Air Service after the Americans entered the war in 1917, becoming an "ace," with five confirmed kills. He was awarded two Distinguished Service Crosses and rose to the rank of lieutenant colonel. Sadly, he died of pneumonia at age forty in 1934.

In February 1915, René Phelizot got into a brawl with a couple of veteran legionnaires over, of all things, a ration of coffee. During the fight he was smashed over the head with an empty wine bottle. After the fight was broken up, Phelizot went back on duty complaining of headaches. In truth, he had a fractured skull. Evacuated to a hospital near Fismes, he died shouting *"Je suis Americain!"* while clutching the tattered remnants of the US flag he had carried through the streets of Paris on his way to the Legion recruiting office.

Bob Scanlon would survive the war, but had been wounded too badly to resume his boxing career. He and Gene Bullard would ultimately have adventures together in not one but two world wars.

Far too many of these brave Americans who volunteered with the French Foreign Legion did not survive the war, but among those who did, they formed a proud fraternity. One of the prime factors in naming the vast and powerful veterans group that became the American Legion was the debt of honor it owed to the French Foreign Legion. In many instances, later in life, when one man was "down," the others lifted him up. Bullard would become both a recipient of largesse and benefactor to others of his Legion mates.

5

DEATH IN THE TRENCHES

After his initial training following his October 9 enlistment, Bullard was not assigned to join the first cadre (Class of '14) of American volunteers but to the 3rd Marching Regiment, bivouacked at the Tourelles Barracks on Avenue Gambetta in Paris.[7] He described the experience there as five weeks of hell. The coarsely woven white fatigues issued to all trainees were rough on the skin and quickly became heavy when soaked with sweat—as all the men were, every day. The *nouvelles* ("new men" as opposed to the veterans, called *anciens)* were up before dawn, when they were required to clean up and do their calisthenics. There was no breakfast, just a cup of strong coffee. Work details and more physical exercises lasted until 10:00 a.m., then they were given a hearty breakfast of bread, cheese, fruit, vegetables—and a cup of wine.

---

7   The Yankees who joined before him were already far ahead in their training and were assigned to the 2nd Marching Regiment.

Long forced marches with heavy knapsacks dominated the initial regimen, followed by issuance of their personal rifles, target practice, first aid, pitching of tents, and crawling under live machine-gun fire. Last but not least was the ominous digging of trenches. The recruits practiced maniacal charges across grounds strewn with obstacles and barbed wire after which they bayoneted hay-filled dummies meant to mimic their German opponents.

Halfway through the regiment's training, Bullard's sergeant pulled him aside and informed him that he had been picked to be one of the unit's machine gunners. The sergeant had been impressed with Bullard's stamina and his excellent physical conditioning. As a "reward," he would get the heavy machine gun to lug around assisted by two teammates, Janus and Mike. One would carry the hefty ammunition belts and the second man would help set up the gun and be the runner, going after replacement ammo when needed.

The staggering losses already being racked up in a war barely four months old accelerated the training of the 3rd Marching Regiment. Their instruction period (which was minimal, at best, by Foreign Legion standards) ended when orders came down to move out to the front by November 28. With "La Marseillaise" blaring, Bullard's regiment marched smartly from the Tourelles Barracks to the cheers of the locals, and headed directly for the front being established along the Somme River. It took over two weeks of slogging in wet and windy weather, but Bullard and his companions finally arrived in the vicinity of Frise on December 15.

The 3rd was part of the Moroccan Division, and as soon as they arrived, Bullard's company was shoved pell-mell into the trenches. It was an unholy shock. The neat, dry, sandy, well-carved, zigzagging cuts of the training grounds were nothing like what greeted Bullard and his confreres. They stumbled into a cesspool of swirling mud, filth, garbage, rats, and the macabre sight of bloody bits of uniform cloth clinging to human bones sticking out of the walls of the trenches. If that wasn't bad enough, the stench was overpowering: a combination of urine, feces, and the odor of rotting meat.

The tableau of horror had barely sunk in when screaming German shells caused every soldier to dive into the stinking morass and burrow into any crevice that could be found. Within moments of their arrival, the new men were covered with the same mud, garbage, and stink as the men they were replacing. Nineteen-year-old Eugene Bullard, recently a carefree young man-about-town in one of the most beautiful cities in the world, had arrived at Hell's front door.

Bullard and the 3rd Marching Regiment first groped with the horrors of war at Frise, then were transferred successively to Dampierre, Harquest-en-Santarre, and Notre Dame de Lorette, all positions along the Somme River. Their movements took up the period from December 1914 to April 1915. The great and notorious Battle of the Somme, which would hungrily devour over a million men as casualties, was still two years away, but the combat Bullard experienced at this early point in the war was chilling enough.

He told the tale, as one of these early battles was about to commence, of a new lieutenant who joined the company directly from St. Cyr.[8] He was the very epitome of the "*beaux sabreur*": his uniform was clean and pressed, his boots polished, his sword shiny and sharp. He carried a whistle on a chain around his neck and when Le Capitaine directed, he took his men boldly over the top of the trench and charged

---

8   St. Cyr, established in 1802, is the French equivalent of West Point in the
    United States or Sandhurst in Great Britain.

the German lines a half mile away, across no-man's-land. When the charge failed, as most did, the brave lieutenant, incredibly, was still alive and he fell back, with the surviving members of his platoon, to the safety of their trench. He had led twenty men out; only eleven returned. It had taken him less than fifteen minutes to lose half his command. He sank into a stinking, muddy hole and wept.

Bullard, too, was shaken by the carnage. As the battles continued to rage around them, the survivors hunkered down, puking in the mud or smoking quietly, filth-covered and unrecognizable. One of his early platoon mates, a Frenchman sheltering ten feet away, was hit squarely by a 77mm shell. In the blink of an eye, the man was completely obliterated. There was nothing left except bits of cloth fluttering down to the ground on a cloud of pink mist. It was as if the man had never existed; and, for his family and friends, he was gone without a trace.

The firing from the Germans was once so intense that Bullard dove into a shell crater. His body slammed into three other soldiers seeking shelter. One of them, George, was the youngest man in the regiment, only seventeen. He had lied about his age and gotten away with it.

George tapped Bullard on the shoulder and shouted above the din, "Sparrow! My friend, my stomach hurts."

Bullard twisted in the muck to see where his friend might have been wounded. George was holding his arm across his midsection. Bullard pried the arm away. George had no midsection: there was only a gaping, seeping hole where his guts should have been.

"Am I going to die, Sparrow?" an ashen-faced George said, pleading for an answer.

"No, you are going to be just fine," Bullard lied. "We'll

get you back to the aid station. Just hold on until the shelling stops."

Thus reassured, George smiled and murmured, "Bless you, Sparrow. You are such a good friend." George's head slowly fell onto Bullard's shoulder and his teenaged fellow Legionnaire was gone.

Under this kind of stress men did strange things. After yet another unsuccessful charge and retreat, a Turkish volunteer named Nedim leaped back atop the parapet and started shouting curses at the Germans, wildly shaking his fist at them. A Portuguese private by the name of Vesconsoledose shouted at Nedim to get down. Nedim raged on as German snipers tried to pick him off. Vesconsoledose jumped up and grabbed Nedim by the collar. As he did so, a Mauser slug slammed into the right side of his head, splitting his skull in half. The Portuguese slid to the bottom of the trench, dragging Nedim with him in a death grip. The Turk tore Vesconsoledose's hand from his collar, got up, and walked away muttering.

Almost every French charge toward the Germans was followed by a response from the Boche. The sergeant would shout for the men to get ready. Sure enough, they would come. This was the signal for Bullard and his machine-gun team to swing into action. When the French charged, the machine gun was too much weight to lug across the battlefield, so Bullard carried only his carbine. When the Germans repaid the favor, he and his crew retrieved their machine gun and set it up on the rim of their trench. Bullard aimed and fired, Janus fed the belts into the gun, and Mike ran back and forth, securing new ammunition. The Hotchkiss chattered in bursts, as Bullard had been taught, so as not to overheat the gun. The Germans fell in clumps. He could see the blood squirting from their bodies as he mowed them down.

The dance of death became the routine played out day after

day, as each side sought some small advantage. The trenches writhed forward and back, like giant snakes, wriggling across a mud-caked landscape, but neither side gained any significant ground. It soon became clear to the Poilus who were doing the dying that their generals were idiots and that the war was all about who would have the last man standing. It also became clear that this "grand adventure" was not going to be over by Christmas.

But, on Christmas Day 1914, something very strange did occur. Amidst all the carnage, the spontaneous singing of Christmas carols broke out on both sides of "no-man's-land." Before anyone really understood what was happening, small white flags fluttered above miles and miles of trenches. Cautiously at first, then by the thousands, then by tens of thousands, men on both sides crawled out of their holes to greet one another. Some even exchanged small gifts, cigars, cigarettes, candy, and chocolate. Men who had been ripping each other apart the previous day were warmly shaking hands. A strange peace settled across the war-torn lines. Bodies of friends and foes alike were finally treated with respect and many who had been dead for days or weeks were laid to rest respectfully at last.

The strange cease-fire became known as the "Great Christmas Truce of 1914." The generals on both sides were appalled and forbade this sort of fraternizing from ever happening again—and it didn't. There were scattered burial parties and brief cease-fires at Christmas in 1915, but nothing like the widespread goodwill gesture of 1914. By 1916, the animosity on both sides and the utter brutality of the war had quashed any holiday humanitarian initiatives for good.

Despite the slaughter and the horrors he witnessed, Bullard was fond of the camaraderie he experienced during his time with the 3rd Marching Regiment. In a very real way, his service in the 3rd granted him another kind of racial harmony, as he had found in Paris after his long sojourn to get to France. He was treated no different in the 3rd than any other man, no matter the race, religion, or nationality of any Foreign Legion member.

The regiment consisted mainly of Belgians, Italians, Greeks, Russians, and, of course, Frenchmen. There were, perhaps, two dozen blacks, mostly American. Jews mixed with Muslims, Catholics with Protestants, atheists with agnostics. The officers came mostly from the Paris police or the Sapeurs-Pompiers (Fire Brigades). The noncommissioned officers, the corporals and the sergeants, were generally men with previous military experience, most of them hard-bitten current or former Legionnaires.

Bullard served with farmers, butchers, firemen, policemen, barbers, bakers, and shopkeepers. He also soldiered with some American idealists who felt the United States should be engaged in the conflict. Kenneth Weeks, an engineer who had graduated from MIT, was one who felt that way. There was a Harvard-educated journalist by the name of Henry W. Farnsworth; Russell Kelley, the son of a very wealthy Wall Street broker; and Edmond C. Genet, a great-great-grandson of "Citizen Genet," the first French Revolutionary minister to the young United States. All of these idealistic comrades served with Gene and all would be dead, killed in action, by the end of 1917.

Along the Western Front (as it was then being called) in the spring of 1915 the Germans held an arrowhead-shaped salient protruding from a line linking Reims to Amiens. This salient had been formed in late 1914 and by the following April its existence was a severe threat to communications between

Paris and all of northern France. General Joffre, commanding all French forces in that sector, along with British General Douglas Haig, believed the salient to be such an obstacle to their future plans that they determined it must be eliminated. Taking back the salient would also give the allies the advantage of being able to cut crucial German rail routes, thereby striking a paralyzing blow to the Central Powers in the region. That was the grand plan, seen from the perspective of the topographical maps spread across the conference table, where the generals strategized, safely ensconced in their châteaux, far away from the ferocious fire of the battlefield.

Seen from the opposite or "grunt's eye" view, the plan that Joffre and Haig concocted seemed to be a relief from the murderous madness of the trenches. As always, of course, the men doing the dirty work had to be careful about what they wished for. Bullard and his comrades were abruptly yanked out of their purgatory and ordered to a large rest area behind the lines. They were allowed to sleep in canvas tents for several days, on cots with real sheets, which may not sound like much luxury, but compared to the trenches it seemed like a suite at the Ritz in Paris.

The men of the decimated 3rd Regiment were given hot food, clean uniforms and replacement equipment, including, for Bullard and his crew, a brand-spanking-new Hotchkiss. This munificence could mean only one thing to the war-wise Poilus: they were being "fattened" for yet another major offensive and the slaughter that would likely come with it.

The historians would dub the follies that occurred over the next three weeks as the Second Battle of Artois. For Eugene Bullard and the men of the 3rd Regiment, it would be their worst nightmare yet.

The Artois Ridge stretched across a wide plain and in the center was the village of Souchez. The Germans had the advantage of months to set up machine-gun positions, intersecting fields of fire, artillery positions and supporting trenches. In retrospect, it was madness to try to take that salient without additional support, such as the type that could be gained from tanks and aircraft. Sadly for the 3rd, the tank would not be put into action on the Western Front until 1916 and the airplane was, at that time, being used almost exclusively for reconnaissance—not bombing or strafing.

In the spirit of putting their best feet forward, and perhaps to enhance the chances of immediate success, the Foreign Legion's toughest veterans, and all the experienced officers, including the colonel commanding the 3rd, went over the top and across the plain in the first wave. The division commander, Colonel Pein, went down immediately, mortally wounded. The commander of the Moroccan Division, Colonel Gaston Cros, fell dead next. Bullard's regiment stayed behind, at first, as a ready reserve, but the German machine guns slaughtered the best of the Legion in vast swaths, so they, too, were soon tossed into the maelstrom.

The commandants of three of the 3rd's four battalions were dead in minutes. Captain Boutin, leading Bullard's company, was nearly cut in half by a burst from a machine gun, and fell across a strand of barbed wire, hanging there like a carcass at the butcher's shop. The bullets ripped the air all around Bullard, but he kept running forward. He expected to die any second.

The survivors grew fewer and fewer. There were no officers to lead them and precious few sergeants remained to guide them. In small knots and tattered groups the soldiers would surge forward a hundred yards, fall flat to the ground behind their packs, and try to catch a breath, using their knapsacks—and the dead—as shields. In this fashion the Legionnaires methodically moved forward, firing as they went. Somehow, by dusk, they had covered seven miles although they had lost more than half the men who had started the day. Thankfully, the Germans had seen enough and began retreating.

The surviving Legionnaires were jubilant, but not for long. Ironically, they had done too well. Their headlong plunge into the hated salient had outstripped their supply lines. Worse, the replacement battalions that were supposed to be moving up behind the main lines were not ready to step off. The Germans, sensing the hesitation by the French, rallied. Supported by their reserves, they pitched back into battle with the exhausted Frenchmen.

The depleted French regiments gave back nearly half their gains. Only total darkness prevented the counterattack from turning into a rout. Gene and his comrades were furious. They had sacrificed so much only to give a great deal of it back. At roll call that night, fifty-eight men answered up. Bullard's company had started the day with two hundred fifty.

At some point during the day, a piece of shrapnel had smacked into Gene's brow. It was a very minor and glancing blow which did little damage, thank goodness, but like most cuts to the head, it bled profusely. Gene hardly noticed during the melee, but later that evening his comrades pointed out that half his tunic was drenched in blood. A bandage was applied and the seepage stopped. Gene was officially and literally bloodied by the war, and his wound would qualify him for the Wound Medal,[9] the first of many decorations he would acquire.

The savage back-and-back combat raged across the Artois Plain and the village of Souchez all through the months of May and June. Neither side gained any appreciable advantage and the slaughter became a brutal war of attrition. During one

---

9 The Wound Medal is akin to and roughly equivalent to the United States military decoration the Purple Heart.

attack in June, which involved storming what had been designated as Hill 119, the French and German forces met each other face-to-face on the western slope. The hand-to-hand combat was desperate. Bullard swung his overheated rifle like a club, and when it shattered, he used his powerful hands to squeeze necks and gouge at eyes. There were so many men fighting in the German trenches that when some died they remained upright until there was room enough to fall.

All through this terrible time, the Legionnaires battled not only the Boche but sleepless nights, terrible food, constant dirt and filth, trench foot, the stench, and unsanitary conditions beyond the imaginable. Yet they had "fuel." Despite the madness of yet another futile charge across machine gun–swept fields, the Poilus did it over and over again. Was it patriotism? Certainly, to some degree, it was. Was it fear of shame or punishment for refusing orders? Those, too, had to be factors, but many of the men, those who managed to survive, gave credit to their "tafia."

Tafia was a type of cheap, distilled rum that had not been aged. It was mostly made from sugarcane and molasses, but also sometimes from grape skins or raisins. No matter, it was well over 100 proof and so powerful that it temporarily boosted a man's morale and his insanity quotient to a level that was off the scales. Eugene Bullard described many instances when he and his fellow soldiers were issued a generous tot of tafia before a charge. Once downed, a man became bold, loud, a little crazy and able to perform the kinds of suicidal acts that were to become commonplace.

The Foreign Legion soldiers also had an esprit de corps that is reflected in one of Bullard's Hemingway-like recollections: "We were just a big family of fifty-four different nationalities, and we kept growing more diverse as the men were shot down. We all loved each other and lived and died for each other as men should."

In mid-July, the 3rd Marching Regiment was finally pulled off the line for good. It wasn't much of a regiment anymore; in fact, there were barely enough men for a full company. It is remarkable that it existed at all—in just two days in May, for example, the fight for the Artois Ridge resulted in the French Army losing 175,000 men killed, wounded, or missing.

The 3rd was given a valorous unit award for its service, then disbanded, with the remaining Legionnaires integrated into the famed and much more prestigious 1st (Regular) Regiment. Bullard was proud but saddened by the enormous sacrifices the 3rd had made.

As his new regiment rested and reequipped, Bullard's previous life in America came into a renewed and unwanted focus. His father, William Bullard, who was still living in Columbus, Georgia, had somehow discovered where his son was and that he was a Legionnaire. It has never been made clear how the elder Bullard found out what his son was doing and where he was. Perhaps the discovery came via a fight card or a poster that filtered back to Georgia, or it could conceivably have been a clipping from an expat newspaper in London or Paris. In any event, the truth about the nineteen-year-old Gene's whereabouts had finally been revealed to his family back home.

William sent a handwritten letter to Secretary of State Robert Lansing at the US State Department in Washington, DC. In it, he pleaded for his son's release from the Foreign Legion on account of him being "under age." William somehow had the mistaken impression that Gene needed to be twenty to enlist. The note was politely answered by a low-level deputy who sent his reply to Columbus, Ohio, where it had to be rerouted to Columbus, Georgia. William was told the State Department would "look into it."

Undeterred, William sent a second letter, this time typed by a local lawyer he had hired, accompanied by proof of Gene's birth date and a picture of the young boy. This time, the letter got to the desk of Lansing himself, who passed it on to William Sharp, the American Ambassador in Paris. Since there was no bar to Gene having enlisted in the Foreign Legion at age nineteen, the matter seems to have been dropped at that point.

For Eugene Bullard, already a grizzled veteran of war, there was no going back. There was only the future, as short as that might turn out to be. For his father, there was only the wondering if he would ever hear from his "lucky" seventh child again.

Gene Bullard mentions this incident in his personal autobiography, but what he does not tell us is whether he responded to his father or to the State Department. Our sense of it is that he preferred to leave his past in the past and move on.

6

THE BLACK SWALLOW OF DEATH

The ebb and flow of battles and the decimation of units continued for the balance of 1915. On October 9, Eugene Bullard celebrated his twentieth birthday. The Legion Marching Regiments had been so badly cut up that it was decided that reconstituting them made no sense. At this juncture, Bullard and all the other Americans in the Foreign Legion were offered a choice: they could stay with the Legion, within the single Moroccan Division remaining; transfer to the North African units that had been left behind;[10] or they could transfer to a regular French line regiment, the 170th Infantry.

Only a handful of the Americans opted for Africa—these men would still have to complete their five-year obligations but at least they would be out of the trenches. About fifty of

---

10 The North African regiments left behind in Algeria and Morocco consisted mostly of Austrians and Germans; therefore, a loyalty risk. The French high command thought it prudent to leave them in place.

the Americans opted to stay with the Moroccan Division. Bullard and about three dozen others decided to transfer to the 170th Infantry Regiment, a storied unit of great reputation and numerous heroic deeds. The soldiers of the 170th had fought alongside the Legionnaires in many of the battles of the last year and a half. With a ceremony and a parade, Bullard and his comrades transferred to the 170th in November and traded their Legion khakis for French Army blue.

The Boche knew the 170th well, having fought against them on numerous occasions. The Germans had even given the regiment its nickname: "The Swallows of Death." In German folklore, the swallow has a significant place in death rituals; thus, the sobriquet. Once Bullard became a member of the 170th, he was instantly dubbed the "Black Swallow of Death," a little twist on ethnic humor, perhaps, but also recognition for his fearlessness in battle.

Bullard was beginning to amass what would become an impressive array of military awards and decorations. For his service in the 3rd Marching Regiment, he earned a four-ragère, which is a distinctive military cord worn on the left shoulder of the uniform tunic. He had the Wound Medal, as previously noted, and the Volunteer Medal. He was promoted to Soldier First Class, a rank just above the very bottom rank of Soldier Second Class, and just under the rank of corporal.

From November 1915 through the following February, the 170th conducted training maneuvers in the area of Somme-Py (today: Somme-Tahure), a region in the Department of the Marne in northeastern France. The ranks were beefed up with replacements and new equipment was distributed. Decent food was available and there was a daily ration of local red wine. For a brief period, Bullard and his brethren could set aside the horrors of war, but they all knew it was only a matter of time until the next call to the front was sounded.

That call arrived on February 20, 1916. The men were told to pack up and move out. The 170th was marched to the local train station and loaded aboard a long string of rail cars. The men were amused that, for once, they weren't marching to their next destination, but when they heard where they were going, the mood became somber. The train's ultimate destination was Verdun.

The Battle of Verdun was almost beyond comprehension in terms of its scope and the casualties it generated. The struggle lasted a grinding eleven months, not ending until December 1916. It was one of the costliest battles in human history, tallying an estimated seventy thousand dead or wounded a month, almost equally divided on both sides.

The Central Powers strategy, as expressed by the chief of the German General Staff, General Erik von Falkenhayn, was to "bleed the French white." Falkenhayn believed that his troops could outgun, outfight, and outlast the French. The Germans massed thousands of artillery pieces on the heights surrounding Verdun, directly opposite France's main battlement, a pentagonal-shaped escarpment known as Fort Duaumont. The artillery fired over a million shells at the French in the first ten hours of the battle.

For the French, and their commander, General Philippe Pétain, the issue was not only strategic, but a matter of national pride. As mentioned previously, the Franco-Prussian War of 1870-71 had dealt the overconfident French a crushing defeat. In a few short months, Napoleon III had been captured and the Germans marched into Paris. The French Army could not—would not—allow itself to suffer another humiliation like that at the hands of the Germans. Besides, a defeat at Verdun would practically guarantee an open road for the Boche to take Paris again, and then gobble up the rest of the country. For the French, this was unimaginable and totally unacceptable, at any price.

As a result, a seemingly unstoppable force met a stubbornly immovable object. The German guns pounded everything. They obliterated the forests surrounding Verdun, they churned the ground into slippery, oozing pools of clay, they killed tens of thousands of French soldiers, and they drove thousands of others stark raving mad.

They didn't destroy everything, however. What the Germans failed to understand was that even tossing millions of shells at your opponent was like using a sledgehammer to swat a fly. The fly was more nimble, so the Poilus survived, many by leaping into shell craters that were still smoking because the likelihood of another shell falling into the exact same spot was low...or, at least, not very likely.

When the German guns stopped firing, the infantry came charging, only to be mowed down by the efficient French 75mm howitzers and thousands of machine guns, like Bullard's. As soon as a French regiment lost 50 percent of its men, it was withdrawn and a new regiment was sent to take its place, bringing renewed firepower. All in all, the ensuing cycle of death was utter madness.

Into this cauldron of fury marched the valiant 170th Infantry, including a machine-gun company commanded by a well-liked officer and ex-fire battalion chief named Captain René Paleologue. The company's ranks included its newest corporal, Eugene Bullard, having been promoted again, and his machine-gun crew of two. The unit was posted in the village of Vaux, on the very front lines, and less than two kilometers from the heavily besieged Fort Duaumont. The 170th was replacing the decimated 42nd and the "Swallows" came up with the 174th which was to replace the 44th. It was February 23, 1916.

The trenches at this section of the line, unlike any Bullard had seen before, were actually made of stone and interconnected, which allowed the linking of dozens of regiments at one time. These masonry works had another distinct advantage: a lack of the loathsome muck. The task of both the 170th and the 174th was simple: hold. They did—for nine straight days of unremitting bombardment, charges, counter charges, and for the first time in Gene's experience, poison gas shells.

On March 1, Bullard's company was ordered back to Vaux to restock their ammunition and exchange their fouled machine-gun barrels for new ones. They were able to grab a hot meal, fresh bread, a bath, and a cot. The following morning, they were to return to the trenches, but along the route they came under fire from the incessant German artillery. The entire company scattered, seeking any shelter available. Twenty, including Bullard, ran into the remains of a large old barn. Bullard grabbed an abandoned mattress and threw himself on the floor, on his back, and pulled the mattress over his body. Moments later, a shell smashed into the roof and exploded on impact, sending red-hot pieces of shrapnel flying everywhere. Four men were killed instantly and another eleven wounded, including Bullard.

A small piece of the shell tore through the mattress and the flat side of the projectile remnant smashed into Bullard's jaw like a sledgehammer. The force of the impact knocked out many of the teeth on the right side of his mouth, top and bottom. Had the mattress not absorbed some of the impact, the wound would likely have been fatal.

Blood streaming from his mouth, and spitting out teeth, Bullard leaped up to see what had happened to his men. The scene was horrific. His lieutenant was missing, one man saying the frightened officer had run away. Despite his tremendous pain, Bullard raced off to get help. His captain was with the regimental commandant at their headquarters a few blocks away. Dodging the screaming shells and trying not to swallow blood, Bullard made his way there. As he dove for the front entrance, another shell exploded nearby which lifted him off his feet and tossed him into the conference room. It was a dramatic but very unceremonious entrance. Through swollen and bleeding gums and jagged remnants of his teeth, Bullard managed to relate the story of his men's plight—and that of the missing lieutenant.

Captain Paleologue and Bullard rushed back to the smoldering barn, along with some stretcher bearers and medical aides to help the wounded. When they arrived the "missing" lieutenant had reappeared. The captain exploded in anger at the shirking young officer, accusing him of cowardice and abandoning his post. Paleologue drew his revolver and aimed it at the lieutenant's head. He had every right to execute the man on the spot, as was French Army policy for desertion. Only Bullard's firm grip on the captain's arm kept him from firing.

The moment passed, and Paleologue stood down, actually thanking the wounded corporal for preventing the execution. The captain ordered the shell-shocked lieutenant to the rear, out of his sight, and out of the war.

For the next two days, the regiment was allowed to stand down, but on March 5 they were ordered up and into the line once more, nearer still to the massive fort. The shelling began again. Regiments charged and countercharged. Bullard's mouth had been sewn back together and bits of the shattered teeth that remained were removed. He was in great pain and his entire face was swollen up like a balloon, but he was not going to let his comrades down. The tafia flowed freely, easing his discomfort. Bullard and his crew fought like demons until the machine gun became so fouled it was useless. The crew buried it in the mud and began to make their way back to get a new one.

As they dodged across the exploding landscape, Bullard heard one of the shells overhead mocking him. To him, it seemed to be calling, in a high-pitched whine, "Gene...een... een!" He swerved to his right and threw himself into a very deep shell hole. As he slid to the bottom, another figure jumped into the same hole. The man was not wearing French blue but German gray—and he was huge!

French machine gunners carried a short carbine as a backup weapon. It was longer than a pistol but shorter than a rifle. Without hesitation, or a word, Bullard shoved the carbine into the man's back and fired, killing the German instantly. The man continued to roll down, landing on him. Wide dead eyes and a gaping mouth spooked Bullard.

He later recalled that "if anyone had seen me come out of that shell hole, he would have not recognized me because I was white. As soon as I was out of the hole, I began to feel kind of bad about having to kill even a Boche. You see, in spite of all the things I have been credited with doing in war and the medals I received for them, I must admit sincerely that I love people. I never in my life wanted to kill anyone. I only wanted to keep someone from killing me."

Later that night, Bullard's captain asked him to take on a very dangerous mission: the company was again in desperate need of resupply, for both food and ammunition. Despite his painful mouth, Bullard agreed. He took thirteen men and off they went, half a mile to the rear. The men zigzagged between shells and machine-gun fire the entire way, out and back. Only three of the fourteen returned unscathed. Five were killed. Bullard lugged a heavy ammunition crate and

critical messages from the colonel for his captain. For leading
the mission, and his bravery, Bullard's captain recommended
him for the Croix de Guerre.

The next day, as he was scampering through a trench,
more shells came raining down. One landed very close by,
and the force of the blast threw Bullard against a trench wall
and knocked him unconscious. A hot sliver from the shell
ripped into his left thigh, opening a gaping and nasty wound.
The shrapnel had missed, by a millimeter, the femoral artery
which, if severed, would have been Bullard's death blow. He
was quickly found by his comrades and crudely bandaged,
but he could not be evacuated until the next morning. The
Red Cross came up and loaded his moaning form into a Ford
ambulance and drove him to a treatment area.

After his thigh was sutured with more than ninety stitches,
clean dressings were applied and a French Army doctor made
the determination that between his leg and his facial damage, the trench war was over for Eugene Bullard. On March
7, he and hundreds of other wounded troops were loaded
aboard a Red Cross train and the entourage chugged away
to the south. Bullard, still groggy from pain medications,
was not sure where they were going, but if it was away from
the trenches, and he was still alive, he would be fine with it.

The slow-moving train wound its way through the French
countryside. After a day, the sounds of the artillery finally
faded. The men who were conscious began to see the unfamiliar sight of green trees and fields of grain and grape vines.
At each stop, women and young girls swarmed aboard the
cars passing out candy, sweets, cognac, wine, cheese, fresh
bread and other treats, while cheering on the men. Nurses
changed bandages. Porters and trainmen discreetly removed

any soldiers who had died since the last stop and buried them in quiet country cemeteries near the tracks.

The train's final destination, after three days of travel, turned out to be Lyon. Bullard was billeted on an airy ward in the Hotel Dieu, a large, castle-like building that had been converted from tourist lodgings into a military hospital. Imagine his shock: after months under conditions that could only have been described as hellish, Bullard had sunshine, fresh air, open windows, and clean white sheets to sleep on.

He would spend three months at the Hotel Dieu, having his thigh wound treated and undergoing extensive reconstructive surgery to replace his missing teeth. Life was beginning to look up again for the brave, young soldier.

It got even better: at the end of the first three months of his rehabilitation, Bullard was picked, as one of only thirty-two recovering veterans, to be sent to a private clinic funded by a Madame Nesmes, the heiress to a family of wealthy silk and fabric makers in Lyon.

He would spend another three months at the Nesmes-funded clinic. These weeks would be a turning point in Bullard's life. First and foremost, the excellent care, country air, good food, and a pair of sturdy crutches would allow Bullard to regain his health, his strength, and his mobility. The one-mile walk from the Nesmes Clinic to the hospital, where he received most of his treatments and his dental surgery, would be undertaken nearly every day. Many of the good citizens of Lyon got to know the determined, smiling, crutch-wielding black soldier as he made his rounds.

He was a bit of an anomaly, and his cheeriness and distinctive countenance—plus the fact he was an American—got him invited into many a drawing room for tea and conversation. When the citizens learned during the summer that

Bullard was to be decorated with the Croix de Guerre for his bravery at Verdun, he became even more of a celebrity.

The notoriety brought him to the attention of the American Consul in Lyon at the time, Dr. John Edward Jones, who happened to be a fellow Georgian. The consul even paid Bullard a visit at the Nesmes Clinic. Along for the meeting was a journalist by the name of Will Irwin who, at the time, was a war correspondent for the *Saturday Evening Post* magazine. The interviews he conducted, followed by more meetings at the consul's office to discuss the war, resulted in several mentions of Eugene Bullard and his wartime experiences in the *Post*. The pieces were widely read back in the United States, but because of wartime security restrictions, Bullard was never fully identified other than as "Private Gene" or "Private So-and-So of the 170th Regiment." Irwin did profile him as "a negroe," but that fact ended up on the editing floor of the *Post*.

On Bastille Day, July 14, 1916, a decoration ceremony was held in Lyon's grand town square. Corporal Eugene Bullard sat with his fellow wounded warriors in the front row of those to be honored with some of France's highest military decorations. Bullard was pinned with the Croix de Guerre amid rousing speeches and wild acclaim from the thousands of citizens gathered for the occasion. It was a proud moment for a black man not quite twenty-one years old, far from home, and recognition he never could have received had he been on American soil.

Among the others to be honored was an officer Bullard had gotten to know while they both convalesced at Madame Nesmes's Clinic. Air Commandant[11] Ferrolino, wounded seriously in the right shoulder, was receiving the Medaille Militaire for his bravery in aerial combat. Prior to that day, he and Bullard had been discussing what they would be doing after

---

11   A French Air Force rank equal to the US Army's rank of major.

their recoveries were complete. The commandant was going back to his squadron, then stationed in Brun. Bullard wanted to go back to the 170th, but the doctors told him he was no longer fit for—and would not be permitted to go into—the trenches where his old regiment was still serving.

Commandant Ferrolino mentioned that the Air Service was in need of aerial machine gunners. Bullard's leg wound would not be a hindrance to machine gunning from the back seat of an airplane. Would he be interested? Bullard was determined not to be posted to a backwater desk among those called *embusqués*, or "slackers," men desperately trying to avoid front line duties. Ferrolino told Bullard that, when the time came for him to be released from the hospital, he would seek a transfer to aviation for him. Brave men, decorated men, would always be welcome in the Air Service, Ferrolino encouraged. Bullard was thrilled with the prospect.

During this same period, he and the other convalescents could avail themselves of a few perquisites of their service and their status as wounded heroes. A Poilus's pay at that time was a paltry single franc (about fifty cents) per day—barely enough to survive on, never mind sufficient for having a little fun. Hero soldiers were given cards good for free train fares, and many private citizens "adopted" soldiers, or sometimes several soldiers, which meant that they could eat and drink at the expense of their patrons. Corporal Bullard requested, and received, several passes to journey from Lyon to Paris on weekends. There he enjoyed his old haunts and joined friends and others who had survived the war so far.

Bullard's closest circle of friends in Paris in 1916 included Moise Kisling, an ex-patriate Polish painter with whom he had served in the Foreign Legion; Gilbert White, an American painter and former student of James McNeil Whistler; and Jeff Dickson, recently arrived from Natchez, Mississippi, with aspirations to become a boxing promoter. It would have been hard to find a quartet more unique, and least likely to succeed as close friends; yet, somehow, they did.

The twenty-six-year-old Kisling had been born in Cracow, then part of Austria-Hungary, today part of Poland. He was raised in a Jewish family of modest means. As a young child, his extraordinary skill at drawing got noticed and at fifteen he was able to enroll in the Cracow Academy of Fine Arts. His principal professor, Jozef Pankiewicz, felt Kisling's enormous potential would best be served in Paris, then the hub of the painting universe.

In 1910, Kisling arrived in Paris with letters of recommendation from Pankiewicz. A friend of Pankiewicz was able to get Kisling a sponsorship from a wealthy Russian patron which afforded him one hundred fifty francs a month. Not having to "starve" as was common among many of the Parisian artists of the day, Kisling had more freedom to paint, exhibit, and spend time in the cafés of Montmartre and Montparnasse. In those bars, he met and caroused with Henri Matisse, Pablo Picasso, Max Jacob, Juan Gris, Kees van Dongen, and many other rising artistic stars.

In the summer of 1911, Kisling accepted an invitation from Picasso to join him, and several other artists, at a rambling artist's conclave outside Paris called "Ceret in the Pyrenees." Ceret was host to artist studios and spaces where Cubism, Fauvism, and Impressionism were being developed. Picasso had a huge studio and it served several of his artist pals, including Kisling, who stayed for about a year.

Kisling missed Paris, however, so he decided to return in 1912 and he rented a spacious apartment and studio atop 3 rue Joseph Bara. The windows were high and wide and allowed the space to absorb the beautiful light that danced across the rooftops of Paris. Kisling would live in this apartment for the next twenty-seven years. Neighbors included Modigliani and Jules Pascin. The local boulevards and cafés seethed with artistic life.

Maybe life "seethed" a bit too much: on June 12, 1914, Kisling and his fellow Polish artist Leopold Gottlieb fought a duel precipitated by a "breach of honor" between the two men (reportedly over a young woman). The duel was seconded by the Mexican artist Diego Rivera, so the fight had a good pedigree, indeed. The duelists paced off in front of a crowd of reporters and onlookers in a field outside of Paris. Neither one of the antagonists was a good shot, apparently, and the first rounds missed. Eventually, after a series of reloads, each man slightly wounded the other. Honor thus satisfied, the two painters shook hands and repaired to a Montparnasse café for drinks.

When World War I commenced, Kisling, like Bullard, wanted to fight for his adopted country, and his only choice was the Foreign Legion. The Jew from Cracow met the boxer from Columbus, Georgia, during their rigorous training together in the 3rd Marching Regiment. Kisling was gravely wounded in the chest during the Battle of Carrency in May 1915. He was pronounced "untreatable" by the harried doctors at the front and sorted out from the wounded and placed with the soon-to-be-dead. Defying the odds, he began to slowly recover. He spent months in a hospital but made a miraculous and full recovery. He was, however, invalided out of the army and awarded full French citizenship and a small pension. By early 1916, he had returned to his bright, airy studio apartment and was happily accepting visitors, especially friends such as his old Legion pal, Gene Bullard.

Jefferson Davis Dickson Jr., then only twenty, sported a great moniker if you were from Mississippi, the home state of your namesake, the president of the ill-fated Confederate States of America. Jeff Dickson grew up in a prosperous postbellum family from Natchez. As a young man, he gravitated to the sport of boxing, even giving it a go himself for a while. He soon determined, however, that promoting fights was much more conducive to a healthy and lucrative life than standing inside the ring.

Hoping to make a name for himself in boxing promotion, he headed for France, fell in love with the country, just as his fellow Southerner Gene Bullard, and elected to stay. Dickson got to meet Bullard through following his matches and he made a pitch to become his promoter just before the war intervened. Bullard introduced Dickson to his comrade from the Foreign Legion, Moise Kisling.[12]

Gilbert White was, at thirty-eight, considerably older than the others in the group. He was a member of Kisling's circle of painter friends. He had come to Paris to study under the renowned James McNeill Whistler. White had been exhibiting his paintings, mostly murals, at the annual Paris exhibitions since 1903. Born in Grand Rapids, Michigan, White had migrated to the East to study art at Columbia University before landing in Paris and Whistler's studio.[13]

A poor black kid who had gotten only through second

---

12   When America finally entered the war, Dickson, still in Paris, volunteered for the Signal Corps. He served as a sergeant in a photo section for the balance of the conflict. After the war, he remained in Paris, promoting fights. He did very well, eventually buying the Palais des Sports in Paris. He nurtured many excellent fighters including the heavyweight champion Primo Carnera. He also promoted hockey, bull fighting, wrestling, bike races, and figure skating. He was reportedly once romantically involved with the skating superstar Sonja Henie. When World War II broke out, he volunteered for the Army Air Corps and was commissioned as a captain in intelligence. The bomber crew he was flying with on July 14, 1943, was shot down near Paris and Capt. Dickson perished in the crash.

13   White, like Jeff Dickson, would sign on with the American Army as it landed in France. He served in an infantry unit, with distinction, and was wounded and awarded the Purple Heart. After the war his fame as a muralist soared, and although he worked mostly in France, he was commissioned to produce murals for the state capitols of Kentucky, Oklahoma, and Utah. He became a commander of the Légion d'Honneur and an officer of the Académie Française.

grade; a Polish Jew who painted with Picasso and Matisse; a white, Southern playboy and entrepreneur; and a Midwest muralist with an Ivy League education: this was the dynamic quartet brought together by the promise of Paris and the call to arms of the "war to end all wars."

In early September 1916, the four friends were up to no good, dining and drinking at La Rotonde, where Kisling sometimes worked as a bouncer, when the subject came up of "What's next for you, Gene?" Knowing that he had assurances from Commandant Ferrolino that he could transfer to aviation, he promptly announced that he was going to become a fighter pilot. It is not known if this was the wine upping the ante, or if Bullard had decided on his own to push for more than he had been promised.

Dickson quickly pointed out, "You know, there aren't any Negroes in aviation."

"Sure I do," Bullard responded. "That's why I want to get into it."

As Dickson continued to pooh-pooh the idea, Kisling rallied behind Bullard, arguing that he knew his man better than Dickson did and insisting that he could make good on becoming a pilot. Bullard pointed out to Dickson that he was in France, after all, not Mississippi. Dickson said he would wager $2000 that Bullard would not make it as an aviator. White backed Kisling and Bullard and the trio made plans to formalize the bet.

The four friends met again the next day and Bullard laid $2000 on the table (loaned to him by Kisling and White). Dickson, not wanting to face the stigma of backing down, opened his checkbook and covered the bet. The challenge was on.

Good for his word, Commandant Ferrolino contacted a Colonel Honore Girod, then Inspector General of all French aviation schools, and secured for Bullard a slot in gunnery school and a transfer to aviation. Bullard reported to his initial flight training base at Caz-au-Lac on October 5, 1916. He was in aviation, but only as a gunner trainee, not nearly enough to win the wager. He had yet to figure out how he was going to make the leap to pilot.

Then, as if on cue, a bit of providential lightning struck: on his first full day of training, Bullard ran into an old acquaintance from the Foreign Legion, Edmond Genet. A fellow American who had also transferred from the infantry into aviation, Genet informed Bullard that there was a special squadron, called the Lafayette Escadrille, that consisted solely of American pilots—and they were being paid much more money than regular French pilots. Could this be the connection Bullard needed? With Genet[14] in tow, he went to see the commanding officer of the gunnery school to request a change in status. The gunnery commander agreed to bump Bullard's petition up the chain of command, back to Colonel Girod. In the meantime, Bullard continued his gunnery training.

On November 15, his request was approved, and he secured a set of orders to begin pilot training at the aviation school at Tours.

Corporal Bullard was viewed no differently than any other flight student, black or white. His treatment among his peers was the same as any other man, with one notable exception:

---

14   Genet was actually in the US Navy in 1915, and when he shipped out to France that year, to volunteer for the French, he technically became a "deserter" from the navy. He nonetheless finished his pilot training and when America declared war, he volunteered to transfer to the American Air Service, which he did, joining the American Escadrille (soon redesignated the Lafayette Escadrille) in April 1917. He was shot down and killed by antiaircraft fire on April 17, just days after his transfer. Although other Americans had already died in action, Genet was officially the first American KIA after the US declared war. His status vis-à-vis the US Navy and the US Air Service was simply ignored and he was buried with honor.

his rank. The French Air Service was not inclined, for reasons of Gallic pride, to offer commissions to any of the American pilots. That would not come until later, when the Americans had demonstrated their worth in the air. Even Norman Prince, who helped start the Lafayette Escadrille and had dual citizenship, was not an officer. All the American pilots were initially made "sergeants," with one exception. Gene Bullard, for reasons unknown, but probably related to his race, remained a corporal.

Designation as a pilot in the French Air Service had no hard-and-fast curriculum and really didn't have a specified timeframe in those very early days. There were a succession of hoops to jump through and a trainee would get his aviator's badge only when the instructors and the commanding officer of the training squadron believed the man was ready, or at least a greater threat to the Huns than to his fellow cadets.

Bullard passed through his flight training in an average amount of time; that is, the six months between late November 1916 and May 1917. He began with the aptly named "Penguin." This French flight-training craft, like its namesake, could not fly. It was essentially an aircraft engine attached to the frame of a biplane without wings. The student used this contraption to practice taxiing and ground maneuvers. When he had demonstrated he could putter around the aerodrome successfully, without crashing into something or flipping the Penguin over (which happened when too much torque was applied to the engine), he would then graduate to training in an aircraft with actual wings.

The French used both an early Bleriot model and the Caudron G-3 biplane for advanced flight training. Both of these aircraft were contraptions made from the proverbial "baling wire, fabric, glue, and sturdy sticks." The engines were loud, cranky, and often spit oil and thick black smoke over their student pilots.

The legendary aviation pioneer and aerial ace Rear Admiral Edwin "Ted" Parsons, who trained at Tours about the same time as Eugene Bullard, said this about his days in flight training: "After the Bleriot and the Caudron G-3, nothing with wings could ever cause any misgivings in my heart. When a buzzard [student pilot] tamed these two ships, if he was still alive and not a nervous wreck, he could fly anything."[15]

Bullard successfully wrestled with these wretched flying machines during the unusually frigid winter of 1916-17. Since all of the training planes at that time were single-seat aircraft, instructors could not accompany their charges on their aerial practices. First flights, therefore, were strictly limited to straight-and-level forays down the runway and three feet off the ground. Once these timid attempts were mastered, the instructors added more and more skills until the rookie pilots could actually make turns in the air, fly as high as two thousand feet, find other aerodromes as far as seventy miles from home, and return safely. After mastering these advanced skills, gunnery practice was added to the regimen.

Sometimes student pilots were lucky enough to come under the personal tutelage of veteran combat pilots. Bullard was extremely fortunate to attract the attention of Jean Navarre, one of France's first air aces. It was Navarre who actually sought out Bullard, having seen him box in a bout in Montmartre before the war. The two soon became pals and Navarre took Bullard all around the Paris "beau monde" scene. Navarre was grounded, recuperating from wounds to the head and body suffered in a bad aerial scrap in June 1916, over Ver-

---

15 Edwin C. Parsons, *I Flew With the Lafayette Escadrille* (New York: Arno Press, New York, 1972), 67.

dun. He was happy to "adopt" Bullard and to teach him all the tricks he knew.[16]

As the terrible winter finally broke into spring, Bullard passed his final flight tests and was duly made Pilot Number 6950 in the French Air Service on May 5, 1917. His designation came with a six-day pass, and Bullard could not wait to get to Paris. Sporting a new sky blue French pilot's tunic, gold aviator's wings affixed to the collar, he strolled into Henri's Bar.

The rendezvous was a setup arranged by his friends Kisling and White. The two pals had invited Jeff Dickson to join them for drinks, but Dickson had no idea that Bullard would be attending, thinking he was still off training somewhere. When the newly minted airman strolled in, Dickson nearly fell on the floor. After recovering his senses he realized his wallet was about to be $2,000 lighter. Dickson was stunned, but still a good sport and a straight shooter: he paid off immediately and the foursome went out for a prolonged—and expensive—night on the town. Bullard, who had never had this much money at one time in his life, was proud to pick up the tab.

Word concerning Eugene Bullard's unique accomplishment got around Paris quickly. He was interviewed by his old Lyon acquaintance, Will Irwin, as well as reporters for the Paris edition of the *New York Herald Tribune*. Articles about the "First Black Fighter Pilot" popped up all over Paris...but news of this singular accomplishment was totally ignored back in America.

In becoming a pursuit (fighter) pilot in May 1917, there is absolutely no doubt that Eugene Bullard was the first Ameri-

16 Navarre would become one of France's leading aces of the war, with twelve confirmed victories and fifteen unconfirmed kills. He was aggressive but also reportedly reckless and undisciplined. He died at age twenty-three, in 1919, while practicing a flight intended to fly through the Arc de Triomphe.

can to be so designated, but he was not the only black military pilot in WWI. Perhaps the first black military pilot, although not a fighter pilot, was Ottoman Empire naval lieutenant Ahmet Ali Celikten (1883-1969). Celikten's father was a Turk and his mother a Nigerian. He received his flight training and completed it in November 1916, six months before Bullard; but, his flying in the war, for the Central Powers no less, was restricted to naval missions and flight observation. After WWI, Celikten stayed in the (new) Turkish Navy, retiring as a captain in 1949.

William Robinson Clarke, from Kingston, Jamaica (1895-1981) served as a mechanic in the Royal Flying Corps starting in 1915. In 1916, still rated as a sergeant, he started pilot training and received his pilot's badge on April 26, 1917. He was assigned to a reconnaissance squadron and flew missions over the Western Front until he was shot down and seriously wounded on July 28, 1917. After his convalescence he was returned to duty as a mechanic and never flew again.

Pierre Rejon (1895-1920) from Martinique became France's first black military pilot in December 1917, seven months after Bullard's designation. An exceptional student, he was studying engineering in Paris when the war broke out. Like Bullard, when he first volunteered, he was sent to the infantry, in his case the 33rd Regiment. In 1915 he was promoted to *sous-lieutenant*, and then, in 1917, posted to aviation training at his own request. Between his rating as a fighter pilot and the end of the war, Rejon was shot down three times but paid back the Germans plus one, shooting down four (and damaging eleven others). At the end of the war he was awarded both the French and Belgian Crosses. He left the Air Service immediately after the war and unfortunately died in an aircraft accident in French Guyana shortly thereafter.

Domenico Mondelli (Wolde Selassie) (1886-1974) was born

in Eritrea and flew for Italy in WWI. He was granted his pilot's license on February 20, 1914, and began immediately flying reconnaissance planes in the 7th Recon Squadron, Royal
Italian Army. A year later, he was in command of the 7th
Bombing Squadron but finished the war as a lieutenant colonel and commander of the 242 Infantry. His service was long
and distinguished, retiring as a three-star general in 1968.

Along with Bullard, these were the remarkable first black
men to become combat pilots, and all flew in WWI, twenty
years before the equally remarkable "Red Tails," the famed
Tuskegee Airmen, of WWII.

ACT III
THE PILOT

7

CAPTAINS OF THE SKIES

On April 6, 1917, a month before Eugene Bullard received his wings, America had finally plunged full force into World War I. Once the United States was in it, tens of thousands of African Americans would serve. Several hundred would, for the first time, receive officer's commissions, but none would serve in nonsegregated units and not a single black officer was accepted for flight training nor were any blacks, of any rank, included in the ranks of any American flight unit.

The only press Bullard received in his home country during the war was a very brief piece in *The Crisis*, the magazine of the NAACP: "Eugene Bullard of Columbus, Georgia, twenty-two years of age, volunteered in the French Foreign Legion in 1914. He was twice wounded at Verdun and has the Croix de Guerre, a much coveted decoration for bravery. After six months in the hospital he was enlisted in the Aviation-Corps."[17]

---

17 *The Crisis*, Foreign News, January 15, 1918. The article did not specify but should have stated Bullard was in the French Air Service, not the American Air Service.

News, generally, of Americans in France was strictly controlled for security reasons, but that aside, the very mention of a black man of extremely limited education mastering the skills necessary to be designated a combat pilot, even under a foreign flag, was just too much for the American Expeditionary Force or the War Department to support. Serious arguments were still being waged in the press in the United States about whether Negroes even had the requisite intellectual skills to master the art of flying, such was the tenor of the times.

All this was meaningless to Bullard, however, as he had more immediate concerns. First among them was completing the advanced flight training necessary to be sent to a front-line squadron, and second was surviving the subsequent aerial combat if and when he was assigned.

After his exuberant week in Paris, Bullard was sent to a succession of "finishing schools" for aviation. At Avord, he learned acrobatic flying, which he found difficult but nonetheless great fun. He also made more friends and was even given some leadership responsibility, though he was still a corporal. Among the pilots, rank didn't mean very much. It was skill in the air that counted—and how many "kills" you obtained. Most of the pilots, as already noted, were mere sergeants anyway. Commissioning pilots would only happen for Americans when they began forming their own squadrons within the actual US Army Air Corps later in 1917. The highest rank Bullard would ever attain during his lifetime would be sergeant, and that would not come until another war.

At Avord, he became good friends and bunk mates with James Norman Hall, future co-author of *Mutiny on the Bounty*, but at that time Hall was a former correspondent for *Atlantic Monthly*. He described barracks life among the young pilots:

There is a fine crew in this school, men from all colleges and men who don't know the name of a college. For instance, there are about a half dozen from Harvard, as many from Yale, some from Dartmouth, a few from Amherst, Williams, etc. We have a couple of ex-All-Americans, a Vanderbilt cup racing driver, men sticky with money in the same barracks with others who worked their way over on ships. This democracy is a fine thing in the army and makes better men of all hands. For instance, the corporal of our room is an American, as black as the ace of spades [Bullard], but a mighty white fellow at that. The next two bunks to his are occupied by Princeton men of old Southern families. They talk more like a darky than he does and are best of friends with him. This black brother has been in the Foreign Legion, wounded four times, covered with medals for his bravery in the trenches, and now uses his experiences and knowledge of French for the benefit of our room— Result: the inspecting lieutenant said we had the best looking room in the barrack.[18]

The last stage of advanced flight training was held at Plessis Belleville Field, near Paris, and that's where Bullard was transferred in late July. At that base he would master the finer points of formation flying and responding to the various hand commands and airplane formation signals required for multi-aircraft maneuvers. (There were still no radios for transmitting communications—they would not come for another decade.)

By early August, Bullard believed that he was finally ready, in every respect, for assignment to a front-line squadron. He was not the finest of the pilots, and he knew that, especially

---

18 James N. Hall and Charles B. Nordhoff, *The Lafayette Flying Corps* (Boston: Houghton-Mifflin Co., 1920), vol. 2, 21.

when he compared himself to the most acclaimed, like his friend Navarre; but he also knew he was better than others. A number of the novice aviators kept getting lost or had more than their fair share of mishaps or even crashes—but not Bullard.

However, when those with lesser records of accomplishment or less time in training began bypassing him and moving up to the front, he began to get suspicious. Was there someone with a negative view of him—someone who was holding him back, behind the scenes? Indeed there was, and his name was Dr. Edmund Gros, a figure of great importance in aviation in the early days of the war, and an American who had powerful connections and an abiding prejudice against blacks.

Dr. Gros, born and raised in the Bay Area of California, received his initial medical education at Cooper Medical College in San Francisco followed by advanced instruction at the École de Médicine in Paris. Electing to stay in France, he helped to establish the American Hospital in Paris. Dr. Gros did contribute to the war effort in several positive ways. First, he was instrumental in starting an ambulance corps, populated mostly by Americans, including, at one juncture, Ernest Hemingway. Secondly, he took a leading role in getting young American men into the air as pilots and observers for both the French and the American armed services. He also collected private contributions from wealthy Americans living in Paris to be paid out monthly, as supplemental income, to the American pilots flying for the Lafayette Flying Corps and the Lafayette Escadrille. This would include, begrudgingly, a brand-new American pilot who happened to be black.

When the Americans finally committed to the war in April 1917, Gros was commissioned a major in the US Army, and later promoted to lieutenant colonel. During all this time he continued his valuable work at the American Hospital. His

prejudice, however, which was well-known, placed a permanent asterisk on his record. Sad to say, in this regard, he was
no different in attitude than the US War Department, the US
Army, or the American Air Service.

Dr. Gros was acquainted with a very wealthy young American lawyer, Norman Prince, whose family had a large estate near Paris. Prince, as mentioned earlier, had graduated
from Harvard University in 1908 and Harvard Law School
in 1911, and as soon as the French went to war, he became
determined to start a unit of American men to fly for France.
Prince had obtained one of the very earliest American pilot's
licenses, completing his qualifications in 1911 while at Harvard Law School. Prince had the money and the ability to
recruit potential pilots. Dr. Gros had the connections to the
French government to make it happen.

In April 1916, the Escadrille Americaine was officially
formed. This would be a unit of American pilots flying as
one cohesive outfit, which was Norman Prince's dream. The
French insisted that the squadron had to be under French
command and control, with French ranks, uniforms, and aircraft. The Americans didn't mind: as long as they could be in
the war, fight the Huns, and fly together as Americans, they
would be happy to operate under French rules.

The Germans did mind: since America was still officially
neutral, the German government protested to the US State
Department. As a result, the Escadrille Americaine under-
went a name change to the Lafayette Escadrille.

This new nomenclature overcame German objections, but
it has caused a great deal of confusion over the years. All
Americans who flew under the banner of France were part of
the Lafayette Flying Corps, named, of course, for the Marquis
de Lafayette, a young French aristocrat who became one of the
great heroes of the American War of Independence. As nearly

as can be determined with fragmented records, some 188 of the approximately 209 American pilots trained in France, by the French, flew in combat. Of these men, 63 died—55 were killed in action and eight perished in training accidents. Eleven of the Corps became "aces," that is, pilots who shot down at least five enemy aircraft. All in all, Corps members destroyed 199 enemy planes, and earned numerous Croix de Guerres, Medailles Militaires, and Légions d'Honneur.

Many American pilots who fought in the Great War were reported as members of the Lafayette Escadrille when they were not. Only thirty-eight Americans served with the actual squadron named Lafayette Escadrille during its two-year history. All the other American pilots who were not assigned to the Lafayette Escadrille were scattered throughout other French fighter, bombing, and observation squadrons, but all were veterans of the Lafayette Flying Corps; thus, the confusion.

The new Lafayette squadron would be commanded by a Frenchman, the very capable and skilled Captain George Thenault, and he was supported by a cadre of five additional French officers. The makeup of the Americans who dominated the squadron had some interesting characteristics: twenty-eight were already serving or had served in the French forces, seven of those in the Air Service; twenty-three were from the Eastern states including nine from New York; their average age was twenty-six; eleven were the sons of millionaires; and thirty of them had attended or graduated from college, including nine from Harvard University.

The merry and ambitious band of American and French pilots who constituted the first men of the Lafayette Escadrille began their active pursuit of the enemy and glory on May 13, 1916, during the Battle of Verdun. Five days later, the squadron shot down its first enemy aircraft. The pilots of the Escadrille would go on to fly over three thousand sorties before the unit was disbanded and absorbed into the Army Air Service on February 8, 1918, as the 103rd Aero Squadron. The daring aviators would lose nine of their own killed in action while racking up forty confirmed and one hundred probable kills.

Dozens of books, several movies, and many documentaries have centered on the Lafayette Escadrille, and why not: this famed squadron produced some of the greatest aerial heroes of the war. Their names are etched in legend. Here is a partial roll call:

- Norman Prince, Dr. Gros's partner in establishing the Lafayette Escadrille, was ultimately credited with 122 combat missions and became an ace. Sadly, in bad weather, on October 12, 1916, the undercarriage of his Nieuport caught a telegraph wire as he was landing. The plane crashed on top of Prince, and he died in a French hospital three days later.

- Gervais Raoul Lufbery was a French-born American who first trained as an aircraft mechanic then went into flying himself. Before he was shot down in 1918, he had chalked up seventeen confirmed kills, but his actual total was probably closer to an astonishing sixty. "Kills" were only credited when they were confirmed by another pilot or observer. Since Lufbery did much of his flying as a "lone wolf" he did not get credit for many of his combat engagements. Lufbery was already a legend in the Lafayette Escadrille when he was picked up for transfer to the American Air Service in April 1917. He was promoted to major and put in command of the fledgling 94th Aero Squadron. One of his star pupils was Captain "Eddie" Rickenbacker.

Deathly afraid of dying in a flaming cockpit (which was all too common among the early pilots), Lufbery decided to jump from his burning aircraft after it was hit on May 19, 1918. He intended to fall into the river directly below his crippled plane. The fall was over 250 feet, so survival was still highly unlikely, but he missed anyway, landing on a spiked iron fence. Incidentally, early pilots did not carry parachutes, even though they were available. Using a parachute was considered an act of cowardice, at least until a wiser commanding officer finally figured out that saving a pilot via a parachute was a lot less expensive than training a new pilot to replace a dead one.

- Victor Chapman was another Harvard graduate who answered the siren call to the skies. His story appeared in these pages earlier; so too the story about Kiffin Rockwell.

Among other notable Americans who flew for the American Air Service or the US Navy included:

- Colonel (later Brigadier General) William "Billy" Mitchell was the first American to fly over German lines and as General John Pershing's initial head of American air operations, he was instrumental in getting the Army Air Service up and operating in France.

- Quentin Roosevelt, the youngest child of former President Theodore Roosevelt, was first assigned as a supply officer for the American Air Base at Issoudon. While working in supply, he continued his training as a pilot, something he had begun at Mineola Airfield on Long Island as a member of the 1st Reserve Aero Squadron. He completed pilot training in December 1917, and was posted next June, after advanced training, to the "Kicking Mules" of the 95th Aero Squadron.

His first combat mission was on July 5, 1918. On July 10, he shot down a German fighter. Unfortunately, on July 14, Bastille Day in France, it was his turn to become the victim: Roosevelt was part of a four-plane photo recon mission when they were jumped by seven Fokkers. Roosevelt peeled away to take on the attackers, against the orders of his flight commander, who had signaled for his men to race for home. Three of the Germans surrounded Roosevelt and one of the Fokkers unleashed a burst, two slugs of which hit Roosevelt squarely in the head. He died instantly. His plane spiraled down to crash behind German lines. When the Boche figured out who the young American was—via love letters from his fiancée found in his flight suit—they respectfully buried him where he had crashed and notified the US State Department.

Quentin's father was devastated. Already in poor health from an expedition he had taken to South America, the news of his "favorite child's" death seemed to be a final blow for the old war horse. He, too, was dead within six months. Mineola Airfield, where Quentin had commenced his training, and also near his family's estate in Oyster Bay, was renamed Roosevelt Field in his honor.

• Edward "Eddie" Rickenbacker was a race car driver before the war and he took that "need for speed" right into the air. Posted to France as a sergeant first class and an aviation mechanic, he was soon commissioned as an engineering officer. While conducting his engineering duties he trained as a pilot in his spare time. He won his wings in June 1918. Within thirty days he was an ace—shooting down five enemy planes. By the Armistice that November he was America's top ace, with a total of twenty-six confirmed kills: twenty-one aircraft and five balloons. For his wartime heroics he was awarded the Distinguished Service Cross which was upgraded later, in 1930, into a Medal of Honor bestowed on him by President Herbert Hoover. He was also promoted to major, but he turned it down. Since he had completed his heroics as a captain, during the war, that's what he preferred to remain, and for the rest of his long life, he was always "Captain Eddie."

• Frank Luke was the second-leading scorer in terms of aerial "kills" for the Americans in World War I. The amazing aspect of his record, however, was that he notched his eighteen shoot-downs in a remarkable eight-day, ten-sortie rampage in September 1918, just two months after he had finished his flight training. The twenty-one-year-old son of—somewhat ironically—German émigrés grew up among the dusty copper mines of the Southwest. This "meteor" of an aviator was dubbed the "Arizona Balloon Buster" in that fourteen of his eighteen kills were German observation balloons. Stationary airships might not seem like challenging targets until you consider that they had machine gunners aboard, and they were almost always surrounded by ground-based antiaircraft and numerous machine guns. They were difficult targets to attack and a number of pilots paid the price for underestimating their lethality. Luke was fearless—and some said reckless.

He usually worked with a wingman, but his favorite partner had been shot down and lost on September 18. On September 29, Luke took off alone, going after three balloons that had been reported aloft behind enemy lines. Under a galling fire, and using acrobatic twists and turns, he managed to shoot down all three targets. Ground fire was still dogging him, however. He ducked down behind a row of hills to avoid the persistent antiaircraft gunners.

There was one machine-gun nest he did not see. Because of his treetop skimming, the gunners were actually above him on the crest of a hill. The crew fired down on Luke. One bullet slammed into his right shoulder and passed completely through his body, exiting at his left hip. Somehow, Luke turned on the gunners and strafed them, destroying their position. Mortally wounded, he still managed to land his Nieuport in a nearby open field. German soldiers rushed forward to capture him, but Luke somehow struggled out of his plane and started staggering away. He did not get very far. As he stopped, turned, unholstered his pistol and fired at the soldiers (missing them all), he dropped dead.

Luke's astonishing war record would be capped with a posthumous Medal of Honor, the first of that war granted to an aviator.

• Ernest Bleckley and Harold Goettler, flying as a team, were to gain immortality for a single mission in a DH-4 DeHaviland observation plane from the 50th Aero (Observation) Squadron. On October 6, 1918, the two young lieutenants, Goettler as pilot and Bleckley as observer, finally found the correct position of the famous "Lost Battalion." This unit, a combination of the 307th and 308th Infantry Regiments of the 77th Infantry Division, had gotten surrounded by Germans in the Ardennes Forest and had been pinned down and fending off dozens of attacks for over a week. Refusing to surrender, the brave doughboys fell one by one until the original contingent of five hundred had less than two hundred. Numerous missions had been flown to try to resupply or at least pinpoint the position of the trapped men.

Goettler and Bleckley were the aviators who finally figured it out, but they had to use their aircraft as a "guinea

pig" target, drawing German fire, in order to properly tri-
angulate the lost soldiers. It worked, but at a high price.
When the pair determined the right location, and turned
to speed away, a German machine gun managed to place
the big lumbering DeHaviland squarely in its sights. Goettler was hit in the head and killed instantly. Bleckley, seated
in the rear, had no aircraft controls in his cockpit and could
do nothing to steer the aircraft. Somehow, with a dead
pilot at the controls, the plane flew lazily ahead, slowly
losing altitude, until it floated over the American lines,
where it finally crashed in a field. Bleckley was thrown
from his cockpit and sustained such ghastly internal injuries
that he died in an ambulance on the way to a field hospital.

Luckily, ground personnel found Bleckley's map and
chart coordinates for the Lost Battalion in his crumpled
cockpit. The information was rushed to the rescue forces
who immediately set out to find and relieve the trapped
doughboys. The incredible bravery and determination of
these two aviators would be acknowledged with Medals
of Honor for each of them.

• David Ingalls was the first ace in the history of the US
Navy—and the only navy ace of World War I. Since the
navy did not operate land bases in Europe during the war
(or yet have operating aircraft carriers), pilots designated
for aerial combat were "loaned" to the Royal Air Force.
Ingalls, who had dropped out of Yale in 1916 to join the
Naval Reserve Flying Corps, finished his pilot training
in 1917 and became Naval Aviator #85. In July 1918, he
was assigned to 213 Squadron of the RAF. By the end
of August he had shot down two observation planes, a
reconnaissance aircraft, a Fokker fighter, and a balloon,
thus giving him the five kills required to reach ace status.

Between World Wars I and II, Ingalls dabbled in law,

politics and government, but after the attack on Pearl Harbor in December 1941, he donned his US Navy uniform again. During the war he commanded the Pearl Harbor Naval Station and rose to the rank of rear admiral.

The fighter pilots[19] of the Lafayette Escadrille and the Lafayette Flying Corps initially flew the Nieuport 11, a single-seat fighter. Later, in October 1916, they would transition to the larger Nieuport 17. The Nieuport 11 was nicknamed *Bébé*, or "Baby" in French. The aircraft was almost eight feet tall, with a wingspan of nearly twenty-five feet, and a length of nineteen feet. The entire plane weighed less than eight hundred pounds, empty, with a maximum takeoff weight of twelve hundred pounds. It was powered by a nine-cylinder, air-cooled rotary engine that could crank *Bebe* up to almost one hundred mph. The effective range was about two hundred miles and the plane could fly as high as fifteen thousand feet. Armament consisted of one Lewis or Hotchkiss machine gun mounted above the wing so that the bullets would not interfere with the propeller.

The Nieuport 17 was slightly longer, taller, and wider. It was a bit heavier and could carry two hundred more pounds. It was a bit faster (110 mph) and could fly higher (17,400 feet). Its main advantage, however, was its armament: early versions had a better Lewis gun, one that could be reloaded in flight more easily, and later models had a synchronized Vickers gun that could shoot in conjunction with the pilot's line of sight and through the rotations of the prop. These were significant improvements.

---

19 American pilots who flew for France who were not fighter or pursuit pilots flew a variety of other aircraft. Some planes were strictly for bombing, or observation or scouting. Besides the Nieuport (series) and a few SPADs, perhaps the next most utilized aircraft were the two-man DeHaviland DH-4 bomber/observation planes.

Both Nieuport models were more advanced than their German competition which, early on, was the Fokker Eindecker mono-wing model. The Nieuports had better controls that gave them improved flight characteristics and maneuverability. It wouldn't take long for the Germans to catch up, however, and even surpass the Nieuports with improved Fokkers.

The Nieuports were soon to be replaced by the SPADs, first with a VII model, then the very versatile and popular XIII. The SPADs were bigger, heavier and faster (two hundred–plus mph). They also had water-cooled engines, better maneuverability, and synchronized guns. The XIII, when it was deployed in May 1917, had twin Vickers machine guns with four hundred rounds of ammunition for each. At that moment, the allies and the French had the best fighter aircraft in the skies.

By the time Bullard got to his first squadron, the SPADs were nearly ubiquitous across the Lafayette Flying Corps, and it would be in a SPAD VII that he would at last take to the air against his enemies.

Unfortunately, he had no weapon to use against a more personal enemy. Dr. Gros made sure that Bullard's monthly stipend for American aviation volunteers was always the last one handed out. He also later withheld from Bullard a special certificate of gratitude from the French Ministry of War presented to every American who flew for France. Whenever Bullard's name came up for inclusion, advancement, recognition, or extra compensation, Gros shot him down. He even went so far as to petition the commanders of the French Air Service to block Bullard from serving at the front.

France was so desperate for trained pilots in 1917 that the requests of Dr. Gros were simply ignored. On August 27, Corporal Eugene Bullard was posted to Squadron N-93, at the front. Also along for the ride, tucked safely inside Bullard's flying tunic, was his pet capuchin monkey, Jimmy. Bullard was not exactly sure how he had come to be Jimmy's keeper. It had something to do with a leave in Paris, a night of excessive drinking, some card playing, and some bets. He woke up the next day "master of the monkey." The two were soon bosom companions, however, and Jimmy went on every flight as Bullard's good luck charm.

8

THE GRAND SKY BALLET

A few minutes before 8:00 a.m. on September 8, 1917, Corporal Eugene Bullard climbed into the cockpit of his single-engine SPAD VII. His mechanic had the aircraft warmed up, engine idling, prop spinning. His double-barreled Vickers gun was primed and loaded. Bullard would have four hundred rounds of 7.7mm ammunition to fire at his adversaries—should he encounter any. Viel, the mechanic, was wiping down the windscreen one last time: a few tiny droplets of oil from the two hundred hp, eight-cylinder, Hispano-Suiza radial engine had flicked off and flown backward, toward the cockpit.

Bullard flew a SPAD VII C1, which was about as much aviation state-of-the-art as a rookie pilot could get. One image exists showing his fuselage painted sky blue with a flashy red engine cowling; another shows his SPAD as banana yellow. It could have been either but probably neither, at least at the start of his flying career. Although pilots did have a great deal of leeway in how their aircraft might be decorated, it was only the accomplished pilots, and mainly the aces—like the famous Red Baron—who could demand a solid color scheme. On a practical basis, the ground crews, aircraft painters, and mechanics would not waste a lot of time lavishing wild paint jobs on untested pilots who might fly only one, fateful, career-ending mission.

It is most probable that Bullard's plane was not painted much at all. Most of the aircraft flown by the allies, especially the French and (later) the Americans, had universally buff or light caramel-colored fuselages (thanks to the varnished canvas). The vertical stabilizer (tail) was almost always painted with three vertical stripes: red, white, and blue, the Tricolor of France. Under and above each wing on both sides were painted three large concentric circles, with white most often the center circle, sometimes blue. Individual escadrilles affixed squadron numbers, and squadrons that had "totems" such as dragons, skull-and-bones, etc., would have them pasted onto the sides of the aircraft as well. Camouflage didn't come into play until very late in the war and many pilots eschewed it entirely in favor of their more distinctive personal colors.

Bullard absolutely had one distinctive decoration, and it spoke volumes about his uniqueness as an aviator and as an individual. He always flew with a large red heart painted on each side of his fuselage, right behind the cockpit. The heart bled, pierced by a dagger. Above the heart was stenciled the following: "*Tout Le Sange Qui Coule Est Rouge*"; in English, "All Blood That Flows is Red." Certainly a testament to his courage, but also a firm statement that no matter the skin colors of the pilots, they all shed the same crimson-hued blood. It was a powerful slogan, and one Bullard adored. He would use a variation as the title to his never-published autobiography.

September 8 weather offered up a chilly late summer morning, but that was not the reason Bullard was bundled into his bulky, thickly-padded flying suit. Should the mission go to 2,000 meters (6,500 feet), as was planned, the outside air temperature would approach freezing. Despite the full-throated power of the big engine, it shared no warmth with its human operator because heating and cooling systems for the pilots had not yet been invented. Warm gloves and fur-lined flying boots were required instead, and Bullard had both.

Jimmy, his faithful companion, scrambled aboard, too, wearing a miniature flight suit. He settled into the cramped space at Bullard's feet that the monkey had been trained to occupy while the duo was in the air. As Bullard was about to make history so, too, may have Jimmy, as perhaps the first flying fighter pilot monkey.

Anyone on their first aerial combat mission is decidedly nervous, excited, terrified. Eugene Bullard was all three. In addition, he clearly understood his place in the annals of aviation. He knew, without question, that he was about to become the first African American fighter pilot in history. He would later recall about that ground-breaking mission:

> In three minutes or less the order was given, *"Partez,"* meaning "Go." The chocks were pulled away. And so we did and fast... I sincerely believe that there has never been a pilot aviator who did not have a funny feeling on his first combat patrol and who wasn't really scared the first time that he faced the enemy in the air or who was flying in formation to meet the enemy. I am not ashamed to admit these facts about myself. Why should I be? I am not an angel, nor am I a hero.
>
> Anyhow, I was determined to do all that was in my power to make good, as I knew that the eyes of the world

were watching me as the first Negro military pilot in
the world. I felt the same way... Lindbergh felt when
he was the first to fly from New York to Paris, France.
I had to do or die, and I didn't [want to] die.

The gods of war went easy on Bullard and his mates that
day. The fourteen Nieuports and SPADs, flying in a V formation, wandered over the German lines and flew as far as
Metz, but encountered no opposition. On the return leg,
German antiaircraft gunners lobbed a few shells skyward,
trying to pick off an unlucky plane or two, but all flew on,
untouched. Pressing for home, the flyers passed over Verdun,
that cauldron of insanity.

Shortly thereafter, over Bar-le-Duc, the flight leader, Captain Pinsard, at the apex of the V, made the swallow-tail
maneuver (waggling his plane's tail side to side) that meant
"prepare for battle." All the pilots in the formation fanned
out, giving each plane space, and all began slipping and sliding from one side to another, which was the way they had
been trained to "look around." Bullard followed the rest and
did likewise. Within a few minutes, though, Pinsard gave
the signal (passed by hand sign from one pilot to another) to
reform the V. Once back together the formation returned to
base, all landing safely and without incident.

Only after landing, with all pilots repairing to the club for
lunch, did Bullard learn that the "prepare for battle" maneuver had been preplanned. All the aviators, except the rookie,
were in on it. It was done to gauge Bullard's reaction to a
battle signal, and to see if he really knew what he was doing.
He had passed with flying colors, having done exactly what
he should have, and all the other pilots offered their congrat-
ulations on a first combat flight well done. It was time for

champagne, and lunch. Perhaps two glasses of champagne: after all, the next sortie wasn't for another four hours.

The afternoon mission would prove to be very different from Bullard's morning baptism. Major Minard (commanding the squadron) would lead this flight which would consist of thirty-three SPADs and Nieuports. If opposition was encountered, the formation would break into groups of seven or eight fighters each. Bullard was told by his commander to stick close to him and not get caught up in any fighting except that which he could not possibly avoid.

Minard joked, "We must not lose you too soon, Bullard, or poor Jimmy will be an orphan!"

Almost immediately after takeoff, four big slow German Gotha bombers were spotted, heading for French positions at Bar-le-Duc. They were accompanied by sixteen German fighters, both Eindeckers and Fokkers. Clearly, this would not be a routine patrol. Minard gave the signal to spread out and attack. Bullard did what he had been briefed to do, but discipline would soon be overcome by events.

Soon the gray skies were filled with snarling engines and the nearly constant *rat-tat-tat* of the clanking guns. Even above the roar of his own engine Gene could hear the enemy's bullets ripping the air as they sought out his fragile crate. There were so many targets, so many aircraft competing for smaller and smaller amounts of space, that it became almost impossible to concentrate on one shape—or to even tell friend from foe. Bullard soon lost track of Major Minard and became enveloped in a whirl of men and machines tearing at one another two thousand feet above the ground.

During those first confusing moments, at least some of his commander's cautions penetrated his consciousness: "Don't forget that there are always three ways to be brought down, or, should I say, to lose your life in the air. The most dangerous way is by your adversary. The second is by artillery from the ground. Then there can be a collision. So please watch out for these three dangers. If you must collide with someone in the air, please let it be a German."

Not colliding with someone at that particular time seemed an impossibility. Dozens of aircraft were spinning and diving, slipping and sliding, dancing and juking in a grand, unchoreographed ballet in the sky. Black contrails began to appear, first here, then there. Bullard could hear an engine sputter then die. For a moment, he panicked, thinking it was his own, but it was not. He pressed the triggers of his own guns and felt, for the first time, the buck-buck-buck of the recoil as it jiggered his cockpit. He had no idea who or what he was firing at, but to do nothing in the midst of that violent maelstrom seemed cowardly. If nothing else, he had cleared his guns, assuring himself that they would fire (often, they didn't). He just hoped that he had not hit one of his pals.

Bullard was no coward. Neither were any of the men whirling around him, French or German. To get into one of these early fighters and take off from the ground was an act of great courage in and of itself. The aircraft, on both sides, were painstakingly manufactured, for what they were, but in reality, as these men knew all too well, they were nothing more than steel wire, varnished struts, lacquered canvas, paper-thin fuselages, and bits of rubber and steel slapped together around an extremely volatile gas tank and a big engine spitting oil and fire.

There was no protection for a pilot from machine-gun bullets or any sort of artillery or ground fire. The 7.92mm Spandau bullets used by most German fighter aircraft guns could rip a man apart if several hit a center mass. One bullet to the head would do the job as well. A single round to an arm or leg would be incapacitating. Nothing on an allied aircraft could stop these rounds, except maybe the engine casing, and even four or five hits could wreck that. These early aircraft had no self-sealing gas tanks either, as would be the case in many World War II planes. Pilots who survived the first war stated that even a handful of rounds could bring down an aircraft if they clipped the right wires, hit the fuel tank or shattered a critical wing strut.

Parachutes, as we have stated, were available, but not a single fighter pilot wore one, or even carried one in the cockpit.[20] You fought and survived, or you went down with your ship. A few men walked away from horrific crashes, but not many. Fire was a serious concern. The early aviators were essentially flying in gasoline bombs that could explode at any moment. A number of World War I pilots perished gruesomely, burned alive in their cockpits before their aircraft struck the ground.

During Bullard's afternoon mission, as the aerial combat waxed and waned, time seemed to stand still, though in reality the entire action lasted less than five minutes. The four German bombers were immediately attacked by the speedy, nimble fighters. One French pilot hit a bomber with a lucky shot that set off the ordnance the plane was carrying, producing a spectacular midair blast that obliterated the aircraft and its three-man crew instantly. The other three Gothas were soon on fire and going down. All three crashed behind the allied lines. Two Fokkers spiraled into the ground, exploding, and two French pilots were shot down as well. Once the bombers were eliminated, there wasn't any more purpose to

---

20   These early parachutes worked well, but they were used principally by the balloon pilots. These intrepid aviators were sitting ducks for fixed-wing aircraft and had no ability to escape a burning gas bag except to jump out of it. These men were forgiven the use of parachutes when needed as they really had no choice.

the mission for the surviving German fighters, so they broke off the engagement and sped toward home.

A muted group gathered at the bar after the mission. They had done quite well, shooting down six enemy planes, but they had lost two pilots of their own. A mechanic reported to Bullard that he had expended seventy-eight rounds, and that there were seven bullet holes in the tail of his aircraft, none of which he had felt or even known about during the flight. He had been "bloodied," in a way, and grateful his SPAD had survived his first serious aerial confrontation.

On September 13, Bullard was transferred to squadron N-85 from N-93. There was nothing more to this transfer than an adjustment to balance out replacements and losses. He began flying under the leadership of Captain Armand Pinsard, a leading French ace with seventeen victories (the total would climb to twenty-seven before the war ended). Pinsard took a liking to Bullard, not quite twenty-two years old, and would often have him fly under his tutelage and alongside him as his wingman.[21]

By the end of October, Bullard had flown twenty combat missions. He had been involved in a number of aerial scraps but he had yet to be credited with shooting down an enemy plane. This was not unusual: hundreds of pilots went without a single victory. Partly this was because of the system, if it can be called such, used to credit victories.

One certain way to score an aerial victory was to have the enemy crash land behind your own lines where the wreckage or the remains of the unlucky pilot could be identified, or if the pilot survived, he could certainly tell the tale him-

---

21 Pinsard would become, after the war, Commander of the Legion of Honor and a general in World War II. He would also be accused of cooperating with the Nazis, for which he was tried and convicted, but later pardoned.

self. Second best was to have an eyewitness back up your claim—someone who was in the sky or on the mission with you. A third way to verify a victory was to have it reported by a balloon crew, who often witnessed the aerial battles and, as trained observers, could keep track of who was blowing whom out of the sky. The World War I years were still an era when a man's word was his bond, so to cheat by faking victories was unheard of and ungentlemanly.

If an enemy target was able to fly back behind his own lines before crashing, which happened very frequently, that could not be counted as a kill, because no one knew the ultimate fate of the aircraft or pilot. If a one-on-one dogfight occurred resulting in a victory, that might not count either since there were no eyewitnesses.

Eugene Bullard was a competent pilot but he was not a Lufbery or Rickenbacker. He never missed a roll call or a mission. He slogged faithfully through the air much the way he had done in the trenches. He could be relied upon, and was a trusted companion. The French were lucky to have him and the Americans would have been fortunate to have him as well…but they didn't want him.

The Americans began arriving in France at the end of April 1917. It was one token regiment at first, but soon the ranks swelled to hundreds of thousands, then millions. By October, a call had gone out for any and all American pilots flying for France to join the American Air Service, commanded by Lieutenant Colonel Billy Mitchell.

Colonel Raynal C. Bolling from General Pershing's staff convened an examining board to review potential pilots for transfer from the French escadrilles to the American Air Service. Bullard and twenty-eight of his fellow pilots were the first eager applicants to rush off to Paris. Army physicians would conduct exams, and then each candidate would be further screened by an examining board consisting of four senior army officers.

The doctors didn't quite know what to do with Eugene Bullard. His previous war wounds had healed so well that they no longer presented any obstacles. His excellent physical shape and overall conditioning, thanks to years of hard work in the gym and strenuous boxing, made him a better candidate than some of his "softer" companions. Several doctors, quite naturally, probed with more than their instruments, peppering Bullard with questions: "How did you learn to fly?"

"Where did you get your training?"

"Who let you into the aviation ranks?"

The doctors found no evidence to deny Bullard from passing their physicals. They rated him "fit for duty." They knew full well, however, that it would never happen. Segregation was still the official policy of the United States Army: blacks were not even allowed into aviation units to perform the most menial of tasks, never mind mechanic, gunner, or pilot. The list of twenty-nine candidates was passed to the examining board, and that was where Bullard ran into a familiar roadblock.

Much to his consternation, one of the four board members was none other than his old nemesis, Dr. Gros. Even the racist doctor couldn't come right out and deny Bullard's application, though. It would offend the sensibilities of the French, even if racial exclusion was official United States policy. Instead, the doctor and his fellow board members took a devious but ultimately effective route. It was required, at the time, that all American pilots had to be commissioned officers and rated at least first lieutenants. The other twenty-eight candidates were rated either first lieutenants or captains and commissioned accordingly. The board rated Bullard only as "sergeant material" and he was therefore disqualified.

It was a bitter blow to his hopes and ambitions. It was also reality. Eugene Bullard truly was a hero of France, and he had gained great notoriety in his adopted country. Even so, Dr. Gros wanted him removed from the air completely, such was his animus toward blacks. The Americans could not afford to have Bullard's fame spread to the home front, but neither could they offend their French hosts. On the other hand, the French couldn't make too many demands of the Americans, such as giving Bullard his due, because they needed the doughboy manpower so desperately. As a result, Bullard was stuck in a regulatory and bureaucratic limbo. All parties decided to do nothing more than ignore Bullard's application.

The dejected candidate returned to his French Escadrille, but at least he had been rated "sergeant," a promotion he still hoped to get.[22] He became determined to shoot down as many Germans as he could. If he could somehow become an ace, he believed the Americans—even the devious Dr. Gros—would finally be forced to recognize his abilities and accept his application.

The day after his harrowing brush with death (as chronicled in the Prologue), Bullard, still nursing a champagne headache, was back in the air. It was November 19, 1917. The weather was sketchy, but a few blue patches among the clouds convinced Major Minard that they needed to at least make an effort.

Bullard's small patrol of seven SPADs and Nieuports drifted lazily toward Verdun at an oxygen-poor twelve thousand feet.

---

22 Even this much deserved advancement was not granted: the paperwork seems to have gotten "misplaced."

It was freezing cold and that, plus the slight hypoxia (which pilots were still ignorant about), caused his mind to wander. The planes sailed through small batches of puffy clouds.

As Bullard punched through one large cloud and came out the other side he found himself alone. His patrol had disappeared. He did not panic, though. He began, as trained, a series of slow port and starboard turns along the patrol's flight path. Nothing. Then something, ahead and below.

There they are, he thought to himself. *I wonder why they dropped down?*

The group of seven aircraft were about three thousand feet below him and two miles off to the left. He goosed his plane to catch up.

Wait a second. There are seven planes. I was the seventh!

What Bullard had in his sights were seven Pfalz scout planes, headed for a mission over Verdun. These biplanes were fairly new to the war and a bit faster than Bullard's SPAD, so he'd have to be careful. Dare he attack? He never really hesitated, even with staggeringly bad odds. The image of Dr. Gros was squarely on his mind as much as the German scouts. He figured he might be able to pick off one or two before they really knew what happened, after which he'd duck into the clouds and run for home. For the moment, high above and behind them, he had the advantage.

He crept along the edges of the clouds to get closer, darting in and out of cover. When he was directly above, he pulled back on the throttle and pushed the nose over, hurtling straight down. He fixed the rear-most Pfalz in his sights, hardly able to believe in his good luck—and that he had not yet been spotted.

Fifty yards behind his foe, he squeezed the trigger. And kept squeezing. With morbid satisfaction he watched the bullets steadily stitch the fuselage, from just forward of the tail all the way to the cockpit. Only at the last split second did the unlucky German aviator realize he was under attack. He swiveled in his seat to look around just as a round smashed squarely into his face. If he even saw the bullet, it was the last thing he ever viewed. A pink mist blew into the wind stream and Bullard released the trigger.

The Pfalz pitched straight up until it stalled, did a wing over to the right, then started a corkscrewing spiral straight down, nine thousand feet. Bullard knew he did not have the luxury of watching the ultimate explosion. The other six Germans had realized he was there. He took a shot at one more scout plane that had turned in his direction, then ducked into the cloud bank. Applying full power, he raced from cloud to cloud, desperate to elude his pursuers. After a few minutes they gave up and returned to their patrol and their mission, whatever it might have been, less one comrade.

Bullard was ecstatic. This time he knew for certain. He had seen the crippling blows he landed knock down his opponent, just like in the boxing ring. It was a full-on KO in the air. Although he felt bad about it, he knew the man was dead. He had seen his head virtually explode. There was no way either he or his aircraft could have survived. The problem, though, was that he had been alone. Maybe one member of his patrol had seen what happened? Perhaps there was an observation balloon nearby, tallying scores? Possibly, a unit on the ground had watched his SPAD with its bright crimson heart and "All Blood Runs Red" logo take down the Pfalz?

No such luck. The remainder of Bullard's patrol had pressed on, uneventfully, figuring their American brother had somehow gotten lost. They were sure he'd turn up. He did, back at home field, full of excitement for his second "victory." Alas, once again, he had no proof. He'd simply have to keep on trying.

9

GROUNDED

Sadly, Eugene Bullard's groundbreaking career as a fighter pilot came to a rather abrupt and ignominious end. Once again, blatant racism raised its hand and swept him from the sky as surely as if he had been downed by enemy bullets. There are two versions to the story as to how this occurred, and only one, of course, can be true. Records to back one claim or the other are nonexistent. The only evidence of Bullard's service as an aviator (in addition to his official license) committed to paper was a single entry in the War Records of France, which simply stated: "Served in Squadron 93 August 27, 1917 to September 13, 1917 and served in Squadron 85 September 13, 1917 to November 11, 1917."[23]

---

23 The end date of November 11 is certainly not accurate. There are squadron records that show Bullard was flying on missions until—as in the last chapter—at least November 19. We also know that the "scrap" described in this chapter that ended his flying career occurred sometime after November 11. Discrepancies like this in official records were very common, most due to the "fog of war."

The tussle Bullard had engaged in with the Pfalz pilot was his last official flight as a fighter pilot, and, as far as can be determined, it was likely the last time he ever sat in a cockpit as a pilot in command. All in all, his career as a combat aviator spanned about ninety days, approximately twenty-five missions, and resulted in two "probable" kills. Compared to some others who flew in World War I, this might not seem to amount to very much, but for the twenty-two-year-old son of a former slave from Georgia with a second-grade education, he had come a very long way, broken several barriers, and accomplished a great deal.

Bullard consistently told one story, for the rest of his days, as to why he was suddenly dismissed from the Air Service. Friends and acquaintances told another, less dignified tale, but no matter which account anyone might accept, both have unfortunate racist overtones and both were ultimately unfair, based on what Bullard had suffered for his adopted country in the war.

Bullard's version went like this: On November 23, thanks to bad weather, he and his chief mechanic, Sergeant Viel, were on one of the frequently granted twenty-four-hour passes. The duo, as well as many of their squadron mates, dashed off to nearby Paris.

Bullard and Viel enjoyed the day in the City of Light, then took a train partway back to their base, stopping at Bar-le-Duc, where they booked a room at the Hotel de Commerce. Their plan was to have dinner, grab some sleep, then catch the first train in the morning. They would be back to the squadron before their passes expired.

The pair dined in the hotel's café, which was jam-packed, mostly with soldiers and officers heading back to the trenches. *A terrible prospect for these men,* Bullard mused, knowing all too well what that was like. After dinner, they were enjoying coffee and brandy when a French officer, dressed in the uniform of a colonial captain, seemed to be making motions for Bullard to step over to his table, where he sat with several other French officers.

Bullard was, of course, dressed in his bright blue aviator's uniform, emblazoned with his pilot's wings, and festooned with his several decorations for bravery in the 170th. He stepped over to the officer's table, came to attention, and saluted the scowling captain. The man refused to return the salute from Corporal Bullard, as French Army protocol—and honor—demanded.

The inebriated and red-faced officer began peppering Bullard with embarrassing questions, such as, "Where did you get that uniform? Who told you that you could wear the wings of a pilot? How did you get those medals? Did you steal them?"

Bullard remained at ramrod attention and mute. Since his salute had not been returned, he was required to do so.

"See?" the captain laughed, gesturing to his tablemates, "I told you the monkey can't even speak French!"

That tore it. Remaining still, Bullard answered evenly, "I cannot answer you, sir, and I cannot consider you as an officer until you learn to return a salute when you are saluted."

The captain leaped to his feet, coiled, ready to strike. He shouted at Bullard, "You are unworthy of those decorations!"

Bullard, ever the boxer, tensed to defend himself. Fortunately, before the confrontation accelerated to physical violence, a major at another table jumped up and shouted to the captain to stand down. The major walked over to Bullard and properly returned his salute. The major then asked the corporal to identify himself, which he did.

"Bullard, eh? I have heard of you!"

He then turned to the startled captain and dressed him down: "This man is a true hero of France! You should be ashamed of yourself. Maybe your service in the colonies of Africa has sun-baked your brain! Your behavior is disgusting."

The major then gave Bullard his card and said if there was any further difficulty with this officer he would be glad to testify on the corporal's behalf. Bullard thanked the major, and all parties went about their business, Viel and Bullard going immediately to their room.

A few minutes later there was a knock on the door. When Bullard opened it, he found the major and two other officers standing there. After inviting them in, the major said, "Bullard, in France we are all the same. That old colonial officer must have thought he was still in Africa. I beg of you to forget what happened downstairs."

Without hesitating, Bullard responded, "It is forgotten, sir."

"Thank you, Bullard. *Vive la France*."

The officers left. When Bullard closed the door, he believed that all involved had put the incident behind them. In this assumption, he was wrong.

Four days later, he received a letter from none other than his constant nemesis, Dr. Gros. The letter accused him of official misconduct for quarreling with a superior officer and that whatever punishment he received it would be totally justified. Sometime at the end of November, he was given orders terminating his service in Squadron 85. The directive dictated his transfer back to his old infantry unit, the 170th.

The second version, which has been mentioned in other accounts and memoirs, is similar, if a bit more ugly. This time, Bullard is hustling back to base after a day and night in Paris and has missed his train. He is jogging down the road back to his airfield, in rain and mud, when a French Army truck rumbles by. Bullard shouts out to the driver, asking him for a lift. The truck stops, and he runs up to the back of the canvas-covered lorry. As he grabs a handle to pull himself up into the back of the truck, a hand thrusts out pushing him down. Perplexed, he tries again. Same result.

Bullard attempts a third time to get in the truck and this time a boot slams into his chest and someone shouts out, "We don't want your kind on this truck," or words to that effect.

Enraged, Bullard grabs the booted foot, yanks hard and drags the man out of the truck and throws him in a ditch by the side of the road. The man jumps up yelling, and Bullard coldcocks him, sending him sprawling in the mud, unconscious.

The other occupants of the truck begin to jump out to the road, and someone produces a battle lantern. The figure lying in the slime is a young French lieutenant. Corporal Bullard has struck an officer, which is a serious, court-martial offense.

Dr. Gros heard about this, of course, and the purge was on, only this time Gros wanted a court-martial and some serious prison time if not a firing squad. Captain Pinsard, Bullard's commander at the 85 Squadron, was able to intervene, but only to the extent that he was not court-martialed, based on his medals and battle heroics. The end result was the same as in Bullard's rendition: he was dismissed from the Air Service and sent back to his old unit.

Thankfully, his old wounds, though they had healed quite well, kept Bullard from being sent back to the trenches. Instead, he was ordered to the service battalion for the 170th, which was located at a French Army base far to the south of Paris, at Fontaine-de-Berger. From December 1917 until the Armistice went into effect on November 11, 1918, Corporal Bullard shuffled paper, stood guard duty, and performed menial janitorial duties far from the sound of the guns.[24]

---

24 Sadly, Jimmy, Bullard's pet monkey, did not survive the war. The sniffles turned into pneumonia, and after two weeks of suffering, the poor little "copilot" passed away. He was given a hero's "funeral" outside the officer's club.

"There was scarcely an American at Avord who did not know and like Bullard," wrote James Norman Hall. "He was a brave, loyal and thoroughly likeable fellow; and when a quarrel with his superiors caused his withdrawal from Aviation, there was scarcely an American who did not regret that fact."

After the end of hostilities, Bullard did not get his release from the French Army until late April 1919. This delay could have been due to the typical sluggish pace of army paperwork, or possibly the ever-wary Dr. Gros could have been at work again. Gros did not want Bullard to have any role in or be part of any celebrations in regard to the end of the war. He was fine with Bullard being kept far away in the obscure hills of the Puy-de-Dome.

Nothing, however, could deny Eugene Bullard's incredible record of wartime service. From the trenches of 1915 through the aerial battles of late 1917, he had been wounded at least three, possibly as many as four times, but certainly seriously twice. He had been decorated with some of France's highest military awards, been designated as an aviator, and was authorized to wear the coveted French Army "fourragère" indicating a unit of distinction and valor in combat (from the old 3rd Marching Regiment).

All in all, Bullard had been awarded the Military Medal (France's second highest honor for bravery), Croix de Guerre, Volunteer Combat Cross, Combatant's Cross, Medal for Military Wounded (twice), World War I Medal, Victory Medal, Voluntary Enlistment Medal, Battle of Verdun Medal, Battle of Somme Medal, and the American Volunteer with French Army Medal.

Out of uniform, the new civilian naturally gravitated to his beloved Paris. Bullard was there by May 1919, back to many of his old haunts, with his old friends—at least those who had survived the war. We do not know how much, if any, of the $2,000 bet to become a pilot still remained in his pockets. Even if penniless, he was about to embark on the next phase of his life, the twenty years between 1919 and 1939, what the Bullard researcher and archivist Craig Lloyd has described as "his golden years." These two decades would prove equal to, in many ways, the amazing experiences of his war years.

ACT IV
THE IMPRESARIO

10

ALIVE AND WELL AND
LIVING IN PARIS

Eugene Bullard could not paint, and he was not much of a
writer. His war wounds had definitely slowed him some, so
going back to professional boxing was an open question. He
was not flush with cash and needed to do something to make
money. He could, for a while, depend on the largesse of his
many friends, but that was not his style—he wanted to give
more than he wanted to receive. What to do?

His easy smile and natural talent for entertaining suggested
the performing arts. Perhaps he could go on the road again,
as a minstrel or pantomime actor, as he had done with Miss
Belle's Picks. He would be due at least a small pension from
France for his service in the war, and he had taken steps to
apply, but it would be a pittance, at best. As he contemplated
all this from his new apartment on the rue Navarin in Montmartre, fate once again intervened on Bullard's behalf.

Montmartre would be the epicenter of the cultural revival of postwar France, providing a home to artists and writers and offering up the nightclubs and restaurants where they would congregate. In November 1919, Sylvia Beach opened the doors of Shakespeare and Company, the bookshop that would become a second home to James Joyce, Ernest Hemingway, Scott Fitzgerald, and other notable authors of the era. The following year, what was called in America the "Roaring Twenties" began; in France, it was *"les années follies,"* or the "crazy years." According to Mary McAuliffe in her book *When Paris Sizzled*, "Whether viewed as crazy, foolish, savage or frenzied, these years flaunted a particularly unabashed rawness and boldness that formed the essence of the postwar modern movement that Parisians already were calling *l'esprit nouveau.*"

McAuliffe continues: "For those fortunate enough to have money and leisure, it became the height of fashion to be witty, decadent and bored. Looking for distraction, everyone who could—whether rich Americans, exiled Russian aristocrats or millionaires from any number of locations—came to Paris. There they could mingle in endless parties and late-night jazz clubs, indulging in a heady mix of booze, drugs and sex."

Bullard could sense the return to glory for the City of Light and he wanted to embrace all of it. He began working out again, to get in better shape and rehabilitate the muscles that had been torn in his left leg. He took on small jobs in a couple of gyms as a sparring partner. There was no shortage of young boxers and rising stars who wanted to go a few rounds with the former "Sparrow" who was then sometimes called by friends "Black Swallow." At night, he would tour the clubs, chatting up friends and looking for work.

What he discovered in the clubs surprised him: the jazz movement was really catching on. People from all over Europe and the States seemed to love the free-form expression of "Negro music," and all the singing, dancing, and gyrating that went with it. Black expression through jazz became au courant, and quite lucrative for those who could sing or play a jazz instrument.

Bullard had made friends with a supremely talented black drummer by the name of Louis Mitchell, who was the leader of a popular group called the Seven Spades Band.[25] Mitchell hooked up his new friend with one of his percussionists, Seth Jones, and Bullard began taking drum lessons at night after his workouts at the gym. If he wasn't a natural he was at least good enough, and he was soon able to sit in with a couple of backup bands.

As in the rising-tide-lifts-all-boats theory, jazz became so popular in Paris at this time that if one was black and owned a pair of drumsticks he could get hired. Even Bullard, years later, often laughed about how bad he was at this stage of his drumming career, but at least he was earnest and loud, and that was all that seemed to matter.

Bullard's first big break in the music world came via the legendary Paris club impresario Joe Zelli. An Italian by birth, Zelli had immigrated to America as a boy with his parents, who settled in Manhattan. As a teen, he took jobs as a waiter to learn the restaurant business from the ground up and the inside out. By 1909, at age twenty, he was already part owner of a bistro at the corner of 43rd and Madison Avenue. When World War I broke out, Zelli, who had not attained American citizenship, was drafted into the Italian Army (allied with America, Britain, and France in this war). He returned to his

---

25 Mitchell came to Paris before the war with the international American stars of dancing, Vernon and Irene Castle. The British-born Vernon flew over three hundred combat missions as a Royal Flying Corps pilot, and died during a training mission in Texas in February 1918. Like Gene, Vernon Castle had a pet monkey, who survived the crash. Devastated by her husband's death, Irene retired from dancing.

native country and served honorably in an artillery regiment for the duration of the Great War.

After the Armistice, Zelli landed in Paris where he soon secured a job as head bartender for the American Officers' Club. His ebullient personality as well as his veteran status soon won him a following among the many officers who were left behind in Paris, stationed there after the war to keep the peace and handle the many duties of the Armistice. Zelli decided to stay, too, and soon formed an ambition to have his own club—but one that differed significantly from the many other jazz spots popping up all over the city.

Zelli had heard—correctly, as it turned out—that there was a quirk in the French bar and restaurant regulations that allowed so-called "bottle clubs" to stay open much longer than regular bars, which typically were required to close at midnight. Bottle clubs could only sell liquor by the entire bottle (typically champagne), which allowed the patron to "own" a table as long as there was liquor in the bottle. (The purchase of additional bottles was, of course, always encouraged.) The challenge was that securing a bottle club license was particularly difficult. Translation: to get permission to open a bottle club you had to "know someone" and that someone or his licensing department had to be handsomely compensated in under-the-table cash. It would also help if you had fought for France in the recent conflict.

To get his foot in the door, Zelli managed to scrape enough money together, with other backers, to buy a traditional club, the Chez Florence, at 17 rue Caumartin in Montmartre. It just so happened that Eugene Bullard was the eager new drummer in the club's band. The two got to know one another and Zelli shared his bottle club ambitions with Bullard.

Zelli spoke Italian, of course, and English. Bullard spoke English, French, and passable German. He was also a decorated and widely admired hero of France. Even better, Bullard had come into the orbit of a very well-known French lawyer by the name of Henri-Robert (also known as Robert Henri). Henri-Robert, an illegitimate child who had been abandoned at birth and sent to an orphanage, was a brilliant criminal lawyer who after the war switched to the practice of civil law. Among his clients were Auguste Rodin, Claude Monet, Pierre Renoir, Camille Saint-Saens, and the actress Sarah Bernhardt. He was a former head of the Paris Bar Association and a Commander of the Legion of Honor.

Henri-Robert had gotten to know Bullard during the war and was taken with the young pilot as another example of someone who had come from nowhere and nothing and accomplished so much (just as he had done). Henri-Robert, who was too old to fight for France by the time war broke out, supported heroes, like Bullard, who did the actual fighting.

Putting two and two together, Bullard came up with the winning combination for his new friend, Joe Zelli. He approached Henri-Robert with the challenge of getting the bottle club license. With Bullard's status as a citizen hero, Zelli's funds, and Henri-Robert's standing, the application sailed through and Club Zelli was born.

Zelli's was an instant hit. Jazz fever had completely transformed the Paris music scene. Jazz made people move. Jazz made people happy. Jazz was so unlike any music form before it that it lifted people's spirits and pushed memories of the recent catastrophic war deep into the recesses of their minds. Nowhere in Paris was jazz performed more enthusiastically—and all night—than at Zelli's. When other cabarets and clubs were required to close at midnight, Zelli's was just opening. Patrons bought their bottles, and unconsciously kept buying bottles, until dawn, at which time Zelli's would serve a robust breakfast then shut down for the remainder of the day.

Joe Zelli packed them in and took their money, yet he never refused anyone a drink because they couldn't pay. He would take their checks if they had no cash. Joe's wife, who was an assiduous bookkeeper and excellent tabulator of records, reportedly had a thick stack of checks that could not be cashed—all from customers whose accounts were empty. Joe never pursued them. He believed that none of his patrons would ever stiff him and if they couldn't settle their tabs currently, well, they would someday. His largesse was well-known and apparently well rewarded. At the end of his first five years in business he would be worth half a million dollars—a staggering sum in those days, especially for someone who had been cashing a barkeep's paycheck only a few years prior.

Eugene Bullard studied his methods and learned from Zelli. When the time would come, as it did, for Bullard to start his own venture, he would copy Zelli's methods, right down to the handshakes for every patron and a free drink if your pockets were empty.

Through the years 1920 and 1921, Zelli's flourished, and so did Bullard. He kept a grueling schedule, though: long workouts at the gym during the day, followed by playing in the band all night. His drumming became better and better. Joe Zelli also gave him the job of booking all the club's talent and managing the acts that were contracted. This put him in contact with the finest musicians, singers, and performers working in Paris during that time.

Yet Bullard still had an itch to fight; he had not gotten the boxing game out of his system. His rise in the ring, as a fairly good middleweight contender on the European circuit, had been interrupted by the war. He had no illusions about his somewhat advanced age of twenty-six or the condition of his body considering his war injuries, but the desire was still strong, and his heart told him he had to give it one more try.

Using connections he had maintained in the boxing profession, Bullard finagled two bouts billed as comeback fights in Cairo, Egypt, slated for early 1922. To pay for the trip and his expenses, he also signed a contract to perform with a five-piece jazz ensemble that had obtained a six-month gig at Cairo's swank Hotel Claridge. With Joe Zelli's blessing, and an open invitation to come back to Zelli's club, Bullard and his band sailed for Egypt in early December 1921. They opened to rave reviews at the Claridge on Christmas Eve.

Bullard went into the ring in Alexandria on February 15, 1922, to fight a fifteen-rounder against an Egyptian fighter who outweighed him by twenty pounds. (Bullard was a lean and muscular 145 pounds.) It was a lively and bruising match that went the distance and ended in a draw. Bullard and his manager, an old army buddy by the name of Opal Cooper, were outraged. They felt they had won on points. They probably had, but they discovered after the fight that the referee was his opponent's brother-in-law.

Two other factors made things worse: First, Bullard hurt his right hand badly in the fight and it swelled to almost twice its normal size. The injury left a permanent, hard knot and the hand was never the same again. Second, the promoter disappeared after the fight, out a back door, without paying Bullard his cut.

A frantic chase down dark unfamiliar alleys ensued, but Bullard was a determined pursuer. He eventually caught up with the scoundrel when he tripped in the dark and went sprawling into a handcart full of dates. Bullard throttled the man and threatened to slice him to ribbons with his pocket-knife if he didn't pay up. The man feigned he had no money, which Bullard knew was impossible, having watched the overflow crowd pay up to see the fight. He promptly turned out the man's pockets and found, hidden in his coat, two large rolls of bills. Bullard peeled away the $600 the man had promised him and returned the rest, leaving the bedraggled promoter squatting in the pile of dried fruit and perhaps grateful that Bullard had not completely emptied his pockets.

His second—and very last—fight also occurred in Alexandria, on April 28. His hand had not healed but a contract was a contract and fifteen more rounds it would be, unless he could knock out the other guy and end it quicker. Four-ounce gloves were used, hardly enough to say it was not a bare-knuckle fight (twelve- to fourteen-ounce gloves were more standard). Bullard's opponent this time was Gabriel Zammar, an Egyptian welterweight of middling distinction, but someone who was durable and tough.

Bullard and Opal Cooper made sure this time there were no hidden agendas and unknown relatives as referees. They also insisted that the prize money be posted up front and held by an independent third party. The match went fifteen rounds, again, and was also scored as a draw, but this time all agreed the result was fair and the crowd agreed, too. In fact, after the fight, a startled Bullard was greeted in his dressing room by none other than a real Egyptian prince, a first cousin of King Faud himself.

The prince had been in the audience during the bout and he said, "Bullard, your fight was the best that my country has ever seen. Here, buy a drink on me," at which moment the prince handed the shocked boxer an Egyptian hundred-pound note (worth about $500 US at that time). This "tip" was nearly equal to the money he made for the bout.

Three weeks later, Bullard's six-month contract with the

Claridge was up. He also knew that his boxing days were over: the right hand would not heal, and even gentle sparring told him that he would never again be strong enough to endure any more fifteen-round-plus matches. He had scratched his itch, however, and without any regret he returned to Zelli's in late spring 1922. He took up with the Paris scene right where he had left off.

His boxing days may have been over but his "fighting" days were not. Sometimes to his regret, Eugene Bullard's personality included having a hair-trigger temper and it apparently was almost impossible to control if he had taken one too many drinks. In short, he was never hesitant to use his fists to settle a dispute or a slight, especially so if it concerned race.

William Bullard had been absolutely right that the racial atmosphere in France in the early twentieth century was much different, and more accommodating, than what existed in contemporary America. Gene Bullard was able to take advantage of the liberality and fraternity of his French compatriots and fellow citizens. The atmosphere changed somewhat after the Great War but not because attitudes in France had morphed but because tens of thousands of "Sammies" (a nickname for the Americans), both black and white, had decided to stay in France and not go back to the States. In addition, the popularity of the postwar Paris art, music, and cultural scene attracted hundreds of thousands more Americans to spend their vacations and money in France.

Many of those who stayed or came to splurge brought their American-born prejudices with them. It rankled many Americans to see a black man walking down the Champs-Élysées with a white girl on his arm. It bothered Southern white men, in particular, to see Caucasian girls snuggling up or dancing with Negro men in the clubs. Accepted in France or not, there were white men in cafés along the boulevards who railed against the fact that these establishments did not have "coloreds only" sections, just like back home in good ol' Mississippi (and elsewhere in the South).

Bullard took these encroaching attitudes particularly hard because he was not just a true American but also a citizen hero of France. He was rooted in both cultures and had to defend each. Nothing represented his dilemma more than an ugly incident that occurred on New Year's Eve, 1922.

This extraordinary headline ran in the *Chicago Tribune*'s Paris Edition on January 2, 1923: "American Felled by Negro Armed with Brass Slug." The smaller, secondary headline beneath said: "Hit As He and British Officer Escorted a Woman." By "brass slug" the paper meant a set of "brass knuckles."

The American was identified as Harry McClellan of Stockton, California, and he was accompanied by Lieutenant Ronald Reuter of the British Army. Reuter was a nephew of Marguerite, Baroness de Reuter, who, in turn, was the sister-in-law of James Gordon Bennett Jr., publisher of the *New York Herald* and the *Paris Herald*, who had died four years earlier. The men had been staying in the Baroness's palatial Paris town house and had been, on that New Year's Eve, out for a grand night on the town, with lady friends.

The story went that the McClellan/Reuter party was finishing a late-night dinner at a luxe restaurant on rue Daunou, had exited, and were immediately accosted by a rowdy group of "drunken Negroes." The article further stated that "Dick" Bullard, identified as a "former jazz band drummer," roughed up McClellan for no apparent reason. McClellan, reportedly, pushed back, at which time Bullard donned a set of brass knuckles and coldcocked McClellan. Other Negroes supposedly went after Reuter, knocking him down and trying to beat him up. The gendarmes soon arrived, and everyone was hauled off to the nearest precinct house.

The *Tribune* then related that "Dick Bullard" managed to present papers identifying himself as a "hero of France" from the recent war, so the French police let him go and didn't even bother to search him for the brass knuckles.

The article then concluded, astonishingly, with this:

> Dozens of Negroes are now said to be infesting Montmartre. It was pointed out by Americans yesterday that American authorities here, cooperating with the police, could see to it that many of these men, nearly all of whom have prison records, were deported.
>
> Bullard was in the Foreign Legion for a time during the war but obtained a transfer to aviation rather than go into the trenches. He was shifted out of aviation on the grounds that he declined to fly. Since the armistice he has frequented Montmartre occasionally playing in jazz bands.

A few salient facts: the *Tribune*'s Paris edition had been established in 1917 to cater to the doughboys pouring into France by the hundreds of thousands. It continued to report to the crowd that stayed behind after the war as well as the huge influx of American tourists. Many in this Parisian subculture wanted the news reported the way it would be reported back home. That meant, in this case, that the "Negroes" became the outrageous aggressors, the possessors of brass knuckles, who "infested"—like vermin—the streets of Paris looking for trouble. The additional comments about "prison records" and "deportations" were used for sensational effect and the aspersions about Eugene Bullard and his war record were clearly beyond the pale. The French would have howled, knowing Gene as they did, but Americans knew little to nothing about his exploits, which were never published in any American press, North or South, during the war, except for the one brief mention in the NAACP newspaper, *The Crisis*, in 1918 (cited earlier).

A second and much more accurate account was reported by Albert Curtis, an African American former soldier who was a correspondent for the *Chicago Defender*. (Founded in 1905, it was considered, at the time, and until well after World War II, one of the most reliable and essential publications in African American journalism.) Bullard had been dining at Ciro's restaurant late on New Year's Eve in the company of several black friends. A French woman at an adjacent table struck up a conversation with him, having overheard his friends talking about some of his exploits during the war. This unidentified woman was apparently McClellan's companion for the evening.

McClellan took exception to Bullard's attention to his lady friend and loudly shouted out that he didn't want "any damn nigger talking to women in his company."

Bullard's short, wine-soaked fuse was lit. He called the man out, inviting him into the street in front of Ciro's. McClellan took a swing, which Bullard easily sidestepped, and then his boxing skill took over. It was no contest—and no brass knuckles needed. McClellan's pal, Reuter, took no part in the fight. When the police arrived, it was already over. Bullard, apparently well-known to the officers who responded, was immediately let go. McClellan and Reuter were hauled off to jail, where they spent the rest of the night.

With Reuter's newspaper connections (he was, indeed, related not only to the *New York Herald* but also the Reuter's News Service) it was easy to get the slanted and totally biased story planted. What neither McClellan nor Reuter counted on, however, was the immediate intervention, once again, of Bullard's old friend, Henri-Robert. Bullard sued, and the attorney won an easy victory on his behalf. Instead of money damages for libel, the plaintiff wanted and won the right to have his side of the story printed in the *Tribune*, on the front page, and in the same position as the original offending story.

On May 24, 1923, the headline "A Letter From Mssr. Bullard" appeared. The paper gave him plenty of column inches to vent his frustration and correct the record. His approach was threefold: to comment on his military record, then his employment status, and finally on the actual facts of the incident. Bullard then closed with some comments on the sad state of affairs in regard to some white Americans and Negroes in France. All in all, the rebuttal was longer than the original libelous piece.

It was important for Bullard to correct the record, and he did so—mostly. For some strange reason, he identified his mother as an "American," which she was, but he did not mention that she was also a full-blooded Native American, and he stated incorrectly that his father was from Martinique. He also added that he had "turned down a lieutenant's commission" offered by the American Air Service in 1917. Bullard knew this was incorrect, and so would have most of his friends. Why make this up? One plausible reason is that he did not wish to expose the prejudice heaped upon him by his countrymen, who had blocked him from getting a commission because of his race.

His letter concluded with the following forceful observations:

> To finish with, let me add that I do not know to whom you refer when you speak of deported negroes who infest Montmartre but be sure that you may tell

your readers that the pilot aviator, a black man and French, Eugene BULLARD, wounded during the war, cited, who has spilt his blood for his country, and for Justice. Alas! Justice is so often denied to his race, is not among those negroes. It is time to finish with these ridiculous prejudices of colors of People who forget too soon the German danger of yesterday and the German threat of tomorrow.[26]

Even with the false claims, the open letter had the desired effect. The publication caused a sensation in Paris, with most French citizens applauding Eugene Bullard while many white American expatriates steamed in silent fury. The whole episode exposed an ugly truth about Americans and Parisian club society. It's also mildly astonishing to note that in his letter, of 1923, Gene was already looking ahead and seeing the "German threat of tomorrow."

Another similar confrontation was resolved without explanations in the press. This incident occurred in mid-1923: of an evening, Bullard was having dinner with his old friend the Dixie Kid, visiting from England. They were dining at the Olympia, a dance hall in the Montmartre section of the city. The two black boxers would be the last people anyone should insult, but a group of white American sailors were not aware of this. There was a shoving match, but before it could escalate, the vastly outnumbered duo of the Sparrow and the Kid decided to vacate the hall by racing up the stairs to the exit. Unsatisfied with this outcome to the fracas, the sailors set off in pursuit. At the top of the stairs, Bullard turned, seized the first sailor below him, and tossed the hapless seaman onto his mates. The two friends waded into the scrum

---

26 *Chicago Tribune* and *New York Daily News*, European Edition, May 24, 1923, pg. 1.

of arms and legs and, according to Opal Cooper, "cleaned out the whole bunch." This TKO does not appear on either man's career boxing record.

In the United States, most Americans were quite content with black musicians entertaining them on stage and in the clubs, but they were not fine with African Americans walking off the stage, mingling with the patrons, sitting down to dine with them or, heaven forbid, dating or fraternizing with them. In France such behavior was accepted, perfectly normal, and quite expected.

Many visiting Americans could not abide this sort of behavior and the raw prejudice fueled by alcohol often boiled over and erupted in fights. Brawls, in fact, became all too common. Bullard reported that there were many times when rowdy Americans were kicked out of his clubs for antagonizing black band members. Typically, the offenders wandered across the street to another club, where the disruptions started all over again.

With Prohibition having become the law of the land in the United States in 1919, even more thirsty Americans were flocking to Paris to drink themselves silly. They represented so much revenue to some Parisian hotel, restaurant, and bar owners that some of them even began a "whites only" policy.

The French newspapers were full of columns about "savage Americans" and their bad behavior. The situation finally came to a resolution when the government began cracking down on those establishments that were exercising reverse prejudice. Licenses were suspended or revoked. Hours of operation were curtailed for those establishments with a prejudicial bent. These financial measures did the trick.

Word spread rapidly concerning the egalitarian-minded French and African Americans were even more persuaded to seek opportunities in France. The exodus of black entertainers and athletes became a flood and Paris, as well as many other cities in France, took advantage of some of the finest talent of that era.

This was a bit of a Golden Age for Eugene Bullard, too. Having the very best connections to many aspects of French society, as well as fluency in the language, made him an invaluable resource. He could translate, make introductions, and set people up with the right contacts. In addition, he offered himself up as a private masseuse and personal trainer.

Bullard was spending time with a large slice of Parisian high society and the entertainment elite. Life was blossoming for him, with a garden apartment, money in his pockets, fabulous friends, great contacts, professional fulfillment, and as much fun as he could pack into his busy life.

It was a heady time for Eugene Bullard, grand impresario of a nightclub he had brought to life with his own hard work and gutsy determination. There is little doubt that his romantic life was active, too, especially in a city undergoing its "crazy years" and without the racial barriers to relationships found in the United States. Yet Bullard, approaching thirty years old, had not taken a wife.

That was about to change.

11

MARCELLE

The story of Eugene Bullard's only marriage is a convoluted tale—or two tales, maybe even three. The possible scenarios of his romantic relationship with Marcelle Eugenie Henriette Straumann are offered here side by side, and the truth probably lies somewhere in between.

During the 1920s, Bullard had continued to remain close with his prewar friends, the painters Gilbert White and Moise Kisling. These two ran with the "art crowd," naturally, and they introduced their dashing drummer friend, and war hero, to many of the leading patrons of the day. Among the families to whom Eugene Bullard was introduced was the Straumanns.

As Bullard told it many times, Monsieur Louis Albert Straumann was married to Helene Heloise Charlotte, the Countess Pochinot. The family, according to Gene, was quite wealthy with a grand home in Paris and another on the French southwest coast at Biarritz. They had only one child, Marcelle, a petite and affable young lady of refined taste and appropriate education. Bullard had been a guest several times at the Straumann home, for dinner parties, and he had even taken the bold step of asking Marcelle out to dance at several of the clubs.

"I began to wonder if I was crazy," Bullard later remarked. "Here I was from a different background and country and even a different color, and yet, it seemed like Marcelle and I just belonged together."

There had been no objection on the part of Marcelle's parents, although she was white, he was black, and she was from money, he was not, though seemingly on his way up financially. While it might have seemed unusual for wealthy Caucasian parents to allow their only daughter to date a black jazz drummer and budding nightclub impresario, it would not have been shocking. This was, after all, Paris in the modern age. Eugene Bullard was also well-known, well connected, and a war hero.

Here is the murky part of the story: The only record of a "Louis and Helene Straumann" family in Paris at that time was one of a bourgeois but fairly prosperous couple in the grocery business, who did, indeed, have a daughter named "Marcelle." They had, however, no known connections to French royalty.[27] This Marcelle helped her family out by working as a seamstress for several of their wealthy grocery patrons. The Marcelle of this version had been born in 1901, and at the time she met Bullard she would have been twenty-one, and he twenty-seven. It would have been entirely possible for them to have met, as Bullard suggested, at a dinner party and for them to have gone dancing. This Monsieur and Madame Straumann, as reported by Lloyd, were not exactly thrilled

---

27   There seems to be no "Pochinot" in the Registry of French Royalty or under the banner of the Bourbon dynasty, which ruled France all throughout modern times up until the advent of La République.

with the color of Gene's skin but they put that aside for all his other qualities and his excellent connections. They were, after all, ambitious for their daughter.

After seeing one another off and on through 1922, Bullard related that he finally began realizing that when he and Marcelle were apart he felt very lonely. It finally dawned on him that he was, at long last, in love. Much to his amazement, Marcelle shared his feelings. With some trepidation, Bullard made his intentions known to Marcelle's parents. According to Craig Lloyd, "The Straumanns laughingly assured him that he was not crazy, as he feared; they knew how much Marcelle, their only child, reciprocated his love."[28]

The happy couple were married at ten o'clock in the morning on July 17, 1923, at the city hall of the 10th Arrondissement in Paris. The Straumanns threw them a huge party and lunch at the Brasserie Universelle. According to Bullard's recollection, "The guests included nobles, artists, boxers, aviators, sportsmen of all kinds and outstanding people in all walks of life and of all colors and religions."[29] Such were the circles the son of a slave traveled in then.

That affair lasted until the dinner hour at which time hired taxis and private cars, in a grand parade, drove up the hills to Zelli's where the festivities—and the flow of champagne— started anew and continued until well after midnight. The newlyweds stayed the night in Paris, after which they took off for a two-week honeymoon in Biarritz.

Upon their return to Paris, Bullard went back to work and Marcelle busied herself with the couple's apartment at 15

---

28 Craig Lloyd, *Eugene Bullard, Black Expatriate in Jazz-Age Paris*, (University of Georgia Press, 2000), 89.

29 Bullard, *All Blood Runs Red*, 133.

Rue Franklin, new digs that came complete with a beautiful view of the Eiffel Tower. Marcelle was also soon preparing for an addition to the family. On June 6, 1924, daughter Jacqueline arrived.

The christening party rivaled the wedding reception as a major social event. Each of Zelli's champagne suppliers donated a case of their finest bubbly. A band of musicians led by the jazz violinist Eddie South played all afternoon and evening in the Bullards' sixth-floor walk-up, though with so many people crowding in, there was not enough space left for dancing. Bullard recalled that the "champagne flowed so freely that the guests were more thoroughly baptized than baby Jacqueline."

He spent much of his time helping inebriated guests get down the six flights of stairs. He was able to squeeze in three hours of sleep, then arrived at Zelli's at midnight. Sitting at the drums on the bandstand, he saw several people who had been guests at the baptism party at the club's jam-packed bar.

In October 1926, Eugene Jr., was born. However, in one of the saddest episodes of Bullard's life, his little namesake did not live very long, dying of pneumonia at only six months.

He would always feel the pain of his son's death, but otherwise, life as husband and father was good, and ennobling: "The sweetness of my high-born French wife and my father-in-law strengthened my trust and respect for most white people. Now, to an even greater extent than before I felt a debt of gratitude for all the kindnesses I have received in all parts of the world from people of all colors. My ambition to repay my debt to humanity by holding out a helping hand to people in trouble grew stronger and stronger."[30]

The couple's last child, Lolita, was born in December 1927. Here, the story divides. For whatever reason, Bullard says

---

30   *Ibid.*

very little about his time with Marcelle after Lolita was born. Marcelle plays no major role in his adventures after about 1928 and what occurs in their lives, subsequent to that time, is for the most part speculation.

Apparently, the couple began to drift apart after 1929. Bullard continued to be laser-focused on running his club, and what little time he had left over he tried to spend with his daughters. His peripatetic lifestyle of being up all night and sleeping or working out all day in the gym was totally opposite Marcelle's normal daily activities of late breakfast, lunches with friends, shopping, and many hours at her favorite pastime, watching horse races at various tracks. It is not even clear that she moved with Bullard in the late twenties when he relocated to yet another apartment at 6 passage de l'Élysée des Beaux Arts, Montmartre. This set of rooms was much closer to a new business venture, Le Grand Duc.

Right about this juncture, Marcelle's father, Louis, passed away. Her mother had predeceased her father by two years. According to Bullard's recollections:

> The trouble between me and my wife started when her father died and left her his fortune. She wanted me to quit working and give all my time to sharing her life as a Parisian society woman. That would mean taking her to horse races at Auteuil or Longchamps every afternoon during the season; escorting her to parties every night; and spending weeks at a time at fashionable resorts like Biarritz and Cannes or Monte Carlo.
>
> Like most American men who aren't sissies, I could not stand the idea of being a gigolo even to my wife. So I told her she could lead the full life of a society woman if she liked but to count me out in my working hours, because I was not going to give up earning my living.

So we were seeing so little of each other that we decided to part company. We were Catholic and we were never divorced. About six years later my poor wife died.[31]

This would mean that, according to Bullard, Marcelle died in 1935. Jacqueline would have been eleven, and Lolita, almost eight.

Several facts belie this narrative. World War II took a devastating toll on public records in Paris, but among those that did survive, one document, unearthed by Professor Lloyd in the city hall archives of the 10th Arrondissement and dated December 5, 1935, clearly showed: "Divorce of Eugene Bullard and Marcelle Eugenie Henriette Straumann."[32] A second record, also uncovered by Lloyd, from the 20th Arrondissement, and dated February 18, 1990, is titled "Death of Marcelle E. H. Straumann."[33]

Why would Bullard make up such an elaborate ruse? One reason may have been to protect his daughters. The tale of separation and death also fit his narrative as war hero, doting father, savior to his children, and emerging "good Catholic." Did Marcelle leave him because the novelty of wedding a black man and having mixed-race children wore off? That would have been sad and very cruel, but it's entirely possible.

Whatever the facts may be in regard to Marcelle, Bullard ended up as the primary parent and guardian of his daughters. He loved them totally, and their welfare was always uppermost in his mind. Either via separation, divorce, or possibly "death" (as told to them by their father), their mother basically left their lives sometime in the early 1930s. Did Bullard

---

31 Lloyd, *Eugene Bullard*, 109.

32 *Ibid.*, 191.

33 *Ibid.*

tell his girls their mother had died to spare them the angst and embarrassment of knowing she abandoned them?

Was infidelity at work? We know with a fair degree of certainty that he became involved with the beautiful and daring spy Cleopatre "Kitty" Terrier, but that wasn't until the late 1930s, long after Marcelle was out of the picture. There were rumors that Bullard might have been involved romantically with one of his favorite singers/dancers, Ada Louise "Bricktop" Smith (whom we'll meet in the next chapter). Neither one of them ever mentions this in their memoirs, but we also know that there were times when their friendship frayed dramatically for business reasons and because Bullard (in Bricktop's opinion) was volatile, especially when drunk. If there was any "spark" between them, it did not last, and neither ever discussed it, not even in writing.

It would also not be uncommon for Bullard to be tempted by the charms and wiles of the many beautiful women who flowed through his clubs over the years. Paris in the 1920s and '30s was wild with sensual pleasures and "modern" women had far fewer of the discretionary urges of the generation before them. Were there flings? Casual assignations? There had to have been temptations. Bullard was much more "gentleman" than "playboy," but the allure, to liberated women, of the dark-skinned French war hero, club owner, and jazz musician had to have offered him plenty of opportunities to play around. He says nothing about this in his memoir, but when he was writing his autobiography he was thinking mostly of his legacy, and his children, and it seems quite unlikely that he would have included any salacious material from those days.

Was Marcelle unfaithful? We have no way of knowing. There simply are no records, and she did not keep any sort of diary that we know of and no letters, notes, or documents have yet surfaced. The most we know for certain is that she lived out her relatively long life (1901-1990) shuttling between Paris and her inherited home in Biarritz. There are no records of her ever remarrying or having any more children. She outlived her ex-husband by over a quarter of a century. Was Marcelle the quiet, reclusive inheritor of a large estate and an extravagant lifestyle along the coast at Biarritz? The records are, here again, incomplete but we do know that if she retained any assets she did not pass them on to her children. There is anecdotal evidence from one of Marcelle's neighbors from her later years in Biarritz that Marcelle assumed that Bullard and her daughters had perished in World War II. If she truly believed that, then she was also deprived of knowing the grandchildren who were born in her lifetime. There is no evidence that the girls were in communication with their mother ever again, which seems logical, since their father had told them their mother was dead.

It's almost hard to believe, though, that she did not know Bullard was alive. There was sporadic press coverage of his activities in Paris as an impresario with high-profile patrons, and it is hard to think that none of it would have reached the newsstands in Biarritz.

In any case, much like the aerial fireworks he and his mates created in the skies over France during the war, the romance and marriage of Gene and Marcelle initially skyrocketed, flourished, then fizzled and fell spectacularly to earth.

12

LE GRAND DUC

Ada Beatrice Queen Victoria Louise Virginia Smith was her given name, but because of a thick shock of bright red hair, she was more commonly known as "Bricktop." Another woman would become Eugene Bullard's wedded wife, but Bricktop, the enormously talented singer and dancer became, for many years, his "business wife." Their relationship was always turbulent yet it was also enduring.

Ada's doting mother was born a slave in 1861, and Ada came along in West Virginia in 1894. Ada's father was an Irishman, which is how she came by the red hair and freckles. "A smallish man, slightly hunchbacked," he ran a barbershop that catered only to white people—somewhat puzzling given that his wife was not. He died when Ada was young, and she and her mother plus three siblings relocated to Chicago. Ada was educated in integrated schools and did well academically, but her natural talent was with her music. Her singing was so astonishingly good that it garnered invitations, at the tender age of sixteen, for her to perform in some of Chicago's chicest clubs.

Bricktop's big break came when she was hired to perform at the Cabaret de Champion, owned by Jack Johnson. "He was a wonderful man," she recalled about the boxer, learning only years later of Johnson's connection to Eugene Bullard. "When he hit the door of the place at night, the millionaires from Lake Shore Drive and everybody else would be screaming, 'Jack, come over here!' He would just stand there with his big, wonderful self and say he'd be right over. Sooner or later he'd hit all the tables, having a drink at each. He never drank anything but champagne."

Through the World War I years and immediately afterward, Bricktop worked many of the popular clubs in the Windy City: "Those days were great days for entertainers in Chicago," she often said.

Alberta Hunter was becoming noticed for her blues singing. The great trumpet player King Oliver came up from New Orleans, and after he had established himself, he brought along a trumpet-playing protégé named Louis Armstrong. Bricktop worked with a dancer named Bill Robinson, soon to be known to millions of cinema goers as "Mister Bojangles."

After Chicago, she performed at clubs in Los Angeles and San Francisco and ended up staying in California from 1919 to 1922. She fell in love there with a man named Walter, but left him when he couldn't kick a heroin habit. Bricktop returned to Chicago, but the enactment of Prohibition had tossed nightlife on the rocks. A visiting club owner named Barron DeWare Wilkins offered her a job in New York City, and Bricktop leaped at it.

"It was 1922 and Harlem was really jumping," she recalled in her autobiography. "Harlem was the 'in' place to go for music and booze, and it seemed like every other building on or near Seventh Avenue from 130th Street to 140th was a club or a speakeasy."

Bricktop sang at her patron's place, Barron's Exclusive Club, and among those who had gigs there, too, was the comedian Frankie Fay, the singer Al Jolson, and a chorus girl named Lucille LeSueur, who would later find Hollywood stardom as Joan Crawford. Regular patrons included the actor John Barrymore, the gangster Jack "Legs" Diamond, the composer Cole Porter, and the young bandleader Duke Ellington.

While Bricktop was performing a guest gig at a club in Washington DC, in 1924, a black entertainer named Sammy Richardson sought her out. His message: come to Paris, an audience waits for you there. The timing could not have been better. About to turn thirty, Bricktop was ready for a new adventure. She booked passage on an ocean liner to Europe and was told a man named Eugene Bullard would be greeting her when she arrived.

The timing was good for another reason: people in Paris were going crazy for black performers from America. In early 1924, there was only a handful, including Richardson, a piano player; plus a cornet player nicknamed Gut Bucket; and a singer named Florence Jones. The latter had been performing in a nightclub called Le Grand Duc but had just announced she was going to switch to a better-paying gig at another club. Bricktop was recruited to Paris because she was black and she was wanted at Le Grand Duc and she was an attractive and proven entertainer.

She gave up her longtime association with Barron's Executive Club at the right moment, and her departure from Wilkins would be the last time Bricktop would see him. There was mounting competition among the bootleggers trying to control the Harlem trade. One night in May 1924,

Wilkins received a shipment of tainted booze and refused to pay for it. Tempers flared, and soon after, Wilkins was shot to death by a junkie named Yellow Charleston. Seven hundred mourners walked through the streets of Harlem for Wilkins's funeral, but soon thereafter, the Executive Club shut down.

Bullard's success at Zelli's, where he observed how much money Joe Zelli himself was raking in, made it inevitable that he would want to emulate his mentor and run his own club. In the spring of 1924, Bullard moved in that direction, leaving Zelli's and relocating a few doors away at Le Grand Duc ("The Great Duke"). This spot had opened a few years prior under the stewardship of the French entrepreneur George Jamerson who reportedly had ties to nefarious types involved with local prostitution, drugs, smuggling, and "protection." The name of the club, which Bullard retained to maintain its clientele, referred to an era some thirty years in the past when French nobility was known for club crawling at all hours of the night.

There is some question as to whether Bullard actually owned the club or simply managed the property. It may have belonged to someone else—with Jamerson still involved, quietly—and Gene simply performing the duties of maître d', talent scout, and accounts manager. He acted as if he owned it, and always wrote and claimed that he did. Like many municipal records from this period (and the 1930s) scads were destroyed in the coming war, and so there is no official means of confirming ownership.

It had actually been Bullard who had tasked Sammy Richardson with recruiting Bricktop to come to Le Grand Duc. Ownership issues aside, Bullard ran the place, and it was his responsibility to book a new act to replace Florence Jones. He had heard about the talented redhead from American ex-pats who were beginning to frequent Le Grand Duc.

Knowing the scheduled arrival date of Bricktop's ship, Bullard took a little time away from his duties to travel to Le Havre to welcome her. He found a woman desperate to regain her "land legs."

"It had taken eleven miserable days," was how the seasick passenger described her journey on the steamship *America*. "I was so happy to see land again that I knew conquering Paris had to be easier than getting there."

They would go about conquering Paris together. Bricktop's first impression of Bullard was of a "tall, handsome American Negro," and she liked him immediately: "He was so self-assured, and I needed to be with somebody who knew what he was doing."[34]

They took the boat train from Le Havre back to Paris. On the way, they emptied the bottle of champagne Bullard had brought along. In the City of Light, he checked Bricktop into a hotel and then they headed to 52 rue Pigalle. Her first impression of Le Grand Duc was not as positive as the one of Bullard. They walked into a small room with twelve tables and a tiny bar. "My, this is a nice little bar," Bricktop said, smiling. "Now where's the cabaret?"

"*This* is the cabaret," Bullard replied. "This is Le Grand Duc."

Bricktop burst into tears. Back in Harlem, she had been backed up by a twelve-piece band. She had come all the way to Paris to perform in something like a closet? She couldn't control her disappointment...until a black busboy emerged from the back, who said, "You need something to eat." He led her to the kitchen and prepared some food and assured Bricktop that she would like Paris and especially Le Grand Duc. This act of kindness made her feel much better.

---

34 "Tall" to describe Gene might have been a matter of perspective, as he was barely 5'11".

The busboy was a young ex-cook and tramp steamer sailor named Langston Hughes. Bullard had hired the twenty-two-year-old a few months earlier not knowing, of course, that he would go on to great fame as a poet, playwright, and novelist. Hughes would become well-known as a leader of the Harlem Renaissance, an explosion of African American art, music, and literature that took place in the late 1920s and '30s. In Paris, however, he was simply a wanderer, having recently departed the ship that had employed him as a crewman as it meandered along the west coasts of Europe and Africa.

Hughes wrote about his carefree days in Paris, including Eugene Bullard and Le Grand Duc, in his 1940 best-selling autobiography, *The Big Sea*. Bullard was always proud of his mention in the book. Like many writers before 1924 and since, Hughes found Paris to be an inspiration. While washing pots and pans in the tiny kitchen of Le Grand Duc, he listened to the singers (soon to include Bricktop) and musicians until the club closed at dawn. Hughes had a room in a tall old house near the Place Clichy. After catching some sleep, he sat at the window overlooking the chimneys of Paris and worked on his poems, influenced by the view and the jazz music still reverberating in his head.

It was during his stint at Le Grand Duc that *Vanity Fair* sent him $24.50 to publish three of his poems. It was the first time Hughes had been paid for his writing. Despite Bullard promoting him to "waiter," Hughes believed his best prospects would be back in America as a poet. He found a job as a deckhand on a ship going to New York, and he left Paris and Le Grand Duc behind in late 1924.

Parisians found Bricktop to be a stunning talent with her singing and marvelous dancing. Soon, she began to draw even more enthusiastic crowds to Le Grand Duc than her predecessor (the aforementioned Florence Jones). Bullard had to turn people away on many nights. The size of the room was indeed a drawback. It had an odd triangular shape with a narrow doorway fanning out to a dance floor and stage, surrounded by tables and banquettes against the walls. In fairness, none of the Montmartre clubs, even the most popular ones of that era, were very large. Le Grand Duc could, perhaps, cram in two hundred people at a time, though most would have to stand.

Le Grand Duc had struggled to be profitable ever since its 1921 opening under Jamerson. It continued to lurch ahead, even with Bullard and Bricktop at the helm. He had to beg for talent, and couldn't pay full price, at first, but several well-known names came forward and performed for free because Bullard had helped them get their starts when he was doing the hiring at Zelli's. Thus, he was able to headline the great jazz drummer Buddy Gilmore and the bandleader and singer Arthur "Dooley" Wilson.

Wilson had his own band in the 1920s, a group called the Red Devils. Though predominantly a singer and drummer, he is, today, best known for his piano playing. He was cast as the piano player in the immortal 1942 film *Casablanca*. Dooley was "Sam" of "Play it again, Sam" fame though, in reality, that specific line was never uttered in the film by any character—not Humphrey Bogart, not Ingrid Bergman, not anyone.[35] Wilson did not even play the piano. In the movie, he does sing the famous song "As Time Goes By," but his piano playing was performed by Eliot Carpenter, with Wilson emulating Carpenter's piano strokes, which he could see a few feet away and behind the cameras.

As Le Grand Duc began to pick up momentum, thanks to gratis performances from famous jazz greats and Brick-

---

35   "Play it again, Sam," was said in a movie, but not until 1972 when a Herb Ross–directed film with that title, based on a Broadway play written by Woody Allen and produced three years earlier, was released.

top's magic, the club started to blossom with a list of famous attendees, a virtual "Who's Who" of Paris cabaret habitués from the 1920s. There was Jack Dean and Fannie Ward, an acting couple of great fame who had starred in several silent movies, most directed by the legendary Cecil B. DeMille. Another frequent patron was Nancy Cunard, heiress to the Cunard steamship fortune. She was also a sometime poet and lover of many, including Aldous Huxley and Ezra Pound, and muse to others, including Ernest Hemingway, Man Ray, and James Joyce. Another patron was the young composer and playwright Noel Coward.

Also squeezing into Le Grand Duc was Anita Loos, the screenwriter, actress, playwright, and author perhaps best known for her comic novel *Gentlemen Prefer Blondes*. The Dolly Sisters, Rose and Jenny, were identical twin sisters, born in Hungary, both actors and dancers with a proclivity for rich men, thereby earning them the label of the "Million Dollar Dollies." A performer who would sub for Bricktop from time to time was Mabel Mercer, the cabaret singer with a velvet voice. Her greatest fan would be a young crooner by the name of Frank Sinatra.

It was not unusual for Bullard to greet Sophie Tucker at the club's front door. The Ukrainian-born comedian, actress, and radio personality, who became the "Last of the Red Hot Mammas," was known as a great supporter of up-and-coming black entertainers. Whenever Charlie Chaplin was in Paris, which was often, he could be found at Le Grand Duc. The same could be said for Gloria Swanson, emerging as one of Hollywood's brightest film stars. Gloria was extremely popular with the Grand Duc crowd, having made several French-themed films and marrying a French Marquis, Henri de la Falaise (her third husband). Another silent film star patron was Roscoe "Fatty" Arbuckle—until his career was overcome by scandal for an alleged rape and murder of a young Hollywood starlet.

Perhaps the most intriguing customer of all was Edward Windsor, Prince of Wales. He even sat in with the orchestra on several occasions, as he was an accomplished jazz drummer. He would break into a broad grin when two of his favorite young performers stopped by, Fred and Adele Astaire. The brother and sister had triumphed in London in 1924 starring in George and Ira Gershwin's *Lady, Be Good*. Side trips to Paris had to include Le Grand Duc, when patrons would push tables up against the walls to make room for an impromptu dance by the Astaires.[36]

---

36 As it turned out, Fred Astaire would portray the dancer and aviator Vernon Castle, with Ginger Rogers as his wife, in the 1949 film *The Story of Vernon and Irene Castle*.

13

"GRAND" GOLDEN YEARS

For Langston Hughes, toiling as a dishwasher in the tiny kitchen at Le Grand Duc, acclaim as a major American writer lay in the future. But in the mid- and late 1920s, there were plenty of emerging and established literary lights who came in through the front door.

One of them was Ernest Hemingway. As he chronicled in his late-life memoir *A Moveable Feast*, he and his (first) wife, Hadley, and their baby son Jack, who they called "Bumby,"[37] were poor but otherwise happy expatriates in Paris. Hemingway was working on short stories that would soon be published in the United States as a collection entitled *In Our Time*. He was simultaneously working on a full-length manuscript that would attract a lot more attention, the 1926 blockbuster novel *The Sun Also Rises*.

---

37 His mother's appellation was "because of his plump teddy-bear qualities."

Despite their precarious finances, the Hemingways scraped together enough francs often enough to become regulars at the cafés and nightclubs. They also took summer vacations in Spain and winter skiing excursions in the Alps. Hemingway always returned with fresh eyes for his adopted city. He wrote, after an excursion in 1925, "When we came back to Paris it was clear and cold and lovely. The city had accommodated itself to winter, there was good wood for sale at the wood and coal place across our street, and there were braziers outside of many of the good cafés so that you could keep warm on the terraces. Now you were accustomed to see the bare trees against the sky and you walked on the fresh-washed gravel paths through the Luxembourg gardens in the clear sharp wind."[38]

Hemingway's acquaintances were Ford Maddox Ford, Gertrude Stein, James Joyce, Ezra Pound, and others involved in advancing literature from beyond the days of Henry James and Mark Twain. When not at the cafés, Hemingway and many of his writer friends frequented Shakespeare and Company, the bookshop owned by Sylvia Beach, who had taken a huge risk in 1922 by publishing Joyce's groundbreaking *Ulysses*.

Although unnamed, Bullard always took great pride in what Hemingway wrote about him in *The Sun Also Rises*: "At Zelli's, a black, southern-accented drummer sings and exchanges pleasantries with Lady Brett Ashley, who acknowledges to Jake Barnes, the novel's protagonist, 'He's a great friend of mine.'"

For Bullard's nightclub, however, another writer outshone even the stellar Hemingway. As Bricktop recalled, "What made the difference was that the Montparnasse crowd of writers discovered Le Grand Duc, led by F. Scott Fitzgerald."

Fitzgerald and his wife, Zelda, were also American expa-

---

38 Ernest Hemingway, *A Moveable Feast* (New York: Scribner, 1964).

triates, and during these years he was newly famous for the novel considered his greatest work, *The Great Gatsby*. When the Fitzgeralds first entered Le Grand Duc in the fall of 1925, "Scott was almost thirty, but he acted like a big, overgrown kid," Bricktop observed. "He was so mischievous, he'd take over the whole place. It was impossible not to like him. He was a little boy in a man's body."

The Fitzgeralds also had a young child at home, so on many occasions Scott came to the club by himself or with friends, without Zelda. He tended to drink copiously and there were times when Bullard or Bricktop had to help him get home. He was a generous tipper, and Bullard was glad to see him because many of Fitzgerald's friends also enjoyed champagne and could easily afford it.

Another notable who became a regular at Le Grand Duc was the songwriter and former Barron's patron Cole Porter. He, too, had wealthy and influential friends, and where Porter went, they followed. Porter owned a home in Paris and spent as much time as he could there during the 1920s when taking breaks from his frenetic Broadway schedule. The first night he entered Le Grand Duc, Bricktop happened to be performing, at that very moment, one of his songs, "I'm In Love Again." Porter fell head over heels for Bricktop's style and her dancing. It was the beginning of a long association and Porter was instrumental in Bricktop being able to open her own club a few years later.

During that heady decade the famous names who found their way or were led to Le Grand Duc were legion, but there was one more that must be added to make the story complete: Josephine Baker.

In 1919, at age thirteen, she was dancing on street corners in St. Louis, living in cardboard lash-ups, working part-time as a waitress and scrounging food from the trash bins behind the restaurant where she worked. Her dancing saved her: she attracted the attention of the director of the St. Louis Chorus and ended up as a dancer in a vaudeville show at age fifteen. Her natural talent, smile and admirably long legs led to other gigs and a move to New York and the Harlem Renaissance. She performed in a number of revues, and when the opportunity came to join La Revue Negre, in Paris, she jumped at it. At that time, Paris was having its own version of the Harlem Renaissance, called *Le Tumulte Noir*.

At age nineteen, Baker was a sensation: she had been convinced to perform on stage all but nude. Her signature costume became a string of oversize pearls and a belt of fake bananas. Her gyrations and the overtly sexual nature of her performances left many customers breathing heavily and thinking thoughts about activities that did not involve the wearing of garments. At the height of her fame, Baker had Parisian women coating their skin with oils that would make them look darker. (Josephine identified as African American but her father was most likely white and she, therefore, was a very light-skinned black woman.) There were Baker robes, pajamas, and banana belts, and for the younger girls, Baker dolls. A special pomade was manufactured to help provide the signature forehead curl "Ba-kir" wore constantly.

In all other respects, she was a complete naïf. She was barely literate and although she had been married briefly, back in America, to a Pullman porter, she was extremely gullible and easily swayed. Thankfully, she had met and come under the protection of Bricktop, who helped guide her through her enormous fame and popularity in France.

"Oh, how she could wear clothes," Bricktop remembered, "although her fame would rest a lot on her ability to perform without them. I became her big sister. She'd come into Le Grand Duc and ask me about everything. She'd say, 'Bricky, tell me what to do.' She wouldn't go around the corner without asking my advice."

Baker became well-known to Eugene Bullard as well, and Baker often babysat for Bullard's daughters. There is a tantalizing wisp or two of evidence that the two may also have been lovers, at some point, but there is no firm proof. Again, as with Bricktop, neither one of them mentioned the other in their separate memoirs as being intimate with one another. They were surely well acquainted and spent a great deal of time together—why ignore their mutual attractions? Was it, perhaps, to keep any affair quiet? It is impossible, now, to know.

There are other intriguing commonalities between the pair. Bullard never renounced his American citizenship, but Baker did. She became a citizen of France in 1937. Bullard had become a citizen automatically upon his being wounded in battle for France in the Great War. Both ended up working for the Deuxième Bureau, an espionage agency, in 1939, and both were honored, post–World War II, by the French government for their work on behalf of France during the war.

Baker and Bullard were also fellow club owners. Josephine opened her nightspot in December 1926. The timing was perfect because during the last half of that delirious decade, there were still plenty of customers and expatriate dollars to go around.

As what the Americans called the Roaring Twenties continued, the money rolled in. Eugene Bullard was able to pay his powerhouse talent and share enough of the proceeds with Bricktop to keep her happy and not interested in going elsewhere to earn more. He could also afford to pay for good staff and top-flight bartenders—and some major muscle: he hired Charlie "Blink" McCloskey, the former heavyweight prizefighter who Bullard had known prewar. "Blink" would be his ever-faithful doorman and bouncer for many years.

Bullard presided over a nightclub that was "the" place for the well-heeled and fashionable to congregate. Like Zelli's, he had the business designated as a "bottle club" so it could stay open all night. Soon he was greeting and in some cases befriending a new wave of celebrities, all of whom wanted to enjoy the cozy and smoke-filled confines of Le Grand Duc. Among these new habitués were Clifton Webb, the actor, dancer, and singer who appeared in numerous movies and stage plays and was twice nominated for an Academy Award; the actress Tallulah Bankhead, who had yet to make the transition from stage to screen star; and James J. "Jimmy" Walker, who in 1926 became mayor of New York City. Pablo Picasso was a regular, too. Although already a world-famous artist, he was nonetheless still struggling financially. Somehow, though, his bills at Le Grand Duc always got paid. His presence and cachet (as far as Bullard was concerned) far outweighed the cost of his champagne.

Picasso was not the only famed artist who drank bubbly at Le Grand Duc. Two other regulars were Man Ray, best known for his portrait photography but also an avid painter, and Moise Kisling, Bullard's old friend and compatriot from the Foreign Legion. Kisling was still living and painting during the day in his spacious loft not far from Le Grand Duc and spending many evenings in Bullard's company at the club.

Even though the money flowed into the nightclub as fast as the champagne flowed out of the ice-cold bottles, the relationship between Bricktop and Bullard could be tense, at times. Bricktop had been raised as a "genteel" sort under the guidance of a struggling yet doting mother. She was well educated, and although not a college graduate, she had gone through high school with high marks in an integrated environment. Eugene Bullard, as we know, came to manhood in the company of Gypsies, sailors, toughs, boxers, Legionnaires, and utter war. He smoked, he drank, he cursed, and had a hair-trigger temper—especially when it came to matters of race and racial prejudice. Hardly a week went by without some sort of confrontation and a bar fight that often spilled out into the streets.

Bricktop witnessed scenes like the following: "I once saw him beat up three sailors with absolutely no help. [Bullard] was drunk, but when one of the sailors knocked him down, he sobered up the instant he hit the floor. One of the sailors was about to kick him, and he said, 'I'm sure you wouldn't hit a guy when he was down.' The sailor said, 'On your feet, nigger.' Gene jumped up swinging. It took five cops to break up the fight."

For Bullard, it was all about maintaining the place he had carved out for himself in the café society of Paris, and protecting his turf. As Craig Lloyd states, "Bullard was undoubtedly a central figure in the dazzling panorama of late-night and early morning Montmartre."

Additionally, beyond the boozy champagne nights and soft jazz wafting over the ritzy crowds, there were local gangs to deal with, payoffs to be made to sticky-fingered suppliers, drunken patrons to toss out, and many starving artists or shell-shocked comrades from the war to support or protect.

Their other rivalry was the business itself. Most likely, to keep Bricktop performing at the club, Bullard had given or sold her an ownership stake in Le Grand Duc. The two owners/managers didn't always see eye to eye, but they made it work, and the partnership was very successful, lasting four profitable years, until each of them courted separate and bigger ambitions.

Before moving on to those ambitions, one more Le Grand

Duc–era item must be mentioned. In July 1928, a monument was dedicated at Garches, outside Paris, to all the American pilots who had flown for France in the Great War. The Lafayette Escadrille Monument became the final resting place of fifty of the sixty-eight American pilots who died in the war. The structure itself was constructed as a half-scale model of the Arc de Triomphe, with a subterranean crypt for the fliers entombed therein.

This edifice would have been a great source of pride for Eugene Bullard, but one of the organizers behind the monument was his old enemy, Dr. Gros. He purposefully left Bullard off the monument as well as the guest list for the dedication. Fortunately, one of his old war buddies, Ted Parsons[39], tracked Bullard down and took him to the ceremony. Dr. Gros was not pleased. Needless to say, Bullard was thrilled—because of the monument, and ruining the racist doctor's enjoyment of the occasion.

As the decade ended, Bullard was ready to move on from Le Grand Duc, its owners, and those who worked there. But there was one more task to do for Bricktop—manage her wedding. In December 1929, she married Peter DuConge, a jazz saxophonist. Bullard was DuConge's best man, and he arranged for the ceremony to be held at the same venue where he and Marcelle had exchanged their vows. Bricktop recalls that Bullard "guided us through the intricacies of a French marriage ceremony and prompted us when to say '*oui*.'"

Then it was back to work. However, it would not be at Le

---

39 Edwin Charles "Ted" Parsons was already an experienced combat pilot when WWI began, having flown for Pancho Villa's forces in 1915-16. He volunteered for France and even remained with the Lafayette Escadrille (where he met Gene) when all American pilots were invited to transfer to the Army Air Service. He finished the war as an "ace" with eight kills. He then became an FBI agent, private detective, film technical advisor for aviation and in WWII a pilot and instructor for the US Navy, ending the war with a Bronze Star and as a rear admiral. When he died in 1968 he was the last surviving ace from the Lafayette Escadrille.

Grand Duc. Bullard sold his ownership share of the club because he was about to preside over a nightclub that was completely his own.

14

L'ESCADRILLE WITHOUT WINGS

The impact of the stock market crash that took place in the United States in October 1929 was not felt right away in Europe, but over time the effects were inescapable. It was probably not the best time for an ambitious nightlife impresario to strike out on his own.

However, that is exactly what Eugene Bullard did. Though he had flourished at Le Grand Duc, he was restless. He'd had a hot and cold relationship with George and Madame Jamerson, who did indeed retain some ownership of the club, and there were continuing spats with Bricktop. His marriage was on the rocks and he needed a distraction to keep his focus on his work. Given his gifts as an impresario and the many people he knew in elite social circles, Bullard wanted to run his own establishment. With the dawn of the new decade, he began to see Le Grand Duc as a vision in his rearview mirror.

By early 1931, he was ensconced in his own establishment,

a bar at 5 rue Pierre Fontaine, not far from Place Blanche and the Moulin Rouge. He named his new club "The Squadron," or, in French, "L'Escadrille," in honor of his aviation service during the Great War, and perhaps also to recapture some of his "glory days" and the special camaraderie he had felt with so many of his pilot friends. In addition to the club, he also purchased a nearby gym at 15 rue Mansart that was named "Bullard's Athletic Club." It offered steam baths, workout facilities, a boxing ring, ping pong tables, and massages. Adding a gym to the night club was an inspiration: each complemented the other. Exhausted club patrons could revive with steam, exercise, and massages and then start the party all over again.

By 1931, though, the Montmartre scene was finally feeling the impact of difficult times. The Wall Street collapse had triggered a worldwide recession as well as a full-blown depression in the United States. Money was tight, and the rich "fat cats" of the 1920s had slunk away to lick their financial wounds or were jumping out of windows. Deep-pocketed Americans no longer filled the pulsating clubs. Even the citizens of Paris were watching their purses and wallets with a great deal of worry.

Like Bullard, Bricktop had branched out and then owned her own club, but by 1931 she would be forced to close it and return to singing for her supper.[40] Even Joe Zelli had given up, returning to New York, where he got into the cheese and salad dressing business—a far cry from hot jazz and chilled

---

40   Bricktop would open another nightspot but it, too, could not endure. She remained in Paris until Germany invaded Poland, and then she sailed for the United States. She continued as an entertainer there, and after the war she returned to being an international chanteuse. After she died in February 1984 at age eighty-nine, in her Manhattan apartment, three hundred friends and admirers attended her funeral, Mabel Mercer and Bobby Short sent letters read at the service, and Ella Fitzgerald and Frank Sinatra sent flowers. Her grave can be found in the Woodlawn Cemetery in the Bronx.

champagne.[41] One by one, other clubs and cabarets closed down. There were simply too many venues for the shrinking pool of patrons who still had discretionary cash.

Bullard, however, seemed to be exempt. He had, of course, made many friends. His fame had spread across the city, and the fact that he spoke French, German, and a smattering of Italian as well as his native English made him much more cosmopolitan than most of his rivals. The gym helped, too, especially since his club patrons received preference for membership and could avail themselves of private lockers and dressing rooms.

Also helping to underwrite the new nightclub was the occasional catering gig: large, society parties for those who could still afford such *affaires magnifiques* were still being held in the best neighborhoods of the city. One such extravaganza, whose entertainment was arranged and produced by Gene, was richly described in Craig Lloyd's book, as follows:

> Bullard's friendship with Parisian Oscar Mauvais, the owner of the club Jardin de Ma Sueur on rue Caumartin, resulted in his being hired for a major social event in the summer of 1931. Knowing of Bullard's familiarity with Biarritz and his connections with African-American performers, Mauvais asked him to arrange part of the entertainment for a party at the Hotel Negresco in honor of King Alphonso XIII of Spain. The deposed monarch, who was still tangling with General Francisco Franco, had taken up residence in Paris after being exiled earlier that year by Franco's Republican political insurgents. An American millionaire whose daughter had been married

---

41   After quitting Paris, Joe Zelli opened clubs in New York and Palm Beach before buying into the wholesale food business. He died in 1971, age eighty-three, in Hillsdale, NY.

into the Spanish royal family was sponsoring the gala. Bullard's task was to put together a troupe of dancers, dress them "in the old plantation costumes of colored folk," and perform the high-stepping cakewalk.[42]

Bullard hired nineteen dancers, including an instructor, Nettie Compton, and since a twentieth was needed, he joined the group in the two-hour rehearsals taking place each of the four days before the affair. Costumes were lent him by another Parisian friend, the ex-producer of the Josephine Baker revue.

Bullard's troupe, "laden with champagne appeased by a lot of hot coffee," cakewalked into the grand ballroom at 3:00 a.m. to the beat of black American Hugh Pollard's band. The king and other guests were delighted, giving them three encores. The entertainers were then treated to a huge supper in the hotel's dining room, which the king visited, toasting and shaking hands with all of them.[43]

That must have been some party, wondrous to behold, and amazing that it could be pulled off, given the constraints of a worldwide depression and the king's abdication.

Even during the difficult years of the early '30s, Bullard was able to book the best acts. When Louis Armstrong came to Paris and encamped there for several months in 1934, he spent numerous nights at L'Escadrille. He was a sensational

---

42 "Cakewalk, couple dance that became a popular stage act for virtuoso dancers as well as a craze in fashionable ballrooms around 1900. Couples formed a square with the men on the inside and, stepping high to a lively tune, strutted around the square. The couples were eliminated one by one by several judges, who considered the elegant bearing of the men, the grace of the women, and the inventiveness of the dancers; the last remaining pair was presented with a highly decorated cake. The cakewalk originated earlier among American black slaves who, often in the presence of their masters, used the dance as a subtle satire on the elegance of white ballroom dances. It contributed to the evolution of subsequent American and European dances based on jazz rhythms, and its music influenced the growth of ragtime." (*Encyclopaedia Britannica*, 2018).

43 Lloyd, 108–109.

Eugene Bullard grew up in a home almost identical to the one next door, shown here, in Columbus, Georgia, circa 1900. *Craig Lloyd/Eugene Bullard Collection, Columbus State University.*

Bullard went only so far as through second grade in this segregated school in Columbus, circa 1902. *Craig Lloyd/Eugene Bullard Collection, Columbus State University.*

1. When Eugene was a child, his father, William "Big Chief Ox" Bullard, worked at the Bradley Warehouse in Columbus, Georgia. *Bradley Co.*

2. The SS *Marta Russ* provided the teenage Bullard with the means of escape to Europe.

3. Bob Scanlon was a friend and colleague of Bullard both in the ring and on the battlefield.

4. Aaron Lister Brown, the boxer known as the "Dixie Kid," befriended Bullard early in his boxing career.

5. Bullard's boxing career benefited from being able to train with Jack Johnson, the first African American heavyweight champion.

6. As a member of the French Foreign Legion, Eugene Bullard (right) first served in the 3rd Marching Regiment (1915).

Shown here in 1913, a svelte Eugene Bullard
was a rising boxing star in the welterweight class.

Top is Fort Douaumont and its immediate surroundings in 1915, and bottom is the same area after the impact of one million shells.

1. Corporal Bullard in the uniform of the 170th Infantry, "Les Hirondelles du Mort," in 1916. Affixed to his left breast is the Croix de Guerre.

National Museum of the US Air Force, Dayton, Ohio.

2. As a pilot in training, Bullard first learns to "fly" the flightless "Penguin."

National Museum of the US Air Force, Dayton, Ohio.

3. The actual license the twenty-one-year-old Eugene Bullard earned that enabled him to become a combat pilot.

National Museum of the US Air Force, Dayton, Ohio.

4. A flight training class at Avord in 1917 gathers for a group portrait. Bullard is standing at the back, fourth from the right.

National Museum of the US Air Force, Dayton, Ohio.

1. This photograph, taken in September or October 1917, shows Bullard in the cockpit about to undertake a mission. Note the distinctive heart and the slogan, "All Blood That Runs is Red."

National Museum of the US Air Force, Dayton, Ohio.

2. Bullard's fellow pilots congratulate him with a "lift" after his first combat mission in the fall of 1917.

National Museum of the US Air Force, Dayton, Ohio.

3. Quickly becoming an experienced combat pilot, Bullard poses in front of a SPAD with his "copilot," Jimmy.

National Museum of the US Air Force, Dayton, Ohio.

Thanks to his bravery and good fortune in not getting killed, Bullard began to accumulate awards from a grateful France. *National Museum of the US Air Force, Dayton, Ohio.*

Among the American pilots who served in France before and after the US entered World War I were:

1. Quentin Roosevelt
2. Eddie Rickenbacker
3. Norman Prince
4. Raoul Lufbery (and Whiskey)

1. Ted Parsons
2. Ernest Bleckley
3. Frank Luke
4. Harold Goettler
5. Victor Chapman
6. David Ingalls

1. The bigoted Dr. Edmund Gros became Bullard's nemesis and was part of his removal from active duty as a pilot.

2. Back in Paris after the war, Bullard enjoyed being a man-about-town.

3. Turning to drumming to make a living, Bullard became a member of the very popular Zelli's Band, seen here in 1922 (Eugene is seated behind the drum, front row).

4. Bricktop (second from left) and Bullard (right) with Joe Zelli (center) and Mabel Mercer (second from right), 1932.

   Courtesy of Manuscript, Archives and Rare Book Library, Emory University.

5. During his nightclub impresario days in Paris, Bullard enjoyed entertaining patrons with an impromptu concert.

   Screenshot courtesy of Critical Past, Reston, Virginia.

Joe Zelli's with the Royal Box Smile

PARIS 1927

1

BULLARD'S ATHLETIC CLUB

(Ex-Entraineur de DIXIE-KID, ex-Champion du Monde, poids Welter
et de AL. BROWN, Champion du Monde, Entraineur de YOUNG PEREZ)

15, Rue MANSART, PARIS-9e
Tél. : PIGALLE 78-05

SON GYMNASE UNIQUE à PARIS

de 8 m. de hauteur, entièrement vitré
AIR, LUMIÈRE, TOUT CONFORT
(Cabines d'habillage et Placards individuels)

CULTURE PHYSIQUE
HOMMES - FEMMES - ENFANTS

BOXE - MASSAGE

PING-PONG -- HYDROTHÉRAPIE

OUVERT TOUS LES JOURS DE 8 H. A 20 H. 30
Location de la Salle et Cours d'ensemble à Sociétés

2

3

1. Seen here in 1927 are musicians on the bandstand at Zelli's nightclub, including (left to right) Glover Compton on piano, Ferdie Allen on banjo, Cricket Smith on trumpet, Frank Goudie on alto sax and Eugene Bullard on drums.

*Courtesy of Dave Radlauer,
Constantine Soo's "Dagogo," February 2018.*

2. Bullard owned and operated a gym that became a popular place for boxers to train and patrons to sweat out a night of partying.

National Museum of the US Air Force, Dayton, Ohio.

3. Ada Louise "Bricktop" Smith began her singing career in Paris thanks to Eugene Bullard, and she became one of the city's most popular performers.

1. Another Bullard import whom Paris patrons enjoyed was Dooley Wilson, later to find fame as Sam in the Oscar-winning classic *Casablanca* (October 1942).

   Courtesy of Warner Bros.

2. Fred and Adele Astaire, seen here in *Lady Be Good* in 1924, enjoyed Le Grand Duc during visits to Paris.

3. The composer Cole Porter was a frequent patron, especially because of his friendship with Bricktop.

   Courtesy of NPR (National Public Radio).

4. The sultry Josephine Baker took Paris by storm in the 1920s and, like her friend and possible romantic partner Eugene Bullard, aided the French Resistance.

1. Ernest Hemingway, shown on the day of his wedding to Hadley in 1921, was a friend of Bullard's and modeled a character on him in *The Sun Also Rises*.

2. The acclaimed poet Langston Hughes worked for Bullard as a waiter and dishwasher in Paris.

3. Louis "Satchmo" Armstrong and Eugene Bullard became fast friends the first time the jazz artist visited Paris in the early 1930s.

   Courtesy of Richard Havers, uDiscoverMusic.com, July 2014.

4. Zelda and F. Scott Fitzgerald in 1924 when they—especially the latter—frequented Bullard's nightclub Le Grand Duc.

5. The Brasserie Universelle in Paris, seen in 1923, where Eugene and Marcelle celebrated their wedding.

1. The interior of L'Escadrille, Eugene Bullard's very popular nightclub in Paris in the 1930s.

   Courtesy of louisjeang.wixsite.com/ allbloodrunsredsite.

2. Eugene Bullard in 1930, when he was opening L'Escadrille and becoming one of the most well-known impresarios in Paris.

   Courtesy of New Georgia Encyclopedia. 31 January 2017.

3. Bullard, seen here in 1936, always made sure the champagne was flowing at L'Escadrille… especially when Nazi officers began to arrive and alcohol fueled loose lips.

   Courtesy of Craig Lloyd/ Eugene Bullard Collection, Columbus State University.

4. Eugene Bullard is overjoyed to be reunited with his daughters, Lolita (left) and Jacqueline (right), in New York in February 1941.

   "Ebony" Magazine, December 1967.

5. Paul Robeson, a popular entertainer before and after World War II, often combined his performances with political causes.

   Courtesy of Office of War Information-1942.

6. Eugene Bullard is shown being beaten when trying to attend a Paul Robeson concert in Peekskill, New York, in 1949.

   "People's Weekly World," September 1949.

1. Louis Armstrong and his wife, Lucille, are on their way to Paris in 1951, accompanied by Eugene Bullard, who was their interpreter as well as friend and occasional studio musician.

   "Ebony" Magazine, December 1967.

2. Bullard in his French Legionnaire's uniform in New York in 1959.

   Courtesy of louisjeang.wixsite.com/ allbloodrunsredsite.

3. Bullard and other French war veterans relight the eternal flame and lay flowers at the Arc de Triomphe in 1954.

   National Museum of the US Air Force, Dayton, Ohio.

4. Eugene Bullard in his Harlem apartment, which was filled with memorabilia dating back to his years in France.

   "Ebony" Magazine, December 1967.

5. One of the proudest moments of Eugene Bullard's life, shared with his daughters, was when he received the Chevalier of the Legion of Honor in 1959.

1. Eugene Bullard's array of medals and decorations, including his pilot's badge (far left).

   National Museum of the US Air Force, Dayton, Ohio.

2. The Rockefeller Center elevator operator Eugene Bullard being interviewed on the *Today* show by host Dave Garroway, who displays the many medals and decorations Bullard earned.

   National Museum of the US Air Force, Dayton, Ohio.

3. Taken in April 1961, this is the last known photo of Eugene Bullard, standing beneath a statue of the Marquis de Lafayette in New York.

   National Museum of the US Air Force, Dayton, Ohio.

4. This bust of the combat pilot Eugene Bullard can be found in the National Air and Space Museum in Washington, DC.

   Courtesy of National Air and Space Museum, NASM #92-13509.

hit, and Bullard enjoyed many lucrative evenings with his club enveloped in "Satchmo's" outsized personality.

Armstrong and his third wife, Alpha, rented an apartment in the rue de la Tour Auvergne, and may have contemplated becoming an expatriate himself. "I just lazied around Paris for three or four months [and] had lots of fun with musicians from the States—French cats, too. And I'd do a concert now and then." In his biography on Armstrong, Laurence Bergreen reports that the trumpet player enjoyed "socializing with other expatriate members of American café society, many of them black—Josephine Baker, Bricktop, Bobby Jones, and Arthur Briggs—taking his ease at Café Boudon, nursing aperitifs, observing the scene. He acquired a stature in Paris that he had never attained at home."

Armstrong and Bullard hit it off as friends, helped by both being black men from the Deep South who had escaped dire poverty. Those who still had the means to enjoy Parisian nightlife and acts like Armstrong, Bricktop, Fats Waller, and Josephine Baker needed a place to congregate and that spot, more and more, became L'Escadrille.

Bullard's Athletic Club flourished as well. His old pal from the war, Jeff Dickson, the man who had put up the bold $2,000 bet that Bullard could not get designated as a pilot, reappeared in Paris as a boxing promoter. He booked many of his contestants into Bullard's gym to work out. The world bantamweight championship boxing match of 1934 was held in Paris between "Panama" Al Brown and Young Perez, and both fighters trained at the Bullard Athletic Club.

Bullard's success had an impending cloud hanging over it, though: the same one causing increasing concern across France. When Hitler came to power in Germany in 1933, Bullard and many of the old hands from the previous war grew very nervous. Here was the same enemy, supposedly taught a lesson in the "war to end all wars," on the rise once again. Nazism was beginning to creep into every corner of Europe, and Paris was no exception.

Bullard's friend and fellow club owner Jocelyn Augustus Bingham, whom everyone called "Frisco,"[44] recalled one day, in 1935, when the two went to their favorite brasserie to have one of their frequent luncheons. Several Germans entered the eatery and made some remarks to Bullard about being black. "Gene looked at them and told them they'd better leave the place or they'd be sorry. They didn't. Instead, they sat down and ordered lunch. When it was served, Gene went over to the table, picked up a plate of spaghetti, and pushed it into the face of one of the Germans."

The resulting row required a number of gendarmes and several bystanders to separate Bullard and the Germans. He was willing to take them on—all of them at once. He held his own against the furious Aryans until the melee got untangled. The Germans were kicked out of the bistro, fuming, with threats of jail if they didn't disperse. Bullard was, after all, a well-known local war hero, and he was practically immune from arrest; still, it was an ugly prelude of much worse yet to come.

There was no escape for Bullard even in his own athletic club. He proudly tacked up the flags of all nations who had boxers and members in his gym. There were twenty-one national flags, including Germany's, on display. One boxer who worked out there wanted another flag flown—the swastika of the Nazi Party. Walter Neusel was the so-called "Blond

---

44 Bingham was originally from Jamaica, but had spent several years as a long-shoreman in San Francisco before migrating to Paris; thus, the nickname "Frisco." Like Bullard, he enlisted in the French Foreign Legion and spent three years in the trenches. After the war he, too, settled in Paris and began entertaining. He was a popular singer and dancer, and with backing from Bricktop and Josephine he opened and ran his own nightclub, "Frisco's," from late 1929 until the Nazis invaded in 1940.

Tiger" of Germany. At his professional apex, in 1934, this heavyweight would take on the world champion, fellow German Max Schmeling, in front of a record one hundred thousand fans in Hamburg. Eugene Bullard, the welterweight who had been known as "Sparrow," proved too much for Neusel, however.

The German pestered Bullard enough times about the Nazi flag that finally the proprietor had enough. Just before the bout with Schmeling (which Neusel would lose in a ninth-round TKO), Neusel finally bugged Bullard one time too many. Bullard was puffing a cigarette at that moment, and he calmly blew smoke in Neusel's face and told him to leave the gym—for good—or else. Neusel backed down, probably more out of concern for his hands and his upcoming fight than taking on the gym owner, but it was a moral victory for Bullard nonetheless. The Nazi flag never went up at the Athletic Club, and Neusel never came back.

Not long after the Neusel confrontation, Bullard and his longtime friend Opal Cooper were having a beverage or two at the Costa Bar. They were drinking and chatting at one end of the metal bar when a large man, who announced he was from New Orleans, approached and asked, "Are you Eugene Bullard?"

After Bullard replied that he was, Cooper reported that "the big guy hauled off and took a big swing at Gene. Gene ducked and the big man hit his fist against the metal bar. If he had ever hit Gene, he would have killed him. As it was, the man broke his hand. Gene jumped on the big guy and almost beat him to death. Gene beat him every kind of way you could think of."

Neither Cooper nor Bullard ever discovered exactly why the Louisianan came after Gene. As the man lay moaning on the floor, there was a mumbled reference to a "lost girlfriend," thanks to Bullard, but no one could quite figure it out.

He was probably safer in his own club with Blink McCloskey keeping a wary eye on him. L'Escadrille was actually smaller than his gym and more of a cabaret than a "grand club." It was wedged in between a *boulangerie* and a branch of Credit Suisse. The comforting aroma of fresh-baked bread on one side mingled with the smell of money on the other. The cabaret contributed the sticky sweet odor of spilled champagne, stale cigarettes, and the brass polish from the band members' instruments. It was a heady mix and it all bespoke good times despite the dawning realization that there could be another war only one generation removed from the last debacle.

To make his cozy space seem much larger, Bullard had emulated a look he had learned to appreciate at the old Zelli's: many of the wall spaces were mirrored, which added almost another full dimension to the space. The restroom doors and walls were completely covered with mirrored glass and the cleaning and polishing of all these surfaces was a daily, nagging chore.

The effect was powerful, however, and many of his well-heeled patrons enjoyed catching glimpses of themselves laughing, chatting, or gliding across the cramped and often crowded dance floor. Had Henri Toulouse-Lautrec still been painting, he undoubtedly would have found the tableau at L'Escadrille perfect for one of his colorful, crowded, dizzying canvases.

On January 30, 1933, Adolf Hitler was named chancellor of Germany. Imagine the irony: the president of Germany, Paul von Hindenburg (who would die the following year), former supreme commander of all German forces in World

War I, was essentially handing over leadership of the country to a formerly obscure German Army corporal from Bavaria. Hitler's rise to international power and his quest for world domination began that day.

In Paris, Bullard picked up a copy of *Le Monde*, with its banner headlines on Hitler, and started a slow, fearful burn. Since 1923, when Herr Hitler first broke into the world's consciousness with his "beer hall putsch," Bullard had been telling anyone who would listen that the Germans would be coming after France yet again. For a decade, many of those who bothered to listen had scoffed. No more.

Some in the French government believed likewise, but early preparations for war took various forms, some productive, some not so much. One effective effort revolved around an organization called the Deuxième Bureau. The French military, prior to World War II, viewed operational intelligence as a key to good preparation. The general staff of the army had two external departments devoted to intelligence collection operations. The first, or Premier Bureau, was responsible for gathering vital information on the strength and capabilities of France's own forces, plus those of her potential allies. The second, or Deuxième Bureau, revolved around counterintelligence: discovering what France's potential enemies were capable of doing, where their spies were located, and all about their cryptanalysis and code-breaking capabilities.

To assist in its efforts, the Deuxième Bureau enlisted the help of many members of both the territorial civilian police forces and the metropolitan police in the major cities. The Deuxième Bureau, history has shown us, did serious and effective work on the home front, especially during the late 1930s as Europe hurtled toward another continental war. It did not embark on its mission a moment too soon. By 1937, over 17,000 Germans, most of them members of the Nazi Party, were living and working in France under various guises, but all, in effect, were spying for either the German intelligence operation reporting directly to the Wehrmacht, known as the Abwehr[45], or the Nazi Party and its notorious spymaster Rudolph Hess. The Deuxième Bureau had most of these intelligence gatherers under surveillance, a huge effort requiring a lot of man (and woman) power.[46]

In June 1938, a metropolitan police inspector by the name of George Leplanquais came into the orbit of Eugene Bullard. By January of '39, Bullard was referring to him as "a dear friend of mine." Leplanquais was more than a local cop. His official title was "Inspecteur Special près des Commissariats de la Ville de Paris" which in Scotland Yard parlance would make him equal to a chief inspector and in New York an officer ranking just below deputy chief. One of Leplanquais's most important, behind the scenes responsibilities, however, was to recruit Parisians to keep an eye on Nazi activity in the city. Aiding him in this mission was a cadre of local operatives scattered throughout Leplanquais's arrondissement (the 18th or Montmartre). The inspector had dearly wanted Bullard to join his network, and he joined eagerly, once he was assured his daughters would be protected if something should happen to him. Assigned to assist Bullard, as well as to coordinate "other activities," was a lovely, seductive, trilingual Alsatian, Cleopatre "Kitty" Terrier.

Born in 1912, Kitty Terrier was the third child, and only daughter, of solid middle-class farmers from the city of Colmar, in northeastern Alsace. The area had been, for centuries, a picturesque French riverfront farming community bordering Germany. After the disastrous (for France) Franco-Prussian War of 1871, Colmar, as well as Metz, Strasbourg, Mulhau-

---

45 The organization, which existed as part of the German Defense Ministry, was active from 1920 to 1944.

46 By contrast, the French counterintelligence effort in Germany in the late 1930s numbered less than five hundred.

sen and Diedenhofen, plus 93 percent of what had once been the Alsace Region (and 26 percent of Lorraine), became German territory. Kitty's grandfather had been the mayor of Colmar before the conflict. The ever-efficient Huns soon began rearranging and erasing all semblance of France in the conquered territory, right down to changing the street names and all municipal regulations. German became the official language, and local magistrates were allowed to fine the citizens for speaking even a single word of French.

As soon as the Great War commenced, in 1914, the Alsace-Lorraine Region became hotly contested territory once again. The French were determined to recover their ceded, sacred soil. Wherever the French Army was victorious within the region, German citizens were rounded up and placed in camps. Special attention was paid to any German veterans of the '71 war, even though these old soldiers were well beyond middle age and of no real threat to warring against the French. The Germans, for their part, where they held sway, were constantly arresting what they termed *francs-tireurs*, or "terrorists." The Germans were not terribly discriminating, which is how Kitty's totally innocent father was arrested one day, tried the next, and placed up against a wall and shot by the end of the week. Kitty was six years old at the time.

The murder of her father engendered in the young girl a lifelong hatred for Germany and all things German. She vowed, someday, to get revenge. She spoke French, of course, but also became fluent in German to aid her cause. In school she also mastered English as well as a bit of Italian. She was extremely bright and once past her secondary school studies she enrolled in the "Centre d'études Diplomatiques et Stratégiques" (Center for Diplomatic and Strategic Studies) in Paris. Her goal was to become a member of the French Diplomatic Corps and fight German expansion and colonialism everywhere she could. She was halfway toward her graduate degree when the Nazi threat to France become all too real. She set aside her studies (at least temporarily) and joined the Deuxième Bureau. Her initial commandant became George Leplanquais.

ACT V
THE SPY

15

THE OBERST

During the spring and summer of 1939, the team of Eugene Bullard and Kitty Terrier were especially cordial to their German "friends" and casually eavesdropped on any and all conversations the Boche had in L'Escadrille. They listened for anything that might be fruitful, plucking all they could for Inspector Leplanquais and the Deuxième Bureau. Apparently, there was a great deal of information to be had, and the pair was kept quite busy.

On the afternoon of June 30, 1939, Bullard was at his gym sparring with a boxer friend when Leplanquais, unannounced, arrived for an "inspection." This was highly unusual. Feigning a need to "see Mssr. Bullard's records," the two repaired to Bullard's private office and shut the door.

"Mon ami," Leplanquais began once he was sure no one

was within earshot, "I have some very interesting news. We have just learned that you are going to be receiving some very important guests tonight."

"Ah, who might they be?"

"You have a reservation, I'm told, for eleven o'clock? Table for ten? Under the name 'Otto Steinwehr'?"

"Why, I believe so, yes. Otto's a regular in our German crowd, as you know. He's dropped some valuable tidbits, that one has."

"Well, he's coming back tonight with a new friend, Colonel Walter Scheer."

"Do we know this Scheer?"

"Indeed we do. He's the newly appointed military attaché at the German Embassy. We also know he's a member of the Abwehr. This is his first week in Paris and he's making the rounds. Tonight, he wants to party, and he's heard of your famous L'Escadrille."

Bullard leaned back in his chair and smiled before responding. "Then we shall make sure he gets our very best champagne—and our most special attention."

"I was hoping I could count on you for that, Gene. Of course, Kitty will be there. It should make for a most interesting evening."

The two comrades stood, shook hands and Leplanquais completed his "inspection" and left. Bullard returned to sparring, his partner noting that the owner's punches had more power to them.

That night, in a display of typical German punctuality, three Mercedes sedans wound their way up the cobblestone pathways of La Rue Fontaine, pulling up in front of L'Escadrille at precisely eleven o'clock. Oberst Scheer, with two aides in tow, emerged from the middle car and strode into the club.

A steel blue tobacco haze hung over the brightly lit center section of the dance floor. Every table was occupied—except the one large banquette reserved for the important party then entering. The band was backing Bricktop as she belted out Cole Porter. The singer's misfortune with her own club had been L'Escadrille's gain, and Bullard was glad to be reunited with her immense talent. As she sang, he banged away enthusiastically on the drums.

This was Paris, not Morocco, but reality was eerily following fantasy that sultry night, foreshadowing the plot of the movie *Casablanca*, which would be released to much acclaim in the United States three years later. With only a few twists of the imagination, L'Escadrille was Rick's Café. It could have been Eugene Bullard as a black Rick Blaine, the role played by Humphrey Bogart, with German spies and Nazi officers in mufti coming through his door. Ilsa, the role that would go to Ingrid Bergman, could be played by the equally mysterious and charming Kitty Terrier. The gallant—and ultimately righteous—Captain Louis Renault's part would fall to Inspector Georges Leplanquais. Colonel Scheer would fill in for Major Heinrich Strasser. In perhaps the oddest twist of all, the role of Sam was being filled that night by Dooley Wilson, who would actually play the part of Sam in the movie. As it happened, Wilson was visiting friends in Paris, and Bullard was only too happy to have him make a guest appearance at L'Escadrille.

As the Germans settled in, Bullard put aside his drumsticks and played, instead, the attentive host to his special guests. Kitty became the coquette and flirted suggestively with the Oberst and his men. The best champagne flowed freely, and the band continued deeper into its playlist. Leplanquais lurked in the shadows of the club, in case "trouble" decided to make a guest appearance.

It nearly did. At two in the morning, the Germans had finally had enough. Colonel Scheer was ready to depart. A group of rowdy Frenchmen and Corsican toughs, from gangs in the neighborhood, had also been in the club and imbibing heavily. Their resentment for the haughty Germans had been building with each round of drinks. A knot of about eight of them got up to follow the German contingent into the street.

Leplanquais grew frantic. The last thing he wanted was a confrontation between regular patrons at the club and the Germans. If there was any nastiness, the Germans might not come back, and that would be a blow to his productive counterintelligence work at the nightclub. Leplanquais signaled Bullard that disaster was afoot. Instantly grasping the severity of the situation, Bullard rounded up several members of the band, all of whom were fiercely loyal to their employer and physically fit thanks to their free privileges at Bullard's Athletic Club. The hulking bouncer "Blink" McCloskey was alongside his boss.

As the Germans began to get into their cars, the toughs hit the door at the front of the club. Bullard and his crew were right behind them. With choreography worthy of the club's dance floor, they placed themselves between the departing Germans and the drunken Frenchmen and Corsicans. Bullard personally thanked Oberst Scheer for coming and helped the unsteady colonel get into his car. Some shoving occurred and some threats were tossed at the Germans as they left, but there was no damage to them, or the spying operation.

Some of the Corsicans involved were members of a local gang called Les Corses, who operated throughout Montmartre and provided "protection services" as well as drugs and prostitutes. Justin Pereti was one of the leaders, and as drunk as he was that night, he still managed to notice how friendly and accommodating Eugene Bullard seemed to be toward the hated Nazis. It did not sit well with Pereti, and he made up his mind then and there that Bullard would have to be made to account for his actions.

16

"REMEMBER YOUR PROMISE!"

So, this is how it ends, Eugene Bullard thought to himself as he squirmed in agony, eyes tightly shut, tears of pain streaming down his cheeks. Having been seriously wounded twice before, in the Great War, he knew the coppery smell of blood, and he could sense his own life ebbing from the wound, puddling on the floor underneath the gurney.

All around him, people were shouting. Nurses were screaming for a doctor. The gendarmes were clamoring to get at him, to question him. Kitty was bent over him, protective, bravely holding back tears. The bullet had probably torn up his insides and his entire gut was on fire.

"Where the hell is the doctor, anyway?" he groaned.

"Be quiet, *mon cher*. He'll be here shortly," Kitty whispered in his ear.

"You must get Leplanquais, Kitty. Now. He made me a promise, if I should die."

"Hush, hush. You're not going to die."

"I know these things, *ma cherie*. I am dying. Please. Go get him. I must speak to him, *tout de suite*."

"Very well." She kissed Bullard firmly on the cheek and disappeared.

Nurses bent over him, fussing, sopping up blood, trying to dress the stubbornly bleeding wound. Each dab placed pressure on his abdomen causing new waves of scream-inducing pain; yet, he did not cry out. *It's best not to seem afraid,* he told himself.

On the morning of the day he was shot, Eugene Bullard followed his usual routine. No matter how late he got back from managing his club, he would get up in time to have coffee with his daughters, Jacqueline, fifteen, and eleven-year-old Lolita. With their mother gone, the girls had been required to take on a great deal of independence given that Bullard was a single parent with a rigorous schedule. Morning coffee was sacred. He wanted to savor every precious moment they could be together.

It was a perfect early July morning in what Bullard thought was the most beautiful city in the world. He and his daughters sat at a table that looked out at a sea of Parisian rooftops. The apartment had a small kitchen parlor with tall double windows that faced south, toward the center of the city. Behind them was an open living room which contained the modest but tasteful furniture his wife, Marcelle, had selected soon after their marriage. Bullard's contributions to the decor could be found on the plastered walls—framed photographs, accumulated over the years, bearing the likenesses of the luminaries and friends (often, they were both) who had patronized L'Escadrille or its predecessor, Le Grand Duc. A casual scan of the pictures would reveal writers like Ernest Hemingway; F. Scott Fitzgerald, with his wife, Zelda; and Gertrude Stein. There were famed musicians such as Duke Ellington and Louis Armstrong; composers and performers such as Cole Porter, "Bricktop," and Josephine Baker; stage and screen stars like Fred Astaire, Gloria Swanson, and Edward G. Robinson; plus, prominent politicians, ambassadors, and even, as Kipling had written, a "man who would be king," Edward VIII of England.

To Bullard, however, there were no more important or beautiful faces in the apartment than those sitting across from him at that moment. As much as Jacqueline and Lolita could, without turning away in embarrassment, the girls tolerated their father's gaze. Bullard reflected that if his own father, "Big Chief Ox" Bullard, were ever to meet them, he would be hard-pressed to believe they were his granddaughters. Unlike the dark, black skin of the Bullard African forebears and Bullard himself, the complexions of Jacqueline and Lolita had been influenced by Marcelle's porcelain white.

Bullard's daughters fully accepted yet found it somewhat fascinating that their grandfather had been born to slaves in a place called Georgia, that their grandmother had been an American Indian and that their father—at an age younger than theirs—had run away to make his way in the world with powerful fists and a strong back. By contrast, with their modest but genteel lifestyle, neither girl could ever dream of running away from the hypnotic charms of the City of Light.

Bullard was then in his forty-fourth year. Marcelle had been gone almost eight years. A decade earlier, poor Eugene Jr., their only male child, had survived for six short months before double pneumonia had taken him. Bullard and his wife had never quite recovered from that heartbreaking experience. So yes, every minute with his remaining children was priceless and could never be recaptured.

Deep in his reverie, Bullard almost missed his daughters kissing him on both cheeks, grabbing their satchels, and dancing out the door with a cheery *"Au revoir, Papa!"* Even on a Saturday in summer, Jacqueline and Lolita attended the academy. It was the best one Bullard could afford, although he was contemplating sending them to England. The threats of war were becoming more strident, and he could not bear the thought of his girls being caught up in that.

Thoughts of war reminded him of the Germans, and that he must get on with his day. After a quick washup, a shave, and a fresh shirt, he left the apartment at noon, off to meet his good friend, "Frisco" Bingham. They rendezvoused, as usual, at the Capital Restaurant where they had, as usual, onion soup and fresh baguettes. Bullard learned from his friend of yet another nightclub closing. Apprehension about the Germans was cutting into the nightlife crowd of Paris with the cruel irony that the one exception happened to be the Germans themselves. They had been flooding into France as though they owned the country, which few doubted they planned on doing.

Bullard hoped his dangerous involvement in espionage would help him learn of any invasion in advance. He also prayed that, with luck, the Nazi war machine would choose a different victim—maybe Belgium, or Poland. The ever-increasing number of Germans who were enjoying Paris didn't offer much for optimists to cling to, however.

The sun shone brilliantly overhead as Bullard took his leave from Frisco and began the stroll that would eventually lead him to L'Escadrille. Early summer in Paris was nearly always sublime, one of the best times of the year. Temperatures rarely rose above seventy-five degrees in the daytime, and the nights were warm and languid. So it was on this particular Saturday, with the citizens of Paris enjoying splendid weather, the street fairs, and shopping. Many were preparing for the evening's fancy dress balls or the clubbing they hoped to do in the cabarets that were still open.

The avenues remained inviting, the cafés were doing their best to carry on, the gardens at Les Tuileries were perfect for daytime or twilight strolls. That month's issue of *Life* magazine contained a stunning series by photographer William Vandivert which clearly showed a city draped in innocence and charm, pushing aside the dark shadows already roiling the eastern frontier.

Despite the ominous signs, there were journalists who chose to ignore the growing apprehensions. "Paris has suddenly been having a fit of prosperity, gaiety and hospitality," reported the American correspondent Janet Flanner, writing as Genet, in her fortnightly "Letter from Paris." Her pieces were published in the *New Yorker* (for fifty years) and absorbed voraciously by readers throughout the United States. "There have been money and music in the air, with people enjoying the first good time since the bad time started at Munich last summer. There have been magnificent costume balls and parties, with dancers footing it till early breakfast."

Meanwhile, Prime Minister Edouard Daladier nervously jousted with the Soviets, the Germans, and his erstwhile ally, England. The year before he had reluctantly sided with Britain's Prime Minister Neville Chamberlain on the Munich Agreement, which essentially ceded Czechoslovakia to Hitler without a fight. Unlike Chamberlain, however, Daladier had no illusions about Hitler's goals—he had even said that Napoleon's efforts to dominate the Continent would someday be seen as "feeble" compared to Hitler's ambitions.

The bands played on, but the storm clouds of war were already enveloping the border towns. Rattled residents from the countryside had begun packing up and streaming to safer regions to the west, many of them inundating Paris. Most Parisians willfully persisted in their routine lives, refusing to believe that months or years of carnage could come again only two decades after the last war.

Even if war returned, the French Army stood behind its vaunted Maginot Line, confident the Nazis could not breach those fortresses. The government of Daladier concluded a contract for thousands of American combat planes to be shipped in early 1940. Even the most pessimistic Frenchmen could not have predicted that it would be too late.

Not believing Janet Flanner's cheery missives, officials at the American Embassy in Paris, the oldest of its brand, dating back to Benjamin Franklin's mission during the Revolutionary War, were strongly urging Americans to leave while they could. Thousands of doughboys had stayed on after the war, settling into comfortable lives in the pleasant arrondissements of the capital city or scattering themselves across bucolic towns and farming areas from the Rhine to Normandy. American Legion Post Number 1, incorporated in Paris in 1919, counted hundreds of former American soldiers among its members, along with a few, like Eugene Bullard, who had served under other flags.

In Montmartre, the carousing became edgy and almost frantic. Nightclub patrons behaved as if nothing would change. Ignorance remained bliss. Transformation became a sad reality, however, as one club after another shuttered, darkening marquees across the district. Some owners simply wanted to get away before it was too late. Others, like the club run by Bullard's dear friend Bricktop, were forced to close as they hosted only empty tables.

L'Escadrille remained a staunch exception, staying open

and as busy as ever. The last determined partygoers had to go somewhere, after all; plus, in Gene Bullard's case, a gym was associated with his club. Bullard's place was also favored because he had an expansive policy on bar tabs: no one was refused at least one drink, even if they couldn't pay. He maintained that, over time, everyone would pony up, and he contended that very few patrons ever stiffed him. Besides, the times were uncertain enough: he was not about to start refusing service to his many friends and loyal customers just because the Germans were rattling their sabers yet again.

L'Escadrille harbored another motive for keeping its doors wide open—the 17,000 Germans in France, most of them in Paris. Many of them were Nazis out of uniform who had come to spy on the French. They had to gather somewhere, and Gene Bullard's club had an excellent reputation and still held many revues.

He was no fan of the Germans, having fought them nearly to the death some twenty years before, but he was happy to take their money. He did not put up with their politics, however—especially the Nazis.

As he strolled through the streets, Bullard marveled at how Paris had turned out to be everything he had hoped it would be, and more. If he had remained in America, especially the South, he could well be nothing more than a laborer, a field worker, maybe a clerk in a shop. Or dead. The night the angry mob of whites had come for his father was just another demonstration that a black man's life was cheap in the South. The drunken rednecks had nearly gotten to "Big Chief," and if they had he would have been swinging from a tree.

That had been the night Bullard made up his mind: he was getting out. He was leaving America and going to France, where his father had told him every man, no matter his race, was free. Leaving home at eleven years old was an enormous risk, but it had gotten him to one of the world's most extraordinary cities—after barely surviving a war, of course. He was quite sure the Boche would insist on another. Bullard wondered if he could survive that one, too. No matter what, his daughters must be out of harm's way. *Damn you, Marcelle,* he thought to himself, *why did you have to go?*

He continued his walk down the streets of Montmartre to the city center, and the warm sun began to relieve the aches and pains in his muscles and bones. *Ah, Gene, you are a tired old bird,* he told himself. He longed for his younger self, the one who had been known, at times, as "the Sparrow," and later, during the war, as the "Black Swallow of Death." He was starting to feel all of his years, the fights, the painful wounds, and the physical and mental wear and tear. He was slowing down, and he knew it, and all the smoking, drinking, and late nights weren't helping any.

One stop, as always when he took these rambles, was to visit his son. Little Eugene was buried far in the back of the Cimetière St. Vincent, against the south wall. A small rectangular marker lay atop the well-tended grass. Bullard could still hear his son's babyish laugh as he tickled him under his chubby chin. Then the crushing silence came, the awful day when fate placed him at St. Vincent's forever.

Bullard had purchased a single red rose along the way, and he bent over to place it on the grave. He was not religious in the least, yet he said a prayer for the boy, even though still bitter and angry with God for taking such a young innocent. Palming away tears, he continued his walk.

He stopped for another coffee at the Brasserie Universelle. Had it already been sixteen years since this grand old palace hosted the magnificent reception his former father-in-law had thrown for Gene and Marcelle? What a happy day that had been—one full of promises and hopes, all dashed over the intervening years.

As Bullard sat quietly at a sidewalk table, he marveled at the crowds. Young couples still smiled as they walked arm in arm. Matrons hurried past, juggling packages from the busy shops. A knot of chattering boys raced by, kicking a soccer ball back and forth. The café was full, the scent of fresh-baked bread was on the air, profusions of flowers bloomed in the sidewalk gardens and the flower boxes fixed to the walls. It was as if no one knew, and no one cared, about the increasing German infestation.

After his coffee he strolled by a large public rally at the Circle Militaire on Place St. Augustin. He was impressed by the fervent patriotism of the speakers and the boisterous singing of "La Marseillaise." Bullard could not help wondering, though, how such enthusiasm would stand up to the artillery and planes of the German military. He had felt the might of the German war machine firsthand, and it appeared, in the early summer of '39, that the Nazis were more powerful and fanatical than the Huns of '14 had been.

Finally, late that afternoon, Bullard stepped through the narrow doorway into L'Escadrille. To his surprise, the house was nearly empty. Though not yet evening, it was a Saturday and that usually meant an almost constant ebb and flow of patrons, with the first wave hitting before five o'clock. Only two customers stood at the bar. His barman was nervous about something, but he would not make eye contact with Bullard. Simone, his cashier, seemed terror stricken. All she could do was point a shaky finger at the restroom, located at the back of the club.

Clearly, something was very wrong. Bullard approached the restroom cautiously and slowly opened the floor-to-ceiling door. Inside stood the local Corsican gangster, Justin Pereti, staggering and drunk. He was shouting curses at the infinite reflections of himself provided by the restroom's mirrored walls.

Pereti was so incapacitated that Bullard could easily lock the gangster's arms behind his back and frog-march him out the front door of the club and into the street. On the way, Bullard discovered that Pereti had hidden a long carving knife inside his jacket. It would seem that the "enforcer" had come for a purpose other than slicing into a steak, though. Bullard took the knife, and when he went back inside he tossed it on the bar. That was when he learned from his barman that Pereti had come in threatening to kill him for some unknown reason, and his belligerent behavior had pretty much emptied the club.

During the scuffle to remove Pereti, a vase full of flowers had been knocked over and into the piano that Dooley Wilson had leaned against while he sang the previous night. Knowing that would not be good for the strings, Bullard set about mopping up the water inside the case. Once that was done, he noticed more patrons had finally started to wander in. Thinking more about Pereti, and not wanting to be on the wrong side of the local Corsican mob, Bullard reasoned the best plan of action would be to tell the gang's leaders what had happened.

The Corsicans hung out at another neighborhood bar, Café Lizeaux, and that was where Bullard found Pereti's two brothers. Explaining what had occurred, and buying a round of drinks, he was assured by the gangsters that there was no problem: Justin had been a big loser at the races, was mad at himself, and had been drinking heavily for days. Thus relieved that there was no lingering discord, Bullard left.

It was close to seven when he arrived back at L'Escadrille. The detour to and from Café Lizeaux had allowed Bullard the pleasure of experiencing *l'heure*, the period between five and seven much loved by Parisians as the time for romance. But it became immediately apparent that there was no romance awaiting him. Blink McCloskey, his beefy doorman, with an accent unchanged from a childhood in Boston, blocked him from entering and said, "Hey, boss, that drunk Corsican is back and he wants to talk to you."

"I've had enough. Tell him to go home and sleep it off."

"Boss, he's chasing away our business tonight. He says if you'll just talk to him, no funny stuff, he'll go away."

Bullard sighed and said, "All right, where is he?"

Blink went inside, and moments later guided the unsteady Corsican out to the street, where Bullard waited, smoking. "What do you want, Pereti? You've caused enough trouble for me tonight. Can't you just go home?"

"Bullard," Pereti slurred, as he wobbled unsteadily on his feet, "how long have we known each other?"

"Why, I guess it's been a few years, why do you ask?"

"Because this is goodbye forever. This is your last night on earth."

Bullard laughed off this statement as an idle threat. Pereti seemed more a danger to himself, in his condition, than he was to anyone else. So, Bullard extended his hand and Pereti shook it. "Adieu," the Corsican said. "Let me kiss you adieu."

He allowed Pereti, as was the custom among male friends, to kiss him on both cheeks. By this time Blink had hailed a taxi, and he poured Pereti into it. As the taxi drove away, the bouncer asked, "The hell with that guy. He wrecked the night's business. I haven't made a sou. Can I go get dinner now?"

Bullard, who would soon regret saying that he could, allowed Blink to stomp away, sulking. Bullard returned to the duties of the club, trying to salvage something from what was continuing to be a listless evening.

A half hour later, Simone screamed, pointing to the front door. Bullard ran toward the entrance, unattended because Blink had not yet returned. There stood Pereti, yet again, but this time the Corsican thug was holding a pistol, a German Luger. He had the gun aimed at Bullard's midsection. Bullard did not know what to do other than to talk softly while slowly moving toward him. "Justin," he said gently, "you know you don't want my kids to be without a father."

Looking far removed from reality and still not steady on his feet, Pereti managed to spit out, "Bullard, I'm going to kill you. You are a dirty scoundrel, a friend to the Germans. You are working for them!"

"Now Justin, you know *you* are my friend," Bullard said, his tone continuing to be smooth and warm. "I'm no German sympathizer. Maybe the war talk has got you so scared that you have to kill somebody. Why not kill Hitler?" He inched closer to the drunken gunman.

Should he tell Pereti about his work with the Deuxième Bureau—that he was actually using his club, in part, to spy on the Nazis, not work for them? Would Pereti even understand in his agitated inebriation? What if Pereti blurted this vital information out to someone else, across the street in the club where he and his men hung out? Life tiptoed on a knife edge as Bullard zeroed in on the gun.

Within an arm's reach of the shaking pistol, he decided to take a chance, hoping his reactions were better than those of the addled Corsican. The skillful ex-boxer made a lightning grab for Pereti's wrist. He pushed the man's hand down… but not before Pereti could squeeze the trigger. Bullard was gut punched by a bullet and felt a pain in his midsection that reminded him of a bad cigarette burn.

He managed to twist Pereti's gun hand behind his back, but the man's finger remained on the trigger, and he kept firing. As the two men fell to the floor, with Bullard on top, Pereti shot himself in the butt. He continued to struggle and fire until he had emptied the gun's eight-round magazine. Most of the rounds slammed into the floor.

Bullard yelled to the bartender to toss him a bottle. When he did, Bullard caught it on the fly and brought it down on Pereti's head. It smashed into dozens of pieces and the gangster went out cold. For a moment, Bullard considered shoving the broken and jagged remnants of the bottle into Pereti's throat. The bartender and Simone managed to pull their wounded boss away.

Blood was running down Bullard's right leg and the pain in his stomach intensified. Simone, her face as white as one of the tablecloths, told him he must get to a hospital. She rushed outside and began shouting for a taxi. Bullard staggered past her and turned up the street. His dazed intention was to return to the Café Lizeaux, to tell Pereti's brothers what had happened, and that they should hurry to L'Escadrille to ascertain what sort of medical attention Pereti needed. After all, they were friends.

Simone and the bartender had other ideas, though, and Bullard was finally thrust into a taxi. Clambering in beside him was Kitty, his companion in espionage and sometime lover. She never seemed to be far away, and somehow she had been alerted. Calmly, she ordered the driver to the nearest hospital—the sooner he arrived, the more he would be paid. With a swift motion Kitty tore off a piece of her blouse and pressed it against Bullard's belly. The bleeding slowed but did not stop. With her other arm, Kitty pulled him in close against her.

Kitty's and Bullard's clothes were covered in blood when they arrived at the hospital. Since it was a quiet Saturday night, the duty surgeon had gone for dinner at a café next door. He was quickly summoned from his soup. In the meantime, the police had been alerted and they were on the way.

As Bullard lay on a gurney being prepped for emergency surgery, two detectives arrived and wanted to know what had happened. The nurses, meanwhile, were trying to shoo the police away. Everyone was yelling as Bullard's blood spilled on the floor in shocking quantities. Kitty was trying to soothe him.

The circus of interests finally abated when the surgeon arrived and restored a semblance of order. The doctor inspected his rapidly weakening patient. The bullet had bounced around in Bullard's insides and exited via his right hip. He was a shredded, bleeding mess. Expecting the worst, the surgeon told Bullard he would do what he could but he also cautioned him to prepare himself for the end.

In the meantime, as Bullard had requested, Kitty had slipped away, desperate to find Leplanquais.

For as long as Bullard could remember, going back to his boyhood in Georgia, he had been prepared to die. That he had lived this long, surviving ghastly war wounds, was already a miracle. Perhaps he was out of miracles. What was different now, though, was something more important than his life—his daughters. His desperate thoughts of his little family became his total focus.

As the doctor scrubbed his hands and the gurney began to roll down the hall to the surgery, Leplanquais appeared at his side.

With what felt like his last ounce of strength, Bullard croaked to him, "Remember your promise!"

17

TOO TOUGH TO DIE

Miraculously, the slug that Eugene Bullard took had wandered around inside his abdomen, ripped up some flesh and muscle, but somehow missed all his vital organs. Even so, just from the loss of blood and shock, most men would have died, but Bullard's strapping constitution coupled with his desire to see his daughters again saved his life. The bullet exited, which also proved a blessing in that the surgeon didn't have to go poking around inside his patient to find it.

After some exploration and suturing, it was determined that Bullard could be classified as in "serious" condition, which was far better than the initial and somber analysis of impending death. The physician, as a precaution, prescribed rest, limited liquids, baby food only, and a prolonged stay in the hospital.

Within forty-eight hours, Bullard was complaining about a lack of "real food." He was already getting restless, and he wanted to see Jacqueline and Lolita, who were being cared for—and kept away from the hospital—by the indispensable Kitty. After having done a little sleuthing, it was she who figured out what had caused the confrontation at L'Escadrille in the first place.

Without telling Bullard, she went to visit Pereti in another hospital where he, too, was recovering. Pereti had a mighty sore ass, since one bullet had plowed through both cheeks, but more seriously he had sustained a fractured skull and had lost the sight in one eye from the blow Bullard had inflicted on him with the champagne bottle. He was, however, lucid enough to talk about the incident.

The explanation was certainly not what Kitty expected. Pereti revealed that he was working for yet another Resistance cell. Even though a common thug, Pereti and his mates harbored deep-rooted patriotic feelings for their adopted land and had powerful anti-Nazi sentiments. Pereti, witnessing how deferentially Bullard had treated Oberst Scheer, had become convinced that the obsequious nightclub owner was a collaborator and, in his drunken haze, determined that he needed to eliminate the "black bastard."

So, there it was, in all its "fog of war" confusion: two teammates mistakenly believed each was on the wrong side. The results of the misunderstanding were nearly fatal for both. When Kitty returned to Bullard, she found Leplanquais at his bedside. She told them both what had happened. It was quite a shock.

Not long after, Pereti's two brothers showed up to visit. In a room full of flowers, food, bottles of champagne, and cards wishing the impatient patient a speedy recovery, the Corsican mobsters pressed several thousand francs into Bullard's hand. It was clearly a bribe—they did not want him to press charges with the police. Bullard refused the money, at first.

"Take it as a gift—a peace offering, to cover the cost of your place being closed because of this incident," the brothers begged.

It was true: L'Escadrille had been forced to shut down for several days while the attack was investigated and its owner incapacitated. Bullard reconsidered, and finally agreed to take the money and drop the charges. The Corsicans departed, smiling, with one last comment: *"On les aura,"* the brothers promised, meaning in regard to the Germans, "We will get them."

"Of all the gin joints in all the towns in all the world, she walks into mine," moans the heartsick, fictional Rick Blaine in *Casablanca*. Rick is, of course, talking about Ilsa, his former lover, then married to another man and on the run from the Nazis. Ilsa begs the piano player, "Play it, Sam." Then later, the two star-crossed romantics, gazing into each other's eyes realize, like Rick whispers, "We'll always have Paris."

Bullard and Kitty "have Paris," too, and would wind up leaving his version of a gin joint and fleeing the Nazis. Was there a crossover story between these two that eerily reflects the fate of Rick and Ilsa? We have only speculation. Bullard reveals nothing during his later years about the fate of Kitty—and their relationship, if any beyond the professional. We do know two things, though: Kitty will, as we shall see, become very important to the survival and fate of Bullard's cherished daughters. There is also one solitary record, post–World War II, awarding one "Cleopatre Terrier, Resistance Fighter extraordinaire, the Legion of Honor." Was she alive to receive it? Was the award posthumous? Whatever her fate, she seems, like Rick and Captain Renault, to have vanished into the mist at the end of her "movie."

In the hospital, Bullard made remarkable progress, and after only ten days, and a couple of loud arguments with his doctor, he was given permission to leave. By late July, he was back at work and L'Escadrille was booming once more. He and Kitty were listening in again on their unsuspecting German patrons, smiling, and pretending they didn't understand anything that was being discussed.

"The Nazis believed their blonde coloring and Nordic ancestry made them superior to anybody else," Bullard wrote, concerning how unguarded the German officers were in their conversations. "Of course, they figured, no Negro could be bright enough to understand any language except his own, much less figure out the military importance of whatever they said in German. So, as the Nazis talked to each other at my tables and I served them, they were not at all careful about discussing military secrets within my hearing."

The intelligence and even gossip he and Kitty gleaned was passed on to Leplanquais. Every night was the same—Bullard effected a "dumb" but smiling face and Kitty pretended to flirt. Both had their ears wide open. Remaining impassive became more difficult to do, however, as what they heard became more alarming.

As Bullard and Kitty relayed to Leplanquais, the Germans were spending a lot of time talking about Poland. Was it the next target? It certainly seemed so. The information was dutifully pushed up the chain of command, where it apparently was ignored—or perhaps not believed, and Poland would pay the price.

On September 1, 1939, the German "Blitzkrieg" smashed into the Polish eastern border. The Poles were so poorly prepared that during the first days of the war they actually sent out a unit of one thousand mounted Lancers to charge against German Panzer tanks. The Panzers sliced through these unfortunates as if they were tissue paper. Mounds of blasted horseflesh and mangled human corpses littered a wide swath of Polish countryside. Poland's entire military capability would be obliterated completely in less than a week.

On September 3, although it was already far too late to save Poland, the mutual defense treaties that France and England had signed with Warsaw went into effect, and the French and the British were at war with Germany. The sons of the survivors of the Great War, and even some who had fought in the trenches, mobilized once again to battle the sons and survivors of their foes across the Rhine.

As Hitler consolidated his gains, the European allies scrambled. The Nazis stood pat, for the most part, and the next six months, from October 1939 to March 1940, was dubbed the "Phony War," wherein not much happened. Although hope could always spring eternal, it could also offer, at times, a false sense of security.

Eugene Bullard, for one, did not believe it was a phony war, and events surrounding him made him only more convinced that another conflagration was about to commence.

18

THE "PHONY WAR" BECOMES REAL

It had been the pride and joy of a penniless kid from Columbus, Georgia. A car—and not just any car, but a 1934 Delahaye. The green two-door coupe had belonged to one of his pals from the Foreign Legion who had purchased it new, but when he fell on hard times as the stock market in America continued to struggle, he was forced to sell it. Bullard had scooped it up in 1937 for the bargain price of $900. A car in Paris was a true extravagance, and with gas rationing and the snarls of civilian and military traffic, a royal nuisance, but Bullard wanted it anyway. He and his daughters took long drives outside the city on those rare days when he could get away from L'Escadrille. They packed picnics in the boot and sped off, full of boundless happiness despite the tensions to the east.

As 1939 turned to 1940, it was Bullard's turn to get rid of

his cherished vehicle. Rationing was bad enough, but gas was almost impossible to find as war materials were being carefully husbanded by a wary French government. The cost of the garage, which was a half mile from his apartment, was an expense beyond his management as revenues from L'Escadrille plummeted. Besides, where could he and his girls go now? Any drive outside of Paris was dangerous as the roads became clogged with troop movements and millions of refugees streaming into the city and to other, safer, parts of France. A friend offered Bullard $700 to take the car with him to America on the same steamer upon which he had booked passage, and Bullard reluctantly accepted.

There would be more sacrifices. He pulled the girls out of the convent school they had been attending. The tuition was not that great, but every sou counted during those uncertain days; besides, he wanted them close to home. They would stay at the apartment with him, and if anything happened, Kitty or Leplanquais would get them to safety.

Bullard had to stop paying his talent again, too, just as in the early days of Le Grand Duc. Most of the good bandsmen and singers were out of work anyway. At least Gene could feed them and pay for their drinks. As Bricktop had done when she first arrived in Paris, many of the musicians literally sang for their suppers.

The war might be phony, but the preparations and precautions were real. Soon after the declarations of war in September 1939, France began imposing blackouts. The famed City of Light, thirty minutes after sundown, became the City of Darkness. Almost all forms of transportation came to a halt after nightfall, and the Champs-Élysées turned into a pedestrian thoroughfare where denizens and tourists alike stumbled around in the gloom. Theaters shut down, their marquees turned off. Cafés weren't even allowed to offer flashlights to provide illumination for their customers. Needless to say, the once-hot cabarets and clubs of Montmartre went cold.

By October 1939, the American Embassy in Paris was urging, practically demanding, that all Americans leave France. With increasing frequency, German bombers flew over Paris. One of them, in broad daylight, dropped a bomb on the embassy. Reportedly, it did not explode but crashed through the ceiling and landed at the feet of US Ambassador William C. Bullitt Jr.

Reluctantly, the African American exodus that had sought liberation from racism in the 1920s and '30s went into reverse. Bookings on the steamship lines from Le Havre and other ports of call skyrocketed. Those without enough money for the fare had to wait for drafts from home, loans from friends, or the outright kindness of strangers.

By this time Bricktop had left[47] but Josephine Baker wasn't going anywhere. She made up her mind to stay; plus, she had renounced her American citizenship and the American Embassy, wearing the snub like a jilted lover, was not of a mind to renew her passport in any case.

Eugene Bullard felt the same about abandoning France, although he was still very much an American citizen. At forty-four, he had been a "Frenchman" far longer than he had been an American. His daughters were French citizens and all that he owned on earth was invested in France. He didn't have a passport either, but he had never had one: as a stowaway, he had snuck into Europe via Scotland, and had never looked back. The only identification papers he possessed were from

---

47 Bricktop hosted a propaganda radio program for the French government in 1939, but when the war finally heated up, she left Paris and moved to Mexico City where she opened another "Chez Bricktop" in 1944. After WWII, she moved back to Rome and opened yet another club there, which she ran from 1949 to 1961. She then moved back to New York where she continued to occasionally perform cabaret gigs and even had bit parts (playing herself) in two Hollywood movies.

his Legionnaire and 170th Infantry days and, of course, his French Air Service pilot's license.

Another reason he refused to abandon his beloved Paris, as he later wrote in his memoirs, "I was never too crazy about walking away from danger."

As a dreary October slipped into an even gloomier November, the French Army was frantically calling up its reserves and organizing its battalions and regiments into divisions and corps. Most of the troops were being positioned in and along the vaunted Maginot Line, France's first bulwark against any invading Nazi hordes.

The Maginot Line, named after André Maginot, French Minister of War from 1915–1920, stretched from Switzerland, all along the German border, through Luxembourg, right up to Belgium. It had been constructed during the 1930s and had cost France the staggering sum of three billion francs. The mostly concrete and steel structures hid all types of artillery and were set up to withstand direct aerial bombardment and also to effectively resist attack by tanks. The underground facilities were air-conditioned, and forts along the line had barracks, dining halls, and all the amenities necessary to support the hundreds of thousands of troops who were stationed within its confines.

The bulwark was a modern marvel of engineering and military might, but it ultimately proved worthless. The northern end of the line was not extended to the English Channel, which would have made it complete, because Belgium objected to having the line on its border. This, of course, gave the Germans a way to conduct an end run around the line; so, anticipating that, the French and British military planners factored that in. The bulk of their blocking forces were stationed along the border of Belgium that abutted France.

Even in this, however, there was one fatal flaw: the line was weakest at the Ardennes Forest which covered parts of Belgium and Luxembourg. The terrain was so thickly forested and so riven with steep hills and deep valleys that it was believed to be impassable—except by a modern, mechanized, armed force. This would be exactly where the spear point of Hitler's offensive would go, and it would be successful.

Bullard was too old to volunteer. He hadn't sat in an airplane cockpit for over twenty years and the last time he did fighter planes had two wings instead of the modern monoplane design. He loosely kept track of where his old 170th Infantry regiment was mobilizing, but he knew they would not take him because of his age. He wasn't exactly itching to go anyway, but he would if he had to.

In the meantime, he had a business and friends to concern him. Even with the blackouts, he kept the gym and the club open. Since L'Escadrille was one of the few clubs still operating Bullard encouraged every patron with any spare money to spend as much as they could. He was not shy about asking them to do so, and he was very open about using their resources to help his many musicians and friends to "get by."

After the sale of his car, he no longer had the means to drive about the city to scrounge for foodstuffs for his kitchen. To make do, he constructed a wooden pushcart out of old crates and bicycle wheels. Every day, he and the cart would be off, right after lunch, to the main food market, Les Halles. During the months of the Phony War, Les Halles was still booming. Farmers, dairymen, livestock producers, bakers, and food producers of all types were still trucking their wares into the city from the countryside.

Bullard hung out until the last half hour or so of the market day; then, as the vendors dropped their prices so as to clear out their goods versus hauling them back home, he swooped in. He would buy up as much in meat scraps, soup bones, and vegetables as his meager purse could afford. He loaded up his cart and pushed it back up the hills to Montmartre. By dinnertime, Bullard's Chinese cook would have a large stew boiling on the stove, and everyone would have at least one hearty meal for the day.

Later that night, the blackout curtains would be deployed, and Bullard would break open packs of cigarettes, placing a few on each table so everyone could have a smoke. The cheap wine flasks would be uncorked so those without funds could at least have one free drink. This cycle repeated itself, day after day, all through the bleak winter—and Phony War— of 1939–40.

The Germans, however, were not idle. After wrapping up business in Poland, Hitler began preparing for the invasion of France. There were some minor skirmishes at sea, and Russia attacked spirited little Finland. In April, Germany launched an offensive against Denmark and Norway. In England, Prime Minister Neville Chamberlain struggled to keep the reins of government in his hands, but was forced to give them up to Winston Churchill in May 1940. Ironically, on the same day Churchill assumed power, the Phony War would end as Hitler, sending a coded signal to his forces, launched his invasion of France and Belgium.

As the German Panzers began smashing into the Ardennes, and tearing up the cobblestone roads of rural Belgium, it became clear to Eugene that continuing to try to operate his clubs was becoming more untenable every additional day. With great regret, he closed and boarded up both establishments. He had hopes of reopening after the war was over, whenever that might be, and only if the French were victorious, of course. He retained ownership of both locations but, sadly, he would never realize any profit from them again.

It was on to the next phase, but Eugene Bullard, hero of

France, had no idea what that might be. He did not expect that being back on the front lines battling the enemy would be part of that scenario, but, as Gene had learned, "life was what happened to you when you made plans."

19

AT WAR ONCE MORE

After World War I ended, hundreds of thousands of dough-boys had remained in France, most of them waiting their turns to travel back to the United States. Logistical quagmires and the need to keep a force of about two hundred thousand in Europe to police the former Central Powers presented General John Pershing and his American Expeditionary Force with multiple challenges, not the least of which was keeping the soldiers busy and sustaining morale.

One of the officers on Pershing's staff, Lieutenant Colonel Theodore Roosevelt Jr., thought he had an idea that might help. He and several other officers, with Pershing's blessing, set about to organize an "American Legion" that would see to the recreational, educational, and repatriation needs of the soldiers who were left behind. From these beginnings, the modern American Legion was born. Post Number 1 was chartered in Paris in February 1919.

Eligibility for the American Legion was extended to all US servicemen who had soldiered overseas in the Great War and was soon extended, in the early 1920s, to all servicemen and servicewomen who had put on the uniform whether they had been sent overseas or not.[48] Membership was also offered to any Americans who had served in the war under any other allied flag; thus, Eugene Bullard had proudly presented his French Army credentials in early 1919 to Post Number 1 and was immediately accepted as a member.

In Paris, the American Legion became a true fraternity and was dedicated to members helping other members. Twenty years later, Post Number 1 was still active, and became even more so in late 1939 when it became clear that most of Europe would be plunging into war again. Legionnaires were busy raising funds to help repatriate old soldiers back to America before they became trapped. The Paris post worked hand in hand with the US Embassy and its consular officers scattered across France to identify and assist those who wished to leave. For those who were staying, like Eugene Bullard, the American Legion tried to find places for their veterans to work, obtain shelter or otherwise avoid the coming conflict.

In May 1940, Bullard fell under the sponsorship of Dr. James V. Sparks,[49] one of the most colorful characters of the interwar period in Paris. Sparks, originally from Indianapolis, graduated from Indiana Dental College (the Indiana University School of Dentistry today) in 1914 and, with war on the horizon, and a yen for military adventure, immediately joined the US Army Dental Corps. The young first lieutenant was shipped to France almost immediately after the American Expeditionary Force was mobilized.

---

48 The Veterans of Foreign Wars, chartered in 1899, is restricted to those who served "on foreign soil or waters" during any declared conflict.

49 *TIC Magazine*, Albany, NY, September 1948.

One of his more intriguing days in France had occurred late in 1917 when the twenty-four-year-old oral surgeon was summoned to General Philippe Pétain's headquarters in the Vosges Mountains. Pershing had recommended his staff dentist to Pétain, who was suffering from an ulcerated tooth. It turned out that Pétain had had the tooth pulled some weeks before, but the dentist had apparently left a sliver of the tooth behind, which became infected.

Pétain, in severe pain, took one look at Sparks and said, "You're too young to be a surgeon."

Sparks immediately replied, diplomatically, "And you, sir, are too young to be a Marshal of France."

Pétain smiled, and Sparks removed the offending piece of tooth with a sterilized pocket knife and no anesthetic. Pétain, greatly relieved, offered his sincerest thanks.

In 1919, Sparks returned to the US to practice dental surgery with an uncle in Oklahoma City. His overseas itch had not been scratched completely, however, and he decided to take a vacation in Paris. While there, through the American Legion, he met another expatriate dentist, Dr. Perry Chance, from Akron, Ohio. The two men decided to open a practice in Paris, and Sparks simultaneously studied for and attained bachelor's and doctoral degrees in dentistry from the University of Aix and the École Dentaire, respectively.

In mid-1924, an American officer on the residual AEF staff in Paris, Colonel Charles Sweeny, approached Sparks with an intriguing offer: a group of American pilots was being recruited to fly for France in Morocco, fighting the Berber tribes in the Rif Mountains. Would Sparks like to go as the attending dental officer? He immediately agreed, and while in Morocco not only did he perform his dental duties but he learned to fly, first as an observer then as a machine gunner, and finally as a full-fledged pilot. After he started flying combat missions with the other pilots he was given the nickname the "Death Dealing Dentist." Also while in Morocco, he met a young French captain who would become a lifelong friend: Charles de Gaulle.

Before leaving Morocco in 1926, Sparks would serve as the honorary captain of the guard of the sultan of Morocco and would be decorated with the Medaille Colonial. The sultan also gave him one thousand acres of land and sixteen wives. Sparks accepted title to the acreage, but wisely left the wives behind.

Back in Paris, he resumed his dental practice, married a beautiful Parisian, and, in 1931, was elected commander of American Legion Post Number 1. For all his work on behalf of France, he was made an officer in the Legion of Honor and in 1939 was elected that organization's commander. Among Sparks's patients over the years he spent in France were Marshal Pétain, General Pershing, the King of Greece, the King of Siam, the Aga Khan, and the Duchess of Kent. Through the Duchess, he met King Edward VIII, who became the Duke of Windsor after his abdication in December 1936.

At the Duke of Windsor's suggestion, an international committee for peace was formed in the late 1930s to try to prevent another world war. Dr. Sparks was chosen as head of the American delegation, and he, with others, met with Hitler, Mussolini, King Emmanuel of Italy, and French Prime Minister Leon Blum. It was all for naught, of course.

When the Phony War morphed into the real thing in May 1940, Dr. Sparks left his work helping Americans escape France and accepted a commission as a colonel in the French Army with responsibility for organizing and equipping a modern ambulance fleet for the troops. One of the principal financial backers for Dr. Sparks's ambulance corps was an American widow by the name of June Jewett James.

She had been married to a very wealthy Englishman who had left her a considerable fortune and a small castle in Neuilly, a suburb to the west of Paris.

Mutual contacts in Post Number 1 brought Eugene Bullard and Sparks together. Bullard, his pockets totally empty after closing up his establishments, needed work and a place to live. He and his daughters were on the verge of having to vacate their apartment because they could no longer pay the rent. Mrs. James needed an all-around handyman, butler, chauffeur, masseur, and experienced waiter for formal dinner parties. Sparks made the introductions, and Bullard, one-time hero of France, was hired and invited to move into the James château along with his two daughters. Paris was still facing uncertainty, but the arrangement was a perfect temporary solution for all parties.[50]

Mrs. James planned an elegant champagne luncheon for all the dignitaries and officials involved in the creation of the new ambulance corps. Bullard would serve as maître d' and for the occasion he donned his old pilot's uniform and wore all of his medals. As luck would have it, one of the invited guests was his old "friend" Dr. Gros, who had been made the head of the American Ambulance Corps, the same post he had held in the previous war.

Gros, who barely deigned to speak to Bullard, although they had known each other for a quarter century, remarked, "I did not know you had the Medaille Militaire."[51]

---

50 Dr. Sparks organized his ambulance corps and led it to the front, but he was forced to flee for Spain after Paris fell to the Nazis. He was captured by the Spanish police and was looking at a firing squad, on the orders of Joseph Goebbels. His old contact, Marshal Pétain, intervened on Sparks's behalf and gave him the choice of evacuation to North Africa or returning to the United States. Sparks chose America, and after he returned, he accepted a commission as a major in the US Army Dental Corps. Illness forced his disability retirement in 1943. He moved to Texas and established an oral surgery practice, and that is where he spent the remainder of his days.

51 France's then second-highest military medal for bravery.

To which Bullard replied, "Oh, I thought you kept all my records, just as you kept the scroll issued me by the French government as it was to every member of the flying squadron."

Gros frowned, reddened, turned on his heel, and strode away without another word. It was the last time the two men ever set eyes on one another.[52]

Soon after the luncheon, Bullard was requested to return to Paris to work for what was then known as "La Résistance." Ironically, there was a metro stop only one mile from Neuilly, so he began a daily commute to the war, in Paris. He met up with his old partner, Kitty, and they stayed together in Kitty's apartment whenever it was necessary for him to spend the night in Paris. Bullard brought with him whatever useful news he picked up by assisting Mrs. James with her regular gatherings at le Petit Château de Neuilly.

For several crazy weeks, Bullard would hop on the metro, when he wasn't needed by Mrs. James, and commute to his old haunts—and Kitty—in Paris. He would bring in any tidbits of information he had gleaned from Mrs. James's guests—information the Resistance might want to have. When in Paris, he and Kitty would work together, most often running information and messages between Resistance cells. In this work, his familiarity with the city was invaluable—but his distinctive "color" was not. It did not take long for the Gestapo to pick up on news about and images of the "black man" possibly working for the Resistance.

Bullard had a couple of very narrow escapes. One day, he was given several rolls of film hidden inside a soccer ball that

---

52   Dr. Gros returned to the United States in late 1940, settling in Pennsylvania. He died there, of a stroke, in October 1942.

he was to take to a British Army colonel soon to be a guest at Mrs. James's château. As soon as he left the office building in Montmartre where the Resistance cell met, soccer ball under his arm, he noticed a "tail" of two suspicious-looking Aryan men following him. His heart skipped a beat. If the men stopped him, they would surely examine the soccer ball, and then it would all be over for Bullard.

Rounding a corner ahead of the men, he ran into a group of six boys playing soccer in an empty lot. Thinking quickly, he traded soccer balls with the boys and told them to meet him three blocks away in ten minutes, and if they did, he'd give them twenty francs.

The ruse worked. Bullard took the "new" soccer ball and continued walking just as the Germans turned the corner. He then started jogging, which caused the men to speed up, too. Another block away, he pretended to panic and tossed the ball down an alleyway. The Germans took off after the ball.

Bullard found the boys, gave them their reward—enough for three new soccer balls and lunch—and trotted off to the metro.

Two weeks later, Kitty and Gene were tasked with smuggling a packet of messages from Resistance HQ to another messenger waiting for them in the Bois de Vincennes park just to the east of the city. It should have been a simple metro ride to the park, and an innocuous handoff. It wasn't.

Once again, Bullard's distinctive face was immediately picked up by a pair of Gestapo "watchers." Gene and Kitty (who was hiding the letters under her skirt) decided on a diversionary stroll, all in very public places so they couldn't be cornered.

Several blocks later, the "lovers" decided to duck into a local church. The two Nazis quickly followed them in—

but the pair was nowhere in sight. The Germans desperately searched every alcove and space—but nothing.

What they missed was the procession of nuns chanting and walking down the central aisle, right out the front door and on their way—including Gene and Kitty hurriedly swathed in black-and-white habits. It was a slick trick, worked to perfection, and helped along by the giggling nuns.

Also doing her bit for France was Bullard's friend—and possible former lover—Josephine Baker. The same month the allies had declared war against Germany, she opened a show in Paris, sharing the bill with Maurice Chevalier. When it closed, as many entertainments did in the Fall of 1939, she put away her skimpy costumes and reported to work at the Red Cross relief center on rue de Châteaudun. According to the biographer Lynn Haney, Baker "did everything from comforting homeless families to helping prepare pot-au-feu for the hungry. On her days off she flew supplies for the Red Cross into Belgium. She wrote hundreds of letters to soldiers at the front and, at Christmas, sent fifteen hundred presents to the troops, each with an autographed photo of herself."

In addition, that spring she and Chevalier took their show on the road, performing for the French soldiers posted along the German frontier. Upon her return, Baker was recruited by the Deuxième Bureau. She told one of the agency's captains, echoing Eugene Bullard's sentiments, "France has made me what I am. Wasn't I the darling of Parisians? They have given me everything, especially their hearts. Now, I will give them mine."

She continued, "Captain, I am ready to give my life for France. You can make use of me as you will." Thus, Josephine Baker, like Gene, became a spy for her adopted country.

★ ★ ★

For Bullard, the day came when he had to say goodbye to the generous Mrs. James. Her teenage daughter was felled by polio. That, plus news of Panzer tanks rolling across France, persuaded Mrs. James to relocate to another estate she owned, this one in Biarritz. She borrowed one of the ambulances she had purchased, driving it herself with her paralyzed daughter in the back. The James women joined the millions of refugees on the road between Belgium and the Spanish border.

There were few Germans going to the clubs; in fact, very few clubs were open at all, so the spying became even more risky since it had to be done pretty much in the open. Bullard's black skin became even more of a liability as far as recognition went.

He and Kitty soon came to the realization that spying was too dangerous for him. This severely limited his options; in fact, his choices really boiled down to two: fight or flee. Kitty knew he would never run. Making Kitty promise to take care of his daughters, Bullard became determined to find his old regiment and rejoin it. He knew he was too old, he knew he'd probably not be accepted for service, but he had to try.

Many veteran Poilus, most of them then old *"grand-pères,"* had dusted off their long blue overcoats and headed for the front. Gene had heard that the 170th was dug in and battling the Germans at Épinal, far to the east of Paris, along the border with Germany.

On June 14, 1940, the Germans triumphantly marched down the Champs-Élysées and through L' Arc de Triomphe. Panic seized Paris and tens of thousands of residents hurried out of the city. Stuka dive-bombers with their paralyzing, high-pitched, screaming engines fell on the mixed columns of soldiers and civilians like raptors on defenseless chickens.

Thousands were killed, their torn and mangled bodies left to litter the roads and ditches.

In a wrenching and tearful scene, Kitty and his daughters helped Bullard pack a big knapsack. He had his old rifle from his French Legionnaire days but carrying that through Paris would be an invitation to disaster, with all the German troops around. He also had a pistol he had picked up along the way, but again, and for the same reasons, his daughters begged him not to take it. If he was stopped and searched by the Germans they could execute him on the spot for having a gun in his possession. If he found his old comrades, he would pick up a weapon from them, or so he hoped.

The backpack was stuffed with tins of sardines, sausages, crackers, cigarettes, a flask of wine, and two volumes on *The Lafayette Flying Corps*—proof, in Bullard's mind, that he was who he said he was, if questioned. Lastly, he stuffed fifteen hundred francs in his pockets. All the rest of his meager funds he left with Kitty, to use on behalf of his girls.

No one spoke the obvious—that this could be their last moments together on earth. The tears and sobs said that for all of them. Bullard's plan was vague but his resolve was firm: if he found his old mates, he would fight with them—if they let him, considering he was an "old man" at forty-four and no longer in fighting shape. Should he survive, all would be good. If not, well, defeating the Nazis was the preferred outcome, no matter the cost. He was confident they would find each other when peace and sanity were restored. Lacking that, and the defeat of the French, they discussed escaping to Spain via Biarritz. Bullard had contacts in Biarritz, including Mrs. James, and was confident that he could get them all out of the country. Kitty's task was to get them to Biarritz when Bullard sent word for her to do so.

After hugging and saying their final goodbyes, Kitty demanded, "Now, get out of Paris as fast as you can."

After one final kiss, Bullard trudged down the stairs and into the streets with his fifty-pound pack. He went to the nearest metro station and boarded a train to Port d'Italie, the southern-most portal of the old city. Outside the station, he found the A-4 main road east, toward Épinal and the Vosges region. He immediately fell in with a handful of old Poilus, like himself, veterans of the Great War. A couple of the men had even donned faded and well-worn remnants of their old uniforms. Grim-faced and determined, they backslapped one another and trudged along—just like the old days.

20

FRIENDS FOUND...AND LOST

For Eugene Bullard and the other old soldiers, their first struggle was trying to swim against the tide of humanity flowing in the opposite direction, frightened exiles desperate not to be overtaken by the German tsunami of troops and tanks. Refugees of all stripes clogged the road, pushing and shoving the soldiers aside. Many of the panic-stricken shouted at them, calling them "old fools" and worse. Some begged the men for food, or water, but there was none to spare.

After a full day and a night with only brief rests, the little band of middle-aged veterans passed Château Thierry, a major battle site of the last war. They trudged on, past Reims, and finally arrived in Chalons, about halfway to their goal. It was there that the men were informed that Épinal and the even closer town of Bar-le-Duc had already fallen into German hands. Worse, for Bullard, was a staggering piece of news: he was told that his old outfit, the heroic 170th, had been wiped out to the last man.[53]

There was nothing to do but turn around and join the surge back to Paris. The grueling return journey took twice as long, three days in all. Once back at Port d'Italie, Bullard planned to duck back into the city, reassure his children he was okay, then try to find another avenue toward the fight. Much to his shock, he was barred from reentering the city. The gendarmes, then taking their orders from the Germans, told him that Paris was too full of refugees already—there was no more room. No amount of coaxing, pleading, bribing or threatening worked.

Bullard began a walk around the walls of the city, looking for a way to sneak in. He found not even a crack unguarded. At the Port d'Orléans, he finally gave up. He heard yet another rumor that the French 51st Infantry was making a stand at Orléans, so he struck out to the south, heading there.

This march was even worse than the one toward Épinal. The crowds were growing more frantic, searching for scraps of food and drops of water. Humanity, to Bullard, seemed to have come unglued. People were doing things that they never would have done in normal society. Men and women openly defecated in full view along the roads, women had babies in ditches, and the stronger preyed upon the weaker, stealing their food, money, their clothes, even their shoes.

---

53 This turned out to not be completely true. At the outbreak of the war, the 170th was stationed on the Franco-German border along a section of the Maginot Line. The regiment was engaged fully from May 16 to June 12, 1940, especially hotly contesting the foe during the Battle of Croutoy on June 9. The area was overrun by the Germans and the 170th retreated to the area around Limoges. The regiment was so badly decimated, having lost over one thousand killed, wounded or missing, that the French Army simply disbanded it on August 6. The proud 170th was reactivated at Épinal on July 1, 1964 and served until 1994, the regiment's 200th anniversary, when it was disestablished once again.

Pitiful cries for help went unheeded, the wounded went uncared for, the dead unburied.

The German dive-bombers were a constant, deadly menace. There was no air cover from the French or any other air force. Although some Luftwaffe pilots refused to carry out orders to strafe unarmed and innocent civilians, other, less-principled pilots did. The teeming crowds were nothing more than target practice and they died in hordes, their twisted corpses sprawled across the roads.

Bullard came under attack on the main highway just outside of Chartres. A Stuka descended, howling, upon the crowds. When the plane finally peeled away, he crawled out of the roadside ditch to witness a horrific tableau. Smashed and broken bodies were everywhere. Pieces of human flesh were still smoldering from the bombs. Shrieks and moans created a cacophony from Hell. As Bullard staggered away he saw a young boy standing in the road screaming uncontrollably, shaking, his eyes crossing and uncrossing. At his feet lay the two halves of a woman, neatly severed at the waist, probably the child's mother. She still held a chicken drumstick, half-eaten, clutched in her right fist.

Bullard tried to comfort the child, to drag him away, but he would not stop screaming and shaking, kicking and fighting. With tears in his eyes, and the loud wail of yet another Stuka gathering speed overhead, Bullard dove back into the ditch he had just exited. The bombs came incredibly close, shaking the earth. When he emerged a second time, there was not a shred of the boy left in sight, nor any piece of his dead mother. He trod on, filled with dread.

Amazingly, just past Chartres, he came upon an old friend. Bob Scanlon and Bullard had served together in the Foreign Legion and he and Scanlon had shared several boxing cards in London and Paris before the Great War. As with Bullard,

Scanlon ended up at Verdun where a shell fragment nearly tore off his right hand. The wound effectively ended his boxing career but after the war, he, too, stayed on in Paris and made a decent living training other boxers and working in and around some of the clubs as a bouncer. He had also secured a small part in a 1918 silent movie, today largely forgotten, called *Doing Their Bit*. Along that terrible road, he was just one more refugee hoping to get out of harm's way.

Amidst the horror, feeling untethered from reality, it was a great comfort for each man to find a kindred spirit. The sense of camaraderie would not last long, however. Shortly after their reunion, and agreeing to march on together, another dive-bombing attack sent each man jumping into shell craters. One bomb landed close enough to Bullard to half bury him in dirt and debris. Unfortunately, that bomb had landed in what he believed was Bob Scanlon's shell hole. When Bullard crawled out, there was no sign of Scanlon anywhere. He was shocked and horrified, but there was no time to grieve. He had to push on, and he did.

Bullard's food supplies were nearly gone—his wine, finished. He had made the mistake of sitting down by the roadside a few days back to have a bite to eat. He was immediately mobbed by a throng of starving people, begging for even the tiniest scrap. They had nearly overwhelmed him, and he, out of the kindness he always displayed for the downtrodden, had shared almost half of his stash. Only a fast jog and his strong physique dissuaded the crowd from robbing him blind of the rest of his resources. From that moment forward, Bullard paused to eat only at night, and in a field or copse of trees far off the road, and even then, only a few furtive bites, lest he be discovered.

Outside of Poupry, north of Orléans, he was out of water. He spotted a fountain in the small village square, still burbling, but nearly dry. He filled his canteen quickly. A crowd trailing behind him saw that he had found some water, and they rushed the square, trampling one another, like an angry herd of beasts, to get to what small trickles were left. Shoving, pushing, and fistfights erupted as Bullard quickly moved away. Several tortured men eyed his canteen enviously, but his face and boxer's posture kept them at bay. He moved on briskly, saddened by what he was witnessing. Images of the last war, the stench of death, the trenches, the desperation of humanity, returned in a flood of unwanted ghostly memories. All of it nearly overwhelmed him. Only thoughts of his daughters kept him pushing ahead.

When Bullard arrived in Orléans, he learned that the 51st Regiment was still fighting, and still in the city. He got directions to its headquarters, near the eastern edge of town, and headed off to find them.

The principal objectives of the German war machine were, at that time, concentrated in the northwest of France and the Low Countries. The Wehrmacht swept over Belgium, Holland, and Luxembourg and completed an end run around the Maginot Line with astonishing speed. In the east, along the Swiss, Italian, and German borders, the Maginot Line held up better than in the north, but the Germans knew that to spend much time smashing into these well-prepared fortifications would be a waste of energy, so their main thrust went around the far western end of the Line and through the Ardennes.

As Bullard searched for the 51st Regiment in Orléans, most French opposition had already been overcome. The battle for France was, in reality, already over, but pockets of resistance, such as the fractured forces in Orléans, refused to surrender. The Germans pressed on, thrusting deeper into the heart of the country, wiping away these uncoordinated and vastly inferior forces wherever they found them.

The German 6th Army Group, which had participated in the capture of Paris, was ordered to proceed south, which they did, battling and sweeping away the French as they went. As they barreled through Chartres, they set their sights on Orléans. The 6th would be the primary German force that Gene Bullard would encounter in the following days. It was an army of 285,000 men facing, perhaps, one tenth that number.

The headquarters of the 51st Regiment was hunkered in a nondescript, stuccoed, single-story building on the eastern side of the city. Soldiers were hustling in and out of the structure, some carrying weapons, others stacks of papers and records, getting ready to abandon the position and move farther south. A harried sergeant came rushing out of the entrance, looking around for a courier to take a message to the front. He spied Bullard approaching and distractedly asked him what he wanted.

"I would like to speak to your commander, Sergeant."

"For what purpose? As you can see, we're a little busy."

"I want to fight."

The sergeant did not laugh. There was little to laugh about those days. He scrutinized Bullard more carefully, perhaps recognizing something in addition to a middle-aged, ragtag refugee. "You were in the last war, I take it," the sergeant asked.

"Yes. The 170th."

"Hah! Les Hirondelles du Mort. Fine outfit. Our commander was in the 170th."

Bullard's jaw dropped, "*Mon Dieu!* What is his name?"

"Major Bader, Roger Bader. Did you know him?"

"Incredible," Bullard nearly shouted. "Yes, I knew him well. He was my lieutenant. We fought at Verdun together."

"Well, he's now our major. He's inside. Perhaps he will see you."

Bullard thanked the sergeant, who had more pressing matters, and rushed inside the dusty building to find his old comrade. It didn't take long for Bullard to spot him. "Major! Major Bader!" he shouted down the hall.

Bader turned, staring, wondering what calamity he needed to address next. His eyes widened. "Bullard! Is that you?"

"Yes, *mon lieutenant*… I am sorry, I mean 'major,' it is me, Corporal Bullard."

The two men shook hands, clearly pleased to see one another.

"Corporal, I wish there was more time to think about old memories, but sadly there is not. We have to pull back to our next line of defense. We're moving out now. Perhaps later?"

"I understand, sir. But I am here to help you. To fight. Please let me help you."

Bader did not hesitate. A volunteer was a volunteer, and men were desperately needed. Plus, he knew what kind of soldier Eugene Bullard had been—a good one—and he still looked to be in shape despite the years he had acquired. "Very well. I have no time to argue." With that, Bader grabbed a nearby sheet of paper and scribbled a quick note.

"Here, Bullard. Your orders. Take them to Capitaine Voiseaux. He commands my machine-gun company. You'll find them on the south bank of the Loire. They are there to hold off the German advance as long as they can. We expect the Boche to arrive tonight. *Au revoir, mon ami. Bon chance.*"

"*Oui, mon commandant. Merci.*"

An hour later, after Bullard had located him, Captain Voiseaux hurriedly read the commandant's message. When he finished he gave the old Poilu the once-over and sighed.

"Very well, Sergeant, the major speaks very highly of you. Are you ready to join in on this madness?"

"*Oui, mon capitaine*, but I am confused. You said 'sergeant'?"

"Yes, that's what the commandant's note says, 'Bullard is an excellent soldier. Give him a section of good men, and the field rank of sergeant, so the men respect him.' So, again, Sergeant, are you ready?"

"*Absolument, capitaine!*" Bullard beamed with obvious pride in his new—and long overdue—rank.

"Here is Corporal Miller, from Alsace. Take him and three others to the left of the line. There's a Hotchkiss there that needs a crew. I'm putting you in charge, Bullard."

"I will not disappoint you, sir."

"All I ask is that you disappoint the Germans—greatly."

Once more, a generation removed, Eugene Bullard made his way toward the front, preparing to repel another German onslaught, with a machine-gun crew.

21

WEARY AND WOUNDED (AGAIN)

The German bombardment of the French positions along the river began shortly after eight o'clock that night. The artillery, primarily light howitzer field pieces, with a range of better than ten thousand yards, far outdistanced the machine guns of the 51st. The shells came raining in at an incredible rate and within minutes it was evident that the French troops would have to move or die. Reluctantly, Major Bader pulled all his men back, including Bullard's small section, which had not yet had a chance to fire even a single round.

This cat-and-mouse battle continued for the next three days. The German artillery would pound whatever position the French set up; then, after they started withdrawing, the storm troopers would rush forward, secure another position for the artillery, and the game would begin again. During the daylight hours, the misery of the 51st was compounded by the Stuka dive-bombers.

There was no French air cover. The French Air Force (L'Armée de l'Air), which, prewar, had been plagued with obsolete aircraft, lack of modern weaponry, poor communications equipment, and too few pilots, was not a factor in this desperate fight. Premier Daladier's thousands of American aircraft, the warbirds he had ordered in 1939 for delivery in early '40, did not arrive in time. Whatever planes and pilots had survived the initial onslaught of the Wehrmacht and Luftwaffe were evacuated to North Africa to "await developments."

In short, acting Sergeant Bullard and his comrades in the 51st were fighting a brave but losing battle every step of the way. On June 18, one hundred miles south of Orléans, his second stint fighting for his adopted country would come to an abrupt end.

The ragged remnants of the 51st limped slowly into the village of Le Blanc. Its main thoroughfare was dusty, deserted, and totally locked up. Most of the population had fled, heading south, and whoever might have remained was nowhere in sight, no doubt hiding in whatever cellars or barns could provide the best cover.

As Bullard and the men in his section came upon the village square, the skies filled with lethal 88-millimeter shells—hungry, seeking targets. One landed on the village church, crushing it like an eggshell, dropping its wooden timbers, brick and shattered stained glass on the handful of parishioners praying inside. No one survived. Another fell directly on the square's fountain, blasting stone and gouts of water skyward.

Bullard heard the shell that was coming for him, but only for two seconds—it roared like a freight train, and seemingly had eyes—tracking straight toward him and his men. The deadly munition could not have landed more than ten yards away from him. The blast and its concussive power swept Bullard into the air and flung him forty feet, where he slammed into the wall of one of the stuccoed houses surrounding the square. Luckily, he struck the building with his left shoulder and side, and not head-on, which would have surely crushed his skull and killed him instantly.

As it was, he was badly injured. One vertebrae in his neck was shattered (later examination revealed). His spine was painfully whacked out of alignment, several ribs bruised and cracked, his left shoulder completely bruised and battered, and a deep cut from a piece of shrapnel had sliced his forehead over his right eye. It would leave a scar he would carry with him for the rest of his days.

The men around him fared much worse. Eleven soldiers were killed outright, and another sixteen were wounded, several critically. One single shell nearly wiped out what was left of an entire company. The square was littered with broken men and shattered bodies. Medics rushed in to help and Bullard was painfully removed, on a litter. That night he was carried off in a truck with several more wounded, as the 51st continued its southerly, fighting retreat.

Ironically, on that very day, General Charles de Gaulle, who was fashioning himself already as the leader of the Free French in exile, made a radio broadcast from London to the French troops remaining in the field. He knew, as did most of those still fighting, that continuing to resist was becoming more and more futile. He also knew that the French government was near collapse and that the military's leaders were close to capitulating. He urged those who wished to remain free and fight against the Nazis to join him, in England. For those who could not escape, he encouraged them to go underground, and join the Resistance. He promised that France would rise again, and free. The battle may have been lost, but the war to defeat the Fascists was just beginning.

Bullard heard the broadcast as he lay in great pain on the litter in a tent. It cheered him as well as the wounded men around him. They did not feel quite so abandoned.

Major Bader sought out Bullard the next day, June 19, and told him that it would be best for him to move on, on his own. He needed better treatment than the local medics could give him, and he was in no shape to continue to fight. Bullard understood, and he did not want to be an impediment to his comrades. The unspoken words were that if he were captured with his unit, the Nazis would undoubtedly execute him without so much as a second thought. A black man fighting for France, and an American at that, would doom any chance for surrender and survival.

"If I were captured with them," Bullard reflected, "I would not just be interned. I would certainly be executed not only because of my color, which put me in at least as much danger as the Jews, but also because the enemy must by now know that I had worked against them in the Underground as well as being a foreign volunteer in two wars."

Bader suggested that he strike out, as soon as he was able, for Angoulême, on the road to Biarritz. The army, Bader had been told, still had a big hospital in Angoulême, and it seemed the best chance for Bullard to get treatment, then work his way to the Spanish border and, hopefully, to freedom. Bullard was determined to start right away, despite his pain. Bader wrote out a safe conduct pass, then the two old comrades embraced, and went their separate ways.[54]

The next twenty-four hours were sheer torture for Eugene Bullard. Using his rifle as a crutch, he hobbled off down the

---

54 Commandant Bader would be captured with the pitiful remains of his proud regiment a few days later. He would be a POW but did escape in 1943 and rejoined the Free French where he fought on, surviving the war, and attaining the rank of colonel. Amazingly, this would not be the last time Bader and Eugene Bullard would see each other.

road toward Angoulême. His uniform and pitiful state garnered a few rides in trucks and cars along the way. Near his
destination he decided to get rid of the rifle. If he were caught
with it, he'd be shot on the spot. He traded it to a farmer for
a stout walking stick. He had also been able, in Orléans, to
exchange his traveling clothes for a proper if sorely used tunic
and uniform trousers, two sizes too big.

Barely able to move because of the agony wracking his
body, Bullard stumbled into the French military hospital in
Angoulême. His tremendous string of luck at running into
old acquaintances continued. One of the doctors on duty
was a comrade, the former medic of the 170th, Dr. H.C. De
Vaux. The doctor had also worked at the American Hospital
in Neuilly (with the detested Dr. Gros) between the wars.
De Vaux gave Bullard a shot of pain-killing medicine and
wrapped his back and spine to immobilize it as much as possible. He also gave Bullard some painkillers to stick in his
pocket. There was nothing more he could do, medically,
with the supplies on hand. De Vaux further advised that he
keep moving, if he could stand the discomfort. The Germans
were expected to capture the hospital any moment. The best
course of action was to get to Biarritz, where there was an
American consul, who was reportedly helping citizens escape the country.

Bullard asked if the doctor was going to go, too, but he said
no. He had too many wounded at the hospital who needed
his help. He was sure he'd be captured, but he was banking
on the Germans needing trained physicians to help with their
prisoners.[55] De Vaux gave Bullard two canteens of water, six

---

55 DeVaux was, indeed, taken prisoner after the Armistice was declared on
    June 22. As to his fate behind enemy barbed wire, no one knows. He dis-
    appears from the pages of history.

tins of sardines and four packs of cigarettes, then sent him on his way.

There were roughly two hundred road miles between Angoulême and Biarritz, where Bullard hoped he could get assistance in getting into Spain. From there, a way to get to America might open up. The thought of "America" seemed strange to him then. Twenty-eight years ago he had put the United States, its racism, deep hatreds for blacks—at least in the South—and the threat of potential lynching behind him. How odd to think that America was his goal then, his potential refuge from the storm that was devouring the Continent.

Had things changed in America since he left? Based on what he knew from his friends, especially black musicians and entertainers, much was still the same; yet, it was home. Georgia was where he had been born. Although he had not seen or heard from any members of his family since his departure as a teen, he wondered if they'd welcome him back. Was his father still alive? What about any of the brothers and sisters with whom he had hid under the bed when the white riders came knocking? Were any of them still in Columbus?

Shoving such thoughts aside, Bullard pushed on. The countryside between Angoulême and Bordeaux is some of the most beautiful in all of France, but that meant little then, as he passed the remnants of humanity littering the highway. The sound of the guns was then still distant, but they would come on soon enough. The frightened people he walked with knew that, and all of them wondered what their fates might be and when they might sleep peacefully once more—if ever.

By noon the next day, having walked nearly all night, Bullard was halfway to Bordeaux. He decided to sit down along the side of the road under the shade of a large elm just ahead and have some sips of water, perhaps a can of fish. As he neared the big tree, he noticed another figure sitting there, a soldier, like himself. This man had a bicycle and wore a tunic indicating he was—or at least had been—in the French Foreign Legion.

The man called out, "Hello. You there, *soldat!*"

"*Bonjour, mon ami.* May I sit and rest with you?"

"Of course, old comrade. Have you anything to eat perhaps?"

Bullard came over, taking off his pack, slowly, wincing with his injuries, and sat with the other soldier.

"You are wounded, my friend?"

"Yes, but I've had worse."

"I tell you what. If you can share a bite of food with me, you can have this bicycle. I will trade you. My unit has been blown to bits, and captured. I have no orders, nowhere to go."

Bullard broke out his supplies. He doled out some of his water and gave the man two tins of his sardines, one of which the soldier hungrily pried open and wolfed down practically in one bite, the oil dripping down his chin.

Licking his fingers, he said, "Ah, if only we had a loaf of fresh bread and a pint of wine. Now that would be a magnificent lunch, would it not?"

Bullard smiled and nodded, slowly biting into a sardine.

"Where are you headed, my friend?"

"America," Bullard replied absentmindedly, still mentally entangled in his recent musings.

"Ah, you are American? Bravo. God bless you. Fighting for my country."

The two men chatted for a while until the other soldier nodded off to sleep in the shade, his stomach at least partly full for the first time in many days.

Bullard stood, put on his pack, tested the bicycle for its new load and stability, and off he pedaled. He started making very good time and was soon near Bordeaux. He decided to press ahead instead of stopping. In the early hours of June 22, he arrived in the coastal city of Biarritz and, he hoped, sanctuary.

22

A HUNTED MAN

In a refugee-choked Biarritz, the American Consul's Office was situated in a nondescript building adjacent to the main post office, near the old Hippodrome. Even at four in the morning, a long line of desperate Americans was huddling outside, and, amazingly, the office was open. Slowly, the candidates for papers moved ahead. After about two hours in line, a bone-weary Eugene Bullard neared the entrance. He propped his bicycle against the wall, next to a large pile of baggage.

A tall, haggard-looking man exited the front door, glancing at the line. He spotted Bullard right away, and motioned him forward.

"Good morning, soldier," the man smiled behind tired eyes. "You're wearing a French uniform. Are you American?"

"Hey!" an angry voice shouted from the head of the line.

"We were here ahead of *him*!" The racial emphasis seemed obvious.

"Yes," the gray-haired official growled back, "but he's in a uniform and appears wounded—and you're not. If you can't wait, go away!"

He turned back to Bullard, concerned: "There are Nazi officers in town already. I saw several having dinner at my hotel last night. You better get out of that uniform quick. Do you have any other clothes?"

"No, monsieur, I do not."

"My name's McWilliams, by the way. I'm the consul here. What's your name?"

"Eugene Bullard. From Paris, but from America first."

"Let me have your passport, Eugene Bullard." The consul extended his hand.

"I do not have one, monsieur. A passport was not necessary when I came to France in 1912."

"Hmm. We may have a problem then. First, you must get out of that uniform."

McWilliams then turned to the crowd and asked, "Does anyone have a spare shirt and a pair of pants for this brave soldier?"

Several of those waiting in line rummaged through their valises and soon an acceptable pair of slacks and a calico shirt appeared.

"Come on, Bullard." McWilliams motioned, taking him inside. The consul gave him use of a private bathroom to change, then he stepped into McWilliams's office, which was piled with files and scattered papers.

McWilliams sat at his cluttered desk, picked up a pen, and grabbed a notepad. "Okay, Bullard, where and when were you born?"

"Columbus, Georgia, sir. October 9, 1895."

By chance, McWilliams had spent a few weeks in Columbus several years before. He began to quiz Bullard on the rivers, towns, and attractions in the Columbus area. Every answer was correct and further proof to McWilliams concerning Bullard's veracity. But there was one more test.

"Wait here, please," at which time McWilliams got up and stepped out of his office. He returned in ten minutes with a stocky, middle-aged gentleman.

"Bullard!" the man boomed. "My God, what are you doing here?"

Bullard could not believe his eyes. It was none other than his friend and former American Legion Post 1 commander, Colonel Sparks, the "Death Dealing Dentist."

"*Mon Dieu!* Colonel Sparks! I'm trying to get a passport."

Behind Sparks, in walked Richard "Craney" Gartz, another old friend from Paris days, and heir to the Crane bathroom fixtures fortune. Bullard had been Gartz's masseur during what then felt like an eon ago.

With his having verified Bullard's account via his own recollections, plus these two witnesses, McWilliams was able to fill out the two-page form entitling Bullard to obtain a passport. The next challenge, however, was that the passports themselves could be issued only over the signature of the consul general, who was 175 miles back up the road in Bordeaux.

What else could he do? Thanking the men most profusely, the wounded, still in pain, and exhausted Eugene Bullard faced the prospect of bicycling to Bordeaux and back. He steeled himself for the trek.

Before he left, Gartz suggested he leave all his other identification papers, his books, and, most importantly, all his precious medals behind. If he were intercepted or captured by the Germans, those possessions could doom him. Gartz promised to wrap them all up and post them to his friend Roger

Baldwin (then head of the American Civil Liberties Union), care of his office in Union Square, New York. Should Bullard, against the odds, make it to America, he could pick everything up there. Reluctantly, Bullard agreed.

Tortuous would be the word to describe the next few days. The best pace Bullard could make in his hungry, weakened, and pain-wracked condition was about ten miles per hour on the bicycle, with a break every hour. Two days later, after a few fitful hours of sleep in a meadow, and fighting the crowds fleeing south, he reached Bordeaux.

He found the Traveler's Aid Society office, where the consul general was temporarily ensconced and issuing passports. It was five in the morning. The main office was closed, but the few Traveler's Aid staffers there who were working through the night pointed Bullard to an open space in the hallway and found a thin blanket for him. He dropped to the floor and was asleep in seconds.

He slept for three hours "and dreamed, I guess, of the horrors that I, like thousands, had witnessed." He would soon learn that another reason for his exhaustion was having lost over twenty pounds since he had left Paris.

He was roused by a tap on the shoulder. Startled, and wrestling with the nightmares of the past few days, Bullard uncoiled like a giant spring. He flailed at the young lady who was trying to gently wake him. He smacked her in the neck, knocking her backward. It was not much of a blow, but when he jerked awake and saw what he had done, he collapsed again, in a heap, sobbing, begging forgiveness.

The girl, who was shaken but not really hurt, assured Bullard that she was fine, and that she understood. She helped him to his feet and told him the consul general was ready to see him.

Henry S. Waterman, a career Foreign Service officer, greeted

Bullard personally. He turned his application from McWilliams into an official passport. He also gave Bullard thirty dollars in American currency, as was the standard issue for stranded Americans in need, and told him to go next door and get the necessary passport photos. A weary Bullard did as he was told, and returned later in the day to have the pictures affixed to his new passport, which Waterman promptly signed.

Though the process had gone more smoothly than he could have expected, it had still cost Bullard precious time. It would be back to Biarritz on roads that could contain German collaborators and possibly German soldiers in disguise, hunting for escaping military men just like himself. As bone tired as he was, Bullard could not afford any delay. He thanked Waterman and left.[56]

When he exited the building, he saw that his next journey might have just become much more arduous: someone had stolen his bicycle. Without hesitation, Bullard swiped another unguarded bike and took off. He mused, "I did unto someone who had done unto me."

Two more grueling days later, he was back in Biarritz, passport in his pocket. He retrieved his other papers from Consul McWilliams's office and spent his last night in the beautiful coastal city wandering the beaches. Did he attempt to look up Marcelle? Did he go to the home where she and he had once enjoyed many blissful days along the Bay of Biscay? If he had tried, would she have even welcomed him? Bullard makes no mention of such thoughts in his unpublished recollections. By this time, of course, he was telling the story that she had died five years prior. Had he convinced himself it was true? Did he want to simply believe it was so and

---

56 Though in his mid-70s and more than eligible to retire, Waterman would stay at his post in Bordeaux for another year, helping Americans escape from the Nazis and the soon-to-be Vichy Government.

move on with his life? Unless she, too, had fled somewhere to avoid the Nazis, she was probably still there.

The French had formally surrendered the previous day, June 25.

The next day, Bullard found a ride in one of Dr. Sparks's ambulances ferrying a handful of American refugees to the Spanish border. The roads were so crowded with French and other refugees that the ambulance could crawl along at only five miles an hour—but for Bullard, it surely beat bicycling, or walking, neither of which he could have done. Still, the slow pace of progress was unnerving. Bullard felt like he was being hunted, and that at any moment the ambulance would be shouted to a halt, the door flung open, and a German gun thrust in his face.

After eighteen hours, they reached the frontier at the French town of Hendaye. There was no immediate relief, however, because everyone was held at the International Bridge, where papers were checked. There were not, as of then, any German guards, which would have made it impossible for Bullard to proceed. The Spanish border guards, being Fascist, might have been problematic, but the amazing Bullard luck held yet again. Bullard recognized one of the Spanish officials as an old comrade from the Foreign Legion, Jacques de la Swaine. He was stationed at Hendaye as a customs inspector, and when he saw Bullard his face lit up with delight. He immediately pulled Bullard out of line and took him to a waterside café where they spent the afternoon dining and drinking and recalling old times.

In the early hours of the next morning, with the bridge still closed from the previous night, de la Swaine personally escorted Bullard across, into Spain, without incident. The two old comrades parted, but not before de la Swaine gave Bullard two more bottles of fine Spanish wine. After walking a short distance, he encountered a group of Americans waiting for the early morning bus to Bilbao and he decided to fall in with them. Despite the early hour, he popped open both bottles and passed them around. All were thirsty and not about to complain about early morning imbibing.

There was one exception, however. A Caucasian woman in the group was horrified to see her companions drinking from the same bottles as a "negro." Bullard winked at her and said, "Only American microbes in here."

The woman smiled nervously, asked for one of the bottles, took a big swig, and everyone laughed.

When it arrived, Bullard and his fellow refugees wearily boarded the bus for Bilbao. Several bumpy, stomach-churning hours later, they were greeted by representatives of the American Red Cross. Spain, at that time, was under the iron-fisted rule of General Francisco Franco. He was in sympathy with the Axis and friendly to Hitler's government, but through a series of deft political and military maneuvers he was able to keep Spain neutral throughout World War II. This status allowed the US State Department to operate cautiously if not freely in Spain during the war. As the conflict began to ramp up, American diplomats and semigovernmental organizations, such as the Red Cross, were given at least tacit diplomatic immunity from potential Nazi depredations under orders direct from Franco. Spain became a vital lifeline for United States citizens fleeing the chaos. Ironically, many Jews, American and otherwise, were finding refuge and unrestricted passage to the United States from a nation with a Fascist leader.

Bullard, along with his new coterie of companions, were put up in Red Cross–sponsored hotels in Bilbao, where they could remain until transportation stateside could be arranged.

On July 4, 1940, the Red Cross held an Independence Day party in the Grand Ballroom of the Hotel Carlton, one of Bilbao's oldest and swankiest hotels. It was a welcome and glorious affair for the many ex-pats still waiting to go stateside. Bullard, with his vast nightclub experience, volunteered to manage the bar and all liquor aspects of the fete.

All went well until about halfway through the planned hours for the dance, when a group of swaggering, obviously drunken Spanish and German officers crashed the party. They insisted on cutting in on the dancing American couples and spouting about their "superiority." It didn't take long for a fistfight to erupt, which began to escalate into a full-fledged brawl. The local police were called and got the situation under control quickly. The unwanted German and Spanish servicemen were escorted from the hotel. What is particularly remarkable about this incident was that the usually hotheaded Eugene Bullard calmly stood behind the bar protecting the bottles of champagne instead of uncorking his fists.

Five days later, the next group of refugees, including Bullard, were called up for exfiltration. They boarded a train in Bilbao for further transport to Lisbon, Portugal. Like Spain, Portugal managed to remain neutral in the war, although under extreme pressure: both sides would have loved military bases in the strategic Azores. On the Spain–Portugal border, Bullard faced one more obstacle.

All through the ordeal of the past several weeks he had managed to keep a beret atop his head. This was not a sentimental or sartorial gesture: the beret had one hundred thousand francs hidden in it.[57] At the border, Spanish customs officials were confiscating currency. When his turn came, Bullard was ordered to remove his clothes. As he did so, he engaged the inspector in a lively discussion about boxing

---

57   Worth about $2,200 US 1940 dollars.

and his career in the ring many years earlier. The distracted inspector never thought to tell Bullard to take off his beret.

On July 12, the chartered steamer S.S. *Manhattan*, with US Navy Commander G. V. Richardson as captain, set sail from Lisbon, bound for New York City, with 798 American citizens and other mixed nationalities, all wanting to "go home."

Six days later, Eugene Bullard stood at the rail as the *Manhattan* glided by Ellis Island. "I can never forget how thrilled I was at the sight of the Statue of Liberty," he later reflected. "I wonder if she ever looked so beautiful to any shipload of Americans as she did that day." He was definitely hoping that the country he had fled almost three decades earlier would welcome him home.

The "burst of brightness from Miss Liberty's torch was quickly clouded," he added, because Bullard could not consider himself truly home until he was reunited with his daughters…if they were still alive. He had heard nothing from them—or Kitty Terrier—since that crowded hour when he had shouldered his pack and gone off to once again fight the Germans.

ACT VI
THE PIONEER

23

CAN YOU REALLY GO HOME AGAIN?

What Eugene Bullard, hero of France, feared most about returning to the land of his birth hit him as soon as he walked off the gangway of the S.S. *Manhattan.*

Jack S. Spector, former commander of American Legion Post 1 in Paris, had been placed in charge of seeing to the immediate needs of all American war veterans—especially Post 1 members—who were being repatriated. If an old soldier didn't have a room to stay in, hotel arrangements were made, and paid for, at least initially. If the veteran had no money, a small stipend to get him on his feet was provided. If there was no family to greet him, there would be a welcome from a former friend or acquaintance in the Post. This was to be provided for all members—except one, apparently, who happened to be the only black veteran who stepped off the boat that day. Spector's excuse? Eugene Bullard "wasn't on his list."

The embarrassed Spector—who, ironically, had been teaching "Americanism" to the children of Post 1 members in Paris before the city fell—managed to pull a few dollars out of his own pocket to give Bullard "food money." Another, better-heeled voyager, Sedley Peck, who had flown briefly for the American Air Service in 1917-18, produced a small wad of cash amounting to about $50. Sharp-eyed readers might ask, "But wait! Didn't Bullard have one hundred thousand francs sewn into his beret?" He did, indeed, but by the time he landed in New York, the "old" French franc under the new Vichy government, was worthless.

Luckily for him, at Dr. Sparks's request, he had been carrying with him a suitcase belonging to a friend of Sparks from Paris. He was asked to deliver the suitcase to the friend's New York City apartment, which he did, and the compensation was a key to the place and the offer to spend a few nights there until he could arrange his own accommodations. That's exactly what Bullard did, landing at 1829 Seventh Avenue in Manhattan.

It had to have been a massive cultural shock for him. Even with the generosity of Spector and Peck, Bullard began his stay in New York with about the same amount of money as he had been given upon arriving in Scotland as a stowaway on the German freighter some twenty-eight years ago. He was also much older, under terrible physical stress with his cracked vertebrae, and covered in scars from two wars. He had spoken more French than English during the past two-plus decades and he was truly more French in dress, manners, and thinking than he was American.

Less than two years earlier, he had been drinking champagne every night, carrying rolls of French francs in his pocket, dining with the elite of French society, mixing with many of the most illustrious names in art, literature, music, and politics, and driving his own flashy sports car around the Parisian environs. That had been a life full of "wine, women, and song," and then, on a New York pier, he was reduced to accepting enough money to buy a few meals and rent a room that he could afford.

Added to all this was the emotional anxiety Bullard harbored over the fate of his children. Since leaving Paris, he had heard nothing from them, or from Kitty Terrier. Were they still alive? Were they in Nazi custody? "Guests" of the Gestapo? All in all, it was quite a comedown from his previous circumstances and it had taken a terrific emotional, mental and physical toll.

Being Eugene James Bullard, however, he would not "break." All he knew—all he had ever known—was that when you got knocked down, you picked yourself up again and moved on. That is what he set out to do that sweltering July day in 1940. As his old pal Ernest Hemingway had written, "The world breaks everyone, and afterward, many are strong at the broken places."

The first few months in America were extremely tough. To make ends meet, Bullard took odd jobs, mostly obtained from wartime acquaintances. He cleaned apartments, ran errands, and waited tables at parties. Whatever money was left after paying for his room and food went to medical expenses, as he tried hard to rehabilitate his back so he could take on more strenuous—and better paying—work. All the while he was waging a constant campaign to locate his daughters and get them to safety in America.

One of the countless friends he had made in Paris was William C. Bullitt. Born into a wealthy Philadelphia family in 1891, Bullitt was raised in society circles, attended Yale, and after graduating in 1913, went to Harvard Law School. He dropped out the next year, however, after his father's sudden death. Turning to journalism, he became a successful European correspondent for a number of years and in 1926 he published a popular novel lampooning Philadelphia society. He worked on Woodrow Wilson's staff during the period when the Versailles Treaty was being drafted, but fell out with Wilson on Soviet relations: Bullitt was very much in favor of closer relations with Soviet Russia, while Wilson was not. Bullitt had another good friend who was on the rise, however: Franklin D. Roosevelt. When Roosevelt became president he made Bullitt the first ambassador to the Soviet Union, a post Bullitt held from 1933-1936.

Once he got up-close-and-personal with Soviet leadership, and witnessed its brutality and perfidy, his opinion was totally reversed. By the end of his tenure, he had turned completely against the Soviet way and became, in fact, a passionate anti-Communist for the rest of his life.

Bullitt's next posting was as ambassador to France. An ardent Francophile who spoke the language fluently, he had a wine cellar stocked with eighteen thousand bottles of fine French wine. He seemed the perfect choice for ambassador. His closeness to FDR also endeared him to the leaders of France who were desperate to court closer ties to the United States in case of war. Bullitt, in fact, in September of 1938, gave a speech in Paris that seemed to imply that the United States would immediately come to the aid of France should she be attacked or if the Germans took control of Czechoslovakia. Roosevelt was aghast and quick to send a denial to Paris. It was the beginning of cracks in the relationship between Roosevelt and his ambassador to France.

Bullitt, who had already been married twice, but a bachelor in the 1930s, had become acquainted with Eugene Bullard via L'Escadrille and did not mind living it up and having a grand old time in the club-crawling years before World War II. When the war broke out, Bullitt refused to quit his post in Paris, which made him a bit of a folk hero among American ex-pats. It did nothing but anger President Roosevelt, however, who wanted Bullitt to leave Paris and move with the Free French government to London. Bullitt was the only allied ambassador still at his post in Paris when the Nazis came marching in. He finally left on direct orders from Secretary of State Cordell Hull. Bullitt came home and went to work as an assistant to Hull, a personal friend of long standing.

It was to Bullitt that Bullard turned in the autumn of 1940, traveling to Washington, DC, for a personal audience with his old pal. Today, it strains the bounds of credulity to think that a private citizen could call up and get an appointment with a prominent former ambassador who is also a chieftain in the State Department. American government has become vast and layered, full of gatekeepers and intermediaries, so much so that even a simple sit-down with your local congressperson requires a herculean effort, in many cases. These were still the days, in late 1940, though, before the global explosion that would vault the United States into its world leadership role, when government was still personal—especially if you "knew someone" or if you had "old friends" who labored in the halls of power. Thus it was that Eugene Bullard, French American citizen, could pick up the phone and quickly arrange a meeting with ex-Ambassador William Bullitt, his old drinking buddy, on a matter of grave personal priority.

Bullard asked if strings could be pulled, and Bullitt did just that. His contacts in the new Vichy government were still good, and after a friend called a friend, in Paris, Bullard's daughters were swiftly located. Miraculously, they were still living with and under the protection of Kitty Terrier.

In January of 1941, a stressed, exhausted, and worried Eugene Bullard received a telegram from none other than Secretary Hull himself. He indicated that Jacqueline and Lolita were then under American protection and that papers were being prepared to allow them to leave France. The State Department would advance the funds necessary for their transport—but the government would have to be repaid.

Bullard was overjoyed. But how to pay back the government? He turned to another old friend, Austen B. Crehore, who was at the time president of the Lafayette Flying Corps Association, headquartered in New York City. Crehore had, in the early days of the Great War, tried to sign on with both the army and navy flying services but had been rejected because he was totally deaf in one ear. Not to be deterred, he booked passage on a steamer and sailed to France where he signed on directly with the French Air Service which cared only if you could fly and shoot straight and not if you could hear the sounds of the German planes shooting back. He acquitted himself superbly, downing at least three enemy aircraft and earning two Croix de Guerre. During one of his successful air engagements he was nearly doubled over in pain from appendicitis but had refused to go to the hospital until he finished his mission.

Crehore put out the word to the members of the association and within no time at all, sixteen of Bullard's former flying pals, including Crehore and Ted Parsons, had raised enough money to pay for all the expenses of getting Lolita and Jacqueline to America. Crehore, who lived in New Jersey, even drove to Harlem to pick up Bullard and took him to Pier F in Jersey City where, on February 3, 1941, the girls arrived safely on the S.S. *Exeter*. They had taken nearly the same route as their father the previous year: Paris to Bordeaux, then Biarritz, Hendaye, and finally Lisbon where they boarded the

Exeter. One has to wonder, as the girls passed through Biarritz, if they gave any thought to their mother.

The reunion between father and children was joyous. Neither girl spoke a word of English, however, so as soon as they were all settled in Bullard's small Spanish Harlem apartment, lessons began. The girls were a great help to their industrious but ailing father. They busied themselves with the necessities and housecleaning while also restarting their education in this strange and complicated land.

As Bullard had anxiously awaited news of his children, he had found a job, through the Flying Corps alumni. He was hired as a security guard at the US Army base in Brooklyn. It was about the best he could come up with, given that he was relearning English and had not enhanced his formal education at all since finishing the second grade in Columbus, Georgia. Unfortunately, there were few jobs for jazz drummers, and owning a club in New York was far beyond his means.

He earned the sum of $40 per week as a security guard. That was barely enough to keep him in food and rent money; adding the support of two teenage girls would make it impossible. He had heard, through his army contacts, that better jobs were open for longshoremen with the navy on Staten Island. He had been a longshoreman once, long ago, in Liverpool, so he elected to give it a try. He recognized that his fractured back might make it both painful and difficult to do that type of work; plus, his age was against him. However, the $100 per week that was being offered was just too good to pass up, so off he went, on the Staten Island Ferry, to apply. He would get the job, but only after a very curious experience that involved a shoving match, a knockdown, and an FBI agent.

As the ferry docked on Staten Island, the crowd surged forward to get off the boat. A white man shoved Bullard aside. He, of course, shoved back. The white guy whirled around and shouted, "You black bastard!" That was all it took for Bullard's hair-trigger temper to take over. He uncorked a right hook which flattened the man to the deck. An ugly, murmuring crowd started to form around the only black man on the boat.

As the man Bullard had coldcocked got up, and the others moved toward him, a voice rang out: "Stop! Get back!"

A tall dark-haired man dressed as a dock worker pushed through the knot of men surrounding Bullard. He raised his hand above his head to show his shiny gold FBI badge.

"I saw what happened. This guy—" pointing to the man Bullard had struck "—shoved the nigger first. He started it. Now move back, all of you."

The show of authority dispersed the angry mob. The FBI agent grabbed the perpetrator by the scruff of his jacket and pulled him close. He growled at him, "This man has more medals for bravery than you'll ever get in your life. He's fought the goddamn Germans in two wars. Now apologize!"

The man did so and was allowed to go on his way. The agent and Bullard walked off the ferry together, the latter in a state of shock.

"So, Bullard, you okay?" the G-man asked.

"*Oui*… I mean, yes. How did you…?"

"These are dangerous times, Bullard. The FBI is just being…careful. Is there anything I can do for you?"

Bullard blurted out, "Sure. I'm here to get a job as a longshoreman. Can you help?"

The agent eyed him with incredulity. "Are you crazy? That kind of work, with your bad back?"

"How did you know about my back? Who are you?"

"Not important. Just doing my job. Are you sure you really want that work?"

"Absolument."

"You're nuts. Okay, let's go."

The FBI man, who never identified himself to Bullard, walked with him to the employment office. With the agent's endorsement, it was a slam dunk. Bullard got the job instantly and went to work the next day.

The records show Bullard did, indeed, get the job but there are still several curious loose threads in this anecdote. Why was an FBI agent tailing Bullard? Or did he just happen to be there, perhaps watching the crowd, or maybe even doing routine surveillance work? Either way, how did he know Eugene Bullard? What interest would the FBI have in a broken-down former jazz drummer, or even a war hero who had fought for "the good guys"? Did they know about his activities on behalf of the Deuxième Bureau? Bullard never said another word about this incident.

It was certainly true that the FBI was engaged in massive amounts of counterintelligence work, especially in the days leading up to America's entry into World War II. It was certainly well-known that the FBI Director, J. Edgar Hoover, was a fanatic paranoid who kept boxes and boxes of secret records on all kinds of persons of interest. Would Bullard fit in that category—and if so, why? Proof, if any, of surveillance on Bullard would have been lost forever in the purge of those FBI spying records, illegal, by the way, which occurred on the same day Hoover died in office on May 2, 1972.[58]

What was the FBI's interest in Eugene Bullard? There is no longer any way to know for sure, but a clue may exist in the

---

58   In an interesting footnote to history, these "secret files" were shredded and burned, as Hoover had ordained, by the Number Two man at the FBI at that time, Mark Felt, who would end up being the "Deep Throat" of Watergate fame.

work he was doing in his spare time. In the summer of 1941, shortly after he had started his new job as a security guard, he joined a group called France Forever. This international organization had been founded by Eugene Houdry, an accomplished mechanical engineer who had been a lieutenant in a French tank regiment in World War I. He was a staunch opponent of the Vichy Regime and an active proponent of the Free French movement and the advancement of General Charles de Gaulle. The Vichy government was so angered by Houdry's efforts that he was stripped of his French citizenship in 1941. He became an American citizen soon thereafter, in early 1942. Houdry's aim, and the goal of France Forever, was to do everything possible outside of France to support de Gaulle and elevate him to the presidency of a restored Free French government.

It would not be hard to imagine that Eugene Bullard would be attracted to such an organization, and he embraced it fully. In 1941, at least until December 7, the United States was still neutral and officially in support of the Vichy Government (but not the Nazis), so any "opposition" group, such as France Forever, would come to the attention of the FBI. It was likely, therefore, that at least a few FBI agents were assigned to monitor the activities of that group. If so, it would not be a stretch to imagine that an active member, such as Bullard, would merit some "watching." This could be one possible explanation for Bullard encountering the agent who rescued him from the crowd on the Staten Island Ferry and helped him get his job as a longshoreman.

It may also have been possible that his previous involvement in the French Resistance was working in his favor. Was Inspector Leplanquais's hand still in the game? Could Bullard's contacts with no less a personage that Ambassador Bullitt and Secretary Hull have brought him under the FBI's protection? All these threads were certainly wound around the life of "Monsieur Bullard, Resistance Spy," as he made his transition back to "Mr. Bullard, American Citizen."

Bullard settled into what would become his final residence, 80 East 116th Street, in July 1941, and began toiling hard on behalf of France Forever whenever he was not loading ships with sacks of war materials. He gave talks to social clubs, church groups, civic associations, hiring halls, and interested gatherings all over Manhattan and Harlem. He often wore his French Legionnaire's uniform, bedecked in medals, which always gave a sterling impression and made the crowds take notice. Interestingly, he never wore either of his French pilot's uniforms. In Paris, he had had one made up out of black and red cloth, with an outsized set of pilot's wings, and there was another of the more regulation khaki and blue. He never explained why he did not wear them. Perhaps it was as simple as they had been lost in his travels out of France and through Spain and Portugal. He did, however, retrieve all his important documents and papers, plus his Escadrille books and medals, from Roger Baldwin, in New York City, as had been promised by Craney Gartz in Biarritz.

Perhaps, too, Bullard preferred to wear his Legionnaire's uniform since it had been in the Foreign Legion where he had won most of his decorations. It could also be that his last assignment in uniform was not as an aviator. After the final Dr. Gros disgracing, he had been sent back to his old infantry unit, the 170th, where he completed the war in khaki.

When Bullard spoke, he emphasized the need to free the French, and to elevate General de Gaulle. He also constantly encouraged the recruiting of young African American men to go and fight for France, as he had once done. These were different times, however, and although racial attitudes had not changed a great deal in the past three decades, young black men did not find it appealing to go to another country and face death for little reason. Young black men in America also were aware that the armed forces of the United States were still segregated—could conditions in France really be that much different?

Bullard wrote to Walter White, president of the NAACP, in 1941, encouraging the recruitment of black men for the Free French, especially as "pilots and mechanics." In the same vein, he also corresponded with Frederick D. Patterson, president of the Tuskegee Institute, insisting that he, Bullard, could be instrumental in getting young black men into nonsegregated Free French aviation units. Bullard was apparently unaware that the US Army Air Corps had, in January of 1941, ordered up a unit of black fliers and that they were, at the time he wrote Patterson, already in training. The soon-to-be-fabled Tuskegee Airmen had been established, although the first group was a paltry thirty-three airmen among the fifty thousand white fliers already in training.

White was not polite enough to return Bullard's correspondence. Patterson did, noting only that "Tuskegee is always happy to support or do whatever it can for the furtherance… of worthwhile causes." Craig Lloyd notes in his book that to him it seemed apparent that neither White nor Patterson had ever heard of Eugene Bullard and therefore did not know that they were being addressed by the first African American combat aviator. If so, what a shame: Bullard could certainly have been a role model to the young men who were already under orders at Tuskegee. No one ever made the connection, so nothing along these lines ever happened.

★ ★ ★

East 116th Street, where Bullard had settled, was squarely within Spanish Harlem. The African American Harlem of that time was a bit farther north, from Lenox Avenue and 125th Street and above. Bullard picked his location, first, because the rents were more reasonable, but also he felt more at home among the broader avenues and open markets of the growing Puerto Rican community than he did in the stacked and crowded tenement houses of the African American enclaves farther uptown.

This would make perfect sense for a man who had spent the last quarter century on the broad boulevards and in the open-air markets of the sprawling City of Light. Even the squat brownstones and flat-sided row houses of Spanish Harlem were more reminiscent of the genteel arrondissements in which Bullard had lived.

Those who visited him in his "headquarters"—and there were many visitors over the years—describe his apartment as neat and organized but also overstuffed. Photographs of the many rich and famous people he had met took up every inch of wall space. Wooden and plastic models of the aircraft he had flown, plus the dozens of other types the French and allies had used in two wars, hung from the ceiling everywhere, suspended by thin strands of wire. Every windowsill and spare bureau top or credenza was filled with potted plants, which Bullard tended constantly and lovingly.

Within the 750 square feet or so, he lived quietly and comfortably with his two daughters. He held court in his tiny living room or dining space when company came calling. There wasn't a wasted square inch, and every piece of furniture, bookcase, and surface was immaculately clean.

Jacqueline and Lolita lived with their father until each married and moved away—but neither daughter moved far while

Bullard was still alive. Lolita, born in 1928, married an African American gentleman eighteen years her senior, Rowland Garnett Johnson, in 1949. They had one child, a daughter, Denise, and lived near Bullard in Harlem. Sadly, Lolita died relatively young, of a heart attack, at age forty-six in 1974. Her husband lived until ninety-one and died in New York City in 2001.

Jacqueline also lived in Harlem for a long time, only moving to Staten Island after her father died. Born in 1924, Jacqueline married a gentleman by the name of Joaquin Hernandez before her father's death. Sometime later, whether widowed or divorced is unknown, she married a gentleman by the name of Charles Reid, by whom she had one son, Richard. Jacqueline died at age eighty-five in July 2009.

History was still not finished with Eugene Bullard. There were more adventures ahead, even as he struggled to pay his bills on a modest and sometimes intermittent income and to make sure his daughters were happy and well cared for. As the battles of World War II raged on, several times Bullard volunteered to fight yet again, for both France and America. He was politely but firmly turned down—every time.

He continued to work diligently on behalf of the Free French, right up to and through the end of the war. On June 17, 1944, eleven days after D-Day, France Forever held a massive parade down Fifth Avenue to honor the anticipated liberation of all of France. Four weeks later, a triumphant General de Gaulle paid a visit to New York where he was hosted by Mayor Fiorello LaGuardia. Six weeks after that, the total liberation of France finally came, and de Gaulle was installed as president. With the goals of Forever France having been achieved, the organization turned from active lobbying to one of fraternal pleasures, meetings, dinners, and swapping stories among old comrades. Bullard participated regularly, wearing his old Foreign Legion uniform.

There were also parties and gatherings for the American-based members of American Legion Post 1 of Paris. Even here, though, Bullard could not escape the ugly shadow of racism. Prior to a Post 1 dinner in 1943, he received an anonymous letter in his mailbox postmarked from Jamaica, New York. The letter read, in part: "Your extended sojourn abroad has perhaps made you forget that in the states [sic] white and colored don't mix at social functions. It would be to your advantage not to attend the dinner on Monday night or to join in any social activities of the Post in the future."

Whether meant as a threat or a warning was not clear. Gene ignored it either way and attended the gathering without incident. He shared a copy of the letter with Jack Spector, the Post liaison officer in New York—the same man who had initially "forgotten" to provide for Bullard when he got off the refugee ship from Portugal. Spector never replied and, given that he lived in Queens, there was at least some suspicion that Spector himself had composed the ugly missive.

At Lafayette Escadrille functions there was never a doubt as to the sole black member being welcomed. Bullard was often the center of attention for his uniqueness and carried with him business cards that contained the line, along the bottom, "First Known Negro Military Pilot."

A year after World War II ended, Bullard thought it was time to return home—not to France, but his original stomping grounds. He made just one trip to Columbus, Georgia, after returning to America. It occurred in 1946, and it was a trek that Bullard made with not a little trepidation. He was so fearful of what he might find that he went alone, leaving his precious daughters in the care of friends back in New York even though he very much wanted to introduce them to any members of his family he might rediscover.

He wondered if a little of his reputation might have preceded him; that is, he had become a highly decorated hero of France, having fought for his adopted country in both world wars. It had not. The news blackout concerning accomplishments of African Americans was still so complete in the Deep South that the deeds of famous native sons and daughters such as Booker T. Washington, George Washington Carver, Frederick Douglass and Harriet Tubman were all but ignored and even scoffed at. As previously noted, only one small piece concerning Eugene Bullard and his war exploits had made it into any American publication—and even part of that was incorrect. He was as unknown and unappreciated in Columbus in 1946 as he had been when he ran away from home in 1907.

When Bullard had left on the odyssey that would eventually bring him to France, his mother had been dead at least five years and his father was still viewed as somewhat of a scoundrel and a fugitive after his run-in with his white stevedore boss at Mr. Bradley's dock. During the ensuing years, Gene's six surviving siblings had scattered to the winds. His older brother Hector had suffered the fate Gene had feared for his father and for himself. Sometime after Gene had arrived in Europe, Hector had sought to attain proper title to a small peach farm left to him (as the eldest child) by his maternal grandmother, a Creek Indian. The white squatters illegally living on the plot trussed up Hector and hanged him from the nearest tree.

Gene's oldest sister, Pauline, had also made good on an escape from Columbus. After World War II, and until her death in the mid-1950s, she lived peaceably and successfully with her husband and children in Newport News, Virginia (ironically, the place where Gene had begun his long European sojourn). Gene was unsuccessful in reuniting with any of his other four siblings: no one, not even his sister, knew where they had gone or what had happened to them. Even the old ramshackle house on Talbotton Avenue where the Bullards lived had been swept away to make room for an urban renewal project.

Big Chief Ox had passed away sometime in the 1930s. However, the "man" Gene feared the most, old Jim Crow, was still very much alive and would be for some decades to come. After taking a rueful look around, Eugene Bullard escaped once more, by hopping on a train headed back to New York. He would never venture across the Mason-Dixon line again.

24

SUDDEN CIVIL RIGHTS ACTIVIST

The heavy burdens of being a longshoreman ultimately proved too much for Bullard's twisted back and old wounds. Shortly after the end of war, he gave up his union card and went into business for himself. He bought a used station wagon and became an independent and itinerant salesman for a range of French perfume manufacturers. Department stores up and down the state, from Manhattan to Buffalo, got used to the smiling "colored man," with his thick French accent and jaunty beret, offering up the latest in Parisian fragrances. Bullard's personality was half the sale, and for several years, although he did not grow rich, he did quite well. His income was enough to support his fraternal activities, apartment, station wagon, and daughters with a little left over for creature comforts and the occasional extravagance.

Still, though, behind the ready smile lurked the hair-trigger temper, as Bricktop had noted long ago. On an early 1950s trip upstate, through the Catskills, Bullard decided to take a bus. After a transfer in Peekskill, the relief driver insisted that he sit in the back of the bus "where the Negroes belong." This was enough to set Bullard's hair on fire, and he threw a punch. The motorman, much younger and bigger than the fifty-five-year-old passenger, fought back.

The confrontation turned into a donnybrook, with the driver and Bullard tumbling off the bus and squaring off in the street. After a couple of rounds, and police intervention, the two men were separated. Bullard was taken to the local hospital and treated for several facial lacerations. One of the driver's fists had landed squarely on his left eye socket and caused real damage. Bullard would ultimately lose most of the vision in his left eye.

This altercation was in the supposedly more liberal North and preceded Rosa Parks's famous December 1, 1955 defiant act on a bus in Montgomery. However, unlike that ground-breaking confrontation in Alabama, Bullard's somewhat pioneering stand received no notice.

This was not the first time, however, that he had stood up for the cause of civil rights. He had been involved in a much more notorious scrap, one that did make the news, in 1949.

Paul Robeson was one of the most intriguing and polarizing figures of the twentieth century. After the passing of Frederick Douglass in 1895 (the year Bullard was born) and before the rise of Dr. Martin Luther King in the 1950s, there were very few more prominent figures on the stage of black activism than Paul Robeson. Often forgotten today, in the wake of Dr. King, Muhammad Ali, Malcolm X, Al Sharpton, and others, Robeson, for several decades, was arguably the most famous black man in America.

He was born in Princeton, New Jersey, in 1898, the youngest of seven children (two of whom did not live beyond childhood). His father was a former slave turned Presbyterian minister. When Robeson was six, his mother, who was nearly blind, got too close to a kitchen stove and her garments caught fire. She was burned so badly that she died soon thereafter. Paul's father, William Sr., did the best he could to raise his children as a single parent, while also tending to his flock at the Witherspoon Street Presbyterian Church in Princeton.

Perhaps Robeson's stirrings as a social agitator came from his father who, in 1901, ended up on the wrong side of a congregational disagreement. The white overseers of Reverend Robeson's black congregation wanted him to stop preaching about "social injustice." The reverend refused and he was voted out after twenty years of steadfast service. The family then moved to Westfield, NJ, where Pastor William became head of the Downer Street Saint Luke African Methodist Episcopal Zion Church. After several years as head of that congregation, he was transferred to the Saint Thomas AME Zion Church in Somerville. This would be the reverend's last parish, as he died, age seventy-three, while still in charge, in 1918.

Young Robeson was a natural athlete who also had, once past puberty, a stunningly powerful basso profundo voice. A star player in several sports in high school, he was offered a scholarship to Rutgers. When he matriculated, in 1915, he became only the third African American student to have attended the state college of New Jersey. Even though an "enlightened" Northern college, Rutgers, at that time, still harbored a great deal of latent racism and Robeson had to battle it the entire time he was an undergraduate. He bore down on his studies, winning many hearts and minds in the process. It did not hurt that along the way he lettered in five sports and led the football team to two championships. He was a first-rate debater, outstanding actor, All-American and member of Phi Beta Kappa. His classmates elected him valedictorian of the Class of 1919.

After Rutgers, Robeson enrolled at New York University Law School, but after a semester he transferred to Columbia University School of Law. He said he "felt more comfortable" living in Harlem and attending a law school that tended to be more liberal. To pay for his education he played professional football on the weekends. He signed on for one year with the Akron Pros (NFL champions in 1920) then started for the Milwaukee Badgers in 1921-22, a team that was a predecessor to the Green Bay Packers. He completed his law degree—and his professional football career—in 1922.

Two years earlier he had met Eslanda Cardozo Goode at the Columbia University summer school. "Essie" was from a long line of slave families but her paternal great-grandfather was a Sephardic Jew whose family had been expelled from Spain in a seventeenth century upheaval. She considered herself to be Jewish and her religion was to become a factor in Robeson's career and public persona. Essie had a bachelor's degree from the University of Illinois and was attending Columbia to pursue a medical degree. The two fell in love and married in 1921 and Essie, seeing her husband's potential in many areas, decided to give up her pursuit of medicine and manage his career. She was the one who convinced Robeson to seriously pursue professional acting and singing, something he often joked that he did to "get her to quit pestering me."

Essie had good instincts. Robeson had a fabulous voice and a wonderful stage presence. Soon, he was singing in major productions on Broadway, producing his own one-man shows, acting in movies, and traveling around the country and most of Europe.[59] Robeson set aside his career as a lawyer to pursue the much more lucrative entertainment gigs he was being offered. Along the way, in 1927, the couple had their one and only child, Paul Jr.

In the 1930s Robeson began to have a political and ideological awakening, and became much more aware of his African heritage. While performing a series of shows in London, he took time to learn a number of African dialects at the School of Oriental and African Studies. During the same sojourn he wrote a widely read essay titled "I Want to Be African."

In 1934, Robeson accepted an invitation to visit the Soviet Union, at the behest of Sergei Eisenstein, the acclaimed Soviet movie director. On the way, he and Essie passed through Nazi Germany. The racist attitudes he encountered there horrified him. By contrast, in the Soviet Union—or at least the society that was shown to him—Robeson felt "liberated." He said of his experiences there: "Here I am not a Negro but a human being for the first time in my life. I walk in full human dignity." His experiences in Soviet Russia made a lasting impression on Robeson, to the point where he began to defend Communism fully (although he never joined the Communist Party).

Like Eugene Bullard, Robeson was exposed to a completely new culture after which he began to fully understand the boundaries of the racial divides in his native country. He brought the ideals of Soviet society back to the United States with him and used them frequently to combat Jim Crow America. It would bring him no end of grief and would shape the arc of the remainder of his career and life.

By the late 1930s, Robeson was among the most widely recognized entertainers in the world and a bankable Hollywood

---

59 Especially praised were his performances in *Showboat* and *Othello*, in both the US and Europe.

star. Gaining great acclaim, he appeared in the film version of the Eugene O'Neill classic *The Emperor Jones* and the adventure flick *King Solomon's Mines*. He was also a ready player in just about any cause to advance labor, anti-Fascism, and racial equality or oppose political oppression. He supported the anti-Franco Republicans in the Spanish Civil War, even traveling to Spain to entertain the Republican wounded. He backed Jawaharlal Nehru's thrust for Indian independence and sided with China against the Japanese. After he learned a patriotic pro-China anthem and sang it in Chinese, the ballad was adopted as (Republican) China's national anthem.

During World War II, while Bullard was fighting in and then escaping France, Robeson pitched in fully in support of America. He gave numerous benefit concerts around the nation to help underwrite the war effort, he sang with shipyard workers as they toiled away building America's fleet, and he hosted a regular radio broadcast of patriotic songs called "Ballad for Americans." He found time to advocate for black players in Major League Baseball and even met with the legendary commissioner of baseball "Kennesaw Mountain" Landis[60] to push for inclusion (to no immediate effect).

In 1946, Robeson met with President Harry Truman to urge antilynching legislation in the wake of four young blacks (two couples) having been hanged from a tree in Georgia. Robeson, somehow, offended the president's native Southern sensibilities, and Truman abruptly ended the meeting. As a result, Robeson enthusiastically supported Henry Wallace for president in 1948, including a risky, life-threatening tour through the South stumping for a candidate labeled a socialist.

In June 1949, Robeson was invited to speak at the Paris Peace Congress. In his electrifying talk he extolled the white

---

60   The very same Judge Landis who sat on the bench during the trial of Jack Johnson.

immigrants and black workers who had built America and declared, "We shall support peace and friendship with all nations, with Soviet Russia and the People's Republic [of China]."

These remarks would have been incendiary enough, but for some unknown reason, the Associated Press reported that Robeson said, "It is unthinkable that American Negroes would go to war on behalf of those who have oppressed us for generations against a country (the Soviet Union) which in one generation has raised our people to the full dignity of mankind."

It has never been determined how his remarks became so mangled. It was later discovered, by looking at the actual time marks, placed by the teletype machines automatically, that the AP's misrepresentation was actually being broadcast at the exact time that Robeson was beginning his speech. Obviously, someone was given a copy of Robeson's remarks in advance (not an uncommon practice, even today) and decided to alter them. The "editor" was never discovered.

Both sets of thoughts, though one was less volatile than the other, were like matches to gasoline. Robeson spent years decrying the false copy, but it never did much good. People believed what they wanted to believe. The immediate result was a hue and cry that reverberated across America. One of the most recognized African American actors in the land was suddenly a pariah to anyone who believed that Communists were infiltrating the American way of life—and millions did. The infamous House Un-American Activities Committee (HUAC) in Congress was immediately on Robeson's back, calling witnesses, like Jackie Robinson, to testify against him. Movie and stage roles began evaporating. Recording contracts vanished. His popularity as an entertainer plummeted.

The firestorm was still raging as Robeson was scheduled

to give an outdoor concert in Lakeland Acres just north of Peekskill, New York, on August 27, 1949. Robeson had performed three times already at Lakeland without incident. The spot was close enough to Harlem to be easily accessible by car or bus and yet away from the sweltering streets of late summer. The August concert was to be a benefit for the Civil Rights Congress, an organization founded in 1946 to primarily speak out against legal injustices against African Americans. This group was quickly labeled "Communist." Although the group had no such affiliation, it, too became a ready target for the HUAC.

On the morning of the scheduled concert, people started arriving early, but few in this crowd were concertgoers. Most of the early arrivals were there to prevent the concert from happening at all: hundreds of local residents showed up with baseball bats and bags of rocks. The local American Legion and Veterans of Foreign Wars chapters turned out their members to prevent the "Commies," "niggers," and "kikes" from holding their show. A likeness of Robeson was strung up on a large oak tree and a group of Klansmen set up a cross on the hillside near the stage and proceeded to set it on fire.

As concertgoers got off the trains and arrived by bus and car, they were pelted with rocks. Several people were dragged from cars and beaten. The anti-Communist vigilantes screamed epithets involving blacks, Jews, and "reds." Robeson's car was hit by stones, and its windows shattered. He tried to get out of his car several times to reason with the protesters but was dragged back in by his friends as cascades of small missiles were hurled in his direction. Neither the local or state police forces detailed to monitor the crowds lifted a finger to break up the riots or help the concert promoters.

After several hours of threats, beatings, and pushing and shoving, it was decided to cancel the event. The concert attendees got back on the trains and buses, many of them bleeding from cuts and scrapes. The mayor of Peekskill deemed it a "peaceful protest." The state police commander huffed and said the whole affair was outside his jurisdiction. The local Joint Veterans Council simply declared it a "parade" held without disorder and "perfectly disbanded."

For Robeson and his supporters, it was a terrible disgrace. They vowed to push ahead and pledged that next time they would be better prepared. Three days later, Robeson spoke to a crowd of over three thousand, including Eugene Bullard, at the Golden Gate Ballroom in Harlem. Robeson pledged to make another attempt, vowing to "be loyal to [the] America of true traditions; to the America of abolitionists, of Harriet Tubman, of Thaddeus Stevens, of those who fought for my people's freedom. Not of those who tried to enslave them. I'll be back with my friends in Peekskill."

The concert was rescheduled for September 4. This time, the early arrivals would be on the side of Robeson and his friends. The newly formed Westchester Committee for Law and Order was put in charge of preconcert staffing and protection. Over 2,500 union workers from the Fur and Leather Workers, the Longshoremen and the United Electrical Workers agreed to form a human cordon around the site for the rescheduled concert. This time the venue was the old Hollow Brook Golf Course in Cortlandt Manor, about four miles from Peekskill, on US 202.

Twenty thousand people showed up and the security contingent directed by the Westchester Committee and the New York Communist Party effectively kept all local protestors, and even the police, far from the concert.

The audience was warmed up by piano performances from the prize-winning Juilliard virtuoso Leonid Hambro and the Russian sensation Ray Lev, playing pieces by Bach, Chopin,

Ravel, and Prokofiev. Pete Seeger and Woody Guthrie were on hand and Seeger performed his ballad (later made famous by Peter, Paul and Mary) "If I Had a Hammer."

As the main act, Robeson belted out several of his favorite songs, to the utter delight of the crowd. He gave a stirring rendition of "America the Beautiful," an aria from "Boris Godunov," several Negro spirituals, and ended with "Ol' Man River," his signature song from *Showboat*. He appealed for funds to support the Civil Rights Congress then closed the show. The concert did not go off without incident, however.

Wearing his ever-present beret, a white dress shirt, and black trousers, Eugene Bullard had arrived on one of the Harlem buses just as the concert was starting, shortly after 2:00 p.m. The protective cordon of union workers and Communist Party men had moved away from the entrance to the concert and onto the golf course to better protect the thousands who were already on the grounds. This left the approximately nine hundred local and state police officers on duty outside the concert to keep the late-arriving concert-goers, Bullard among them, from the hundreds of baseball bat–waving veterans, anti-Communist locals, Klansmen, and anti-Semites who had gathered—once again—to disrupt the performance.

As witnessed by Paul Robeson Jr., one of the protestors spat on Bullard as he walked by, striding toward the entrance. Bullard, of course, could not let the slight pass without reacting. He spat back. This brought an instant reaction by a Westchester County deputy sheriff, who was standing three feet away. As documented clearly by photographers there at the time, the deputy began shouting at Bullard then beating him with his nightstick. Bullard raised his arms above his head to wield off the blows, then he staggered back and fell to the ground. Other police joined in on the beating, which lasted almost a minute.[61]

Bullard was bruised, and also received a couple of scrapes, but he was not deterred. When the police moved on to other victims, the proud war veteran and Resistance fighter got up, recovered his beret, placed it back on his head, brushed himself off, and continued on into the concert, with others following him inside, defying the glares of the police and protestors.

After the concert, those who had attended took buses and private cars back to Harlem and elsewhere in New York City. Since one-third of the crowd had been African American, they became easy targets. Most of the vehicles were forced down the two roads available—and both were lined with thousands of angry locals, VFW members, anti-Communists, and American Legionnaires. They threw rocks and insults at every vehicle that looked "black" or "Communist," including one bus of schoolchildren from Harlem returning from a summer camp. They had nothing to do with the concert, but the bus driver had gotten lost and ended up in the concert traffic. Twelve children were injured by broken glass and flying stones.

Pete Seeger and his wife and children rode along with Woody Guthrie and their car was pelted with hundreds of stones. Seeger tacked up a shirt on one of the windows to prevent flying glass from harming anyone. Later, using the old saying, "If life sticks you with lemons, make lemonade," Seeger used the rocks that landed in the car in the construction of his chimney at the cabin he built in Fishkill, New York. For decades, they provided a reminder of the Peekskill events.

---

61   Robeson Archive, video entitled "Peekskill Outrage." Also on YouTube: https://www.youtube.com/watch?v=1pgyACdT1rM (accessed 12/08/2018).

25

NOT-SO-SENTIMENTAL JOURNEYS

The beating inflicted on Eugene Bullard in Peekskill was painful, and it further insulted a body that had experienced more than its share of injuries. He felt some pride, though, that it had not occurred during a back-alley brawl but in defense of civil rights. The *Pittsburgh Courier* had declared the Peekskill incidents among the "blackest and most shameful spectacles in American history."

Amazingly, the newly inflicted injuries did not slow him down. On the contrary, it revived, for a short while, the interest of the American public in the story of the "first Negro fighter pilot."

Pictures of Bullard, on the ground, after being struck by the troopers, appeared on the front pages of the *New York Daily Mirror* and the *New York Amsterdam News*. Captions correctly identified him and several lines were written about his status as a former pilot and his gallant service in two world wars.

For Bullard, it was the first time his legend, or any part of it, had been told accurately in any American newspaper. The story created a minor flurry of interest in Eugene Bullard but was soon subsumed in the general disinterest of the American public in any positive news about what were routinely referred to as "colored people."

The Peekskill Riots, as they became known, were indeed an ugly blot on American racial history. However, despite the bravery of those who attended—including that of Eugene Bullard, rising from the ground after a beating to lead others forward—the violent incidents were merely a blip on the civil rights radar. Paul Robeson called a general press conference the day after, September 5, at the Council of African Affairs on 26th Street in Manhattan. Professor Lloyd reports that Bullard "appeared with fifteen other people, most of them, like him, bandaged, to testify against police brutality aimed especially, in their view, at African Americans. Bullard said he was a disabled veteran of two foreign wars and that he had been knocked down and beaten by police for trying to enter the grounds."[62]

Westchester County District Attorney George Fanelli (later a New York State Supreme Court judge) issued a complete whitewash of the affair two days later in a report sent to Governor Thomas Dewey. Despite direct photo evidence to the contrary, some of which landed on Dewey's desk the next morning, Fanelli's report claimed that Robeson's coterie had been responsible for initiating the violence that occurred and that the police had used admirable restraint.

Several days after Fanelli's report surfaced, Robeson and his followers organized a march on Albany. Over three hundred people gathered outside Dewey's office door. The rattled governor refused to meet with any of the leaders, proclaiming

---

62 Lloyd, *Eugene Bullard*, 138.

that they had been organized and the violence initiated by "Communists." Civil lawsuits were filed against Westchester County and the veterans groups who had participated in the disturbances. None of them were successful, and by three years later all twenty-seven of the lawsuits had been dismissed.

The adventures in Peekskill, plus the later bus trip that half blinded him, left a very bad taste in Bullard's mouth. He knew that racism and Jim Crow were still very much alive in his native Georgia, but to have seen the outpouring of pure hatred in the North, especially among American veterans, was a stunning blow to his hopes for a more enlightened United States—or at least something echoing his beloved France.

Bullard made one more journey that turned out not to be what he had hoped. In early 1950, he began to wonder if returning to France might be possible. With his daughters grown and married, he looked once again to the beacons of the City of Light.

With much anticipation, Bullard returned to Paris in late 1950. His old friend "Frisco" Bingham had survived the war, during which time he had been interned in Paris and constantly watched by the Nazis. The old Jamaican and former trench fighter, like Bullard, had been a very popular dancer and club owner before the war. He, too, had mentored Josephine Baker as well as Bricktop. The two old comrades were overjoyed to see each other, and Frisco invited Bullard to stay with him as long as he wished.

Bricktop was back as well. A number of her old friends and club-goers from the halcyon days had pooled some cash and gotten her back in business, with her own eponymous club, in Montmartre. Unfortunately, the tables were not full, the action was not robust and the rich folks—those who were left anyway—were not pursuing the old prewar lifestyle. Whether Bricktop's would survive was an open question. (It did not.)

As soon as he settled in with Bingham, Bullard began a campaign to recover his old properties. When he walked away in 1940, he had simply shuttered the gym and club. He had not sold either business, but neither had he taken precautions to protect his interests. His old pal Henri-Robert, the eminent lawyer who had helped both Zelli and Bullard untangle the byzantine French property and nightclub laws, had passed away in 1936.

Over the ensuing years, other "owners" had popped up, or they were at least operators willing to possess and fix up the abandoned properties. They were given a sort of "squatter's rights" first call on assets which made it hard for former owners, like Bullard, to establish a valid claim. After all, in the old Gallic sense of "loyalty," the squatters had at least stuck around and toughed it out.

Bullard filed petition after petition, claim after claim, but got nowhere. Neither did he have the financial resources—or the contacts—to endure indefinitely the expensive process of trying to reestablish his rights. The best he could do, and it was certainly better than nothing, was to get the rejuvenated government of France to recognize his valiant sacrifices and battle awards. Such recognition entitled him to a very modest second pension as well as a small lump-sum payment to use on "housing," which would be applied to the rent of his Harlem apartment.

After several months of wearying and expensive legal battling, Bullard knew when he was beaten. He could also see that the atmosphere had changed. Paris was no longer a favored destination for postwar Americans, and the feeling was mutual as far as the citizens of Paris were concerned. The Era of de Gaulle was firmly entrenched and France was already forgetting, in its stiff-necked pride, that America had saved their bacon not once but twice. With reluctance, Bullard said his goodbyes and returned to Spanish Harlem and the only family he had left.

Bullard would not live in France again, but he was not through with the Continent just yet, thanks to Louis Armstrong. In the early 1950s, his friend from L'Escadrille days needed an advance man to help arrange the entertainer's European bookings and travel. Bullard's facility with French and German—plus a smattering of Italian—was of great help to Satchmo and his entourage. And in New York, during recording sessions, Bullard revived his drumming skills to help out as a studio musician during rehearsals when Armstrong's regular drummer was not available. Gene can still be heard on some of Armstrong's early 1950s recordings, such as the tape made at the Dunbar Hotel in Los Angeles in 1951, in particular, on track 4, entitled "Baby Don't Baby Me."[63]

Working with the ebullient genius of Armstrong was a joy, but Bullard could do it for only a couple of years. He hopscotched the country with Armstrong in 1950 and '51, making travel arrangements for the group and sometimes sitting in on jam sessions as well as recording studios. He went on a couple of trips to Europe with Satchmo but the grind of extensive travel was too much for his rebelling body, so the aging warrior set about searching for less strenuous work.

He would not turn up his nose at any legitimate, steady position, and that was why he responded to an offer suggested by an old buddy and took on the job of being one of the elevator operators at Rockefeller Center. The original fourteen

---

63   Louis Armstrong House Museum Online Catalogue, tape number 1987, 3.0131, 2016.

buildings of the complex were constructed in the 1930s in what remains the largest totally private building project ever attempted. The elevators were state-of-the-art for the time, but they were not yet automated. They still needed human operators to tend to the many passengers and respond to the buzzing requests made thousands of times per day.

Bullard was assigned to 10 Rockefeller Center, the building that housed, among other tenants, the newly popular television phenomenon, *The Today Show*. He showed up for every shift on time and ready, and was, in all respects, a model employee. His only quirk, and one that went on for years, was that he would usually wear one or two of his many wartime medals on his neatly pressed elevator operator's uniform. If nothing else, it was an opportunity for Bullard to engage his many passengers in gentle repartee as they flew up and down the elevator shafts. It helped to pass the time.

It would also lead to one final brush with fame.

26

RECOGNITION AT LAST

Although America never seemed to want to know much about its homegrown hero, France never forgot him. Eugene Bullard was, and would always remain, far better recognized in his adopted country than the land of his birth.

One example of this was an invitation extended, in 1954, to Bullard and a group of American veterans who had fought for France. Those who were invited had all their expenses paid to attend a ceremonial relighting of the eternal flame in honor of France's Unknown Soldier. The flame burns underneath the Arc de Triomphe (still) and on display there is an iconic photograph of Bullard and several other old soldiers relighting the flame and laying a wreath at the base of the flame over sixty years ago. Bullard wears a long trench coat adorned with his medals, and he is also wearing a pair of thick-rimmed black glasses. He had not worn eyeglasses at all until his unfortunate encounter with the pugilistic bus driver in Peekskill in the early '50s.

A final and personal high-profile honor recognizing Bullard's life and his service to France was not bestowed upon him until his sixty-fourth birthday, October 9, 1959. On that day, the French Consul in New York, Raymond Laporte, pinned the Legion of Honor to the suit coat of a beaming Eugene Bullard. The flashy medal and ribbon represent France's highest honor. The award had originally been proposed for Bullard in Paris in 1933. The malignant Dr. Gros had still been around, however, which made bestowing this singular honor impossible. Later in that decade the war intervened, and the proposal languished until revived by friends of Bullard's, in Paris, in 1959.

The ceremony elevating him to Chevalier (Knight) of France was attended by his proud daughters, many friends, and the actor Charles Boyer (who had also been active in France Forever). A number of his old pals from the Lafayette Flying Corps and the Foreign Legion showed up as well. The day was topped off by a champagne party hosted by Violette Marzan, a wealthy French socialite in New York, who had served as a nurse in General de Gaulle's First French Army during World War II.

Bullard offered a few remarks at the ceremony, and his concluding thoughts, delivered in French, were: "I have served France as best I could. France taught me the true meaning of liberty, equality and fraternity. My services to France can never repay all I owe her." A reporter from the *New York World Telegram* who covered the ceremony asked Bullard to sum up his many accomplishments. He replied, "You might say I touched all the bases. Not much more you can do in sixty-four years."

Any newspaper columnist would be thrilled to get a twenty-seven-year contract, and if any columnist did, it would be very rare. One of the most famous First Ladies in American history, Eleanor Roosevelt, actually had that opportunity. From December 30, 1935, to September 26, 1962 (two months before her death at age seventy-eight) Mrs. Roosevelt wrote a syndicated column for ninety newspapers that were read all across America and reached over four million people a day. It was called "My Day" and in roughly five hundred to one thousand words she waxed eloquent on any subject that struck her fancy. Mrs. Roosevelt never kept a private diary, but "My Day," in effect, became a very public one. Many columns were serious, others were much lighter. She covered thousands of themes and many hundreds of topics.

On October 31, 1959, Mrs. Roosevelt's "My Day" reported (in part):

> NEW YORK—A very interesting little ceremony took place on October 9 at the office of the Consulate General of France in New York City. On this occasion Eugene (James) Bullard, the grandson of an American slave, was made Chevalier of the Legion of Honor of France... In World War I he enlisted in the Foreign Legion and then transferred to the 170th Infantry, and he was later the first Negro aviator.[64] He was a member of the French underground during World War II... I think we in America should be proud of this man who now lives in our country after his long service to the French and the France he loved.[65]

Upon publication, this warm, chatty column made its way to her four million readers. It was the first time in all of Eugene Bullard's sixty-four years that he was turned into some-

---

64 Actually, the first African American fighter pilot. The first black aviator was Emory Mallick, in 1912.

65 Eleanor Roosevelt, "My Day," New York, NY, syndicated column, October 31, 1959.

thing like a household name. Eleanor Roosevelt's voice was a powerful one, and if she said it, people believed it. It did not necessarily create a groundswell of interest in Bullard, but it certainly created some national recognition for an accomplished African American whose life and adventures had been too long overlooked.

That same year, Dave Garroway was a forty-six-year-old television host at the height of his fame. Every weekday morning the enormously popular program *The Today Show*, headquartered in Rockefeller Center, and entering its ninth year, placed him in front of, and had him heard by, millions of Americans. Those who watched and listened saw a bright, beaming, ebullient man who projected a positive energy about life in America. Only a handful of his closest friends and associates knew that Garroway's broadcasting success could sometimes be undercut by the chronic depression that he had suffered his entire life. Unhappy events could make the depression worse, and Garroway was, in 1959, coping with such an experience.

One of his most popular co-hosts, and a personal friend, Charles Van Doren, the plucky Columbia professor with the engaging smile, was deep in controversy and up to his eyeballs in scandal. Van Doren had risen to national fame as the long-running champion of one of television's all-time hit quiz shows, *Twenty One*. His run had been the most successful ever, and he had knocked off another longtime champ, Herb Stempel, to gain his title. Viewers tuned in by the millions to watch these brainy titans battle, and when Van Doren defeated Stempel, they continued to watch as Van Doren knocked off one smart challenger after another.

There was only one problem: it was all rigged. The producers of the show were later to admit they had provided Van Doren with some of the questions and answers in advance. Ironically, it was Stempel who unveiled the scheme in a jealous fit over having been kicked off the show. Even more astonishingly, it was also revealed the producers had given Stempel many answers, too.

Garroway was devastated by the news, not only with concern for a friend, but by proxy for his own show, which Van Doren had co-hosted many times. It seemed like *Today* and Garroway were being tarred by the same negative brush although they had nothing to do with the *Twenty One* debacle.

At 7:30 a.m. on Wednesday, December 16, Garroway and his producer were rushing for the elevators at Rockefeller Center, headed upstairs to the *Today* suite for a production meeting. The men stepped into elevator number three, the one manned by Eugene Bullard that particular morning.

Garroway had a certain casual familiarity with the friendly, bespectacled colored man in his neatly pressed Rock Center uniform. They had ridden up and down together hundreds of times over several years. Garroway had also grown used to seeing Bullard's uniform decorated with one bauble or another, usually a pendant of some sort festooned with a multihued ribbon, much like a military decoration. He automatically—and wrongfully—assumed that these doodads were membership badges for some fraternal organization or another, or perhaps commemorative pins for one of the many colorful "Negro marching bands" or societies that were popular in Harlem.

As usual that December morning, Bullard greeted the popular host with his patented smile and a cheery hello: "Good morning, Mister Garroway."

"Good morning, Gene. How are you?"

"Fine, sir, just mighty fine. And you?"

"Excellent," Garroway responded automatically, without a second thought.

Something was different that morning, though, and the fine-tuned reporter's sense that Dave Garroway had so carefully nurtured over the years was tinkling little alarm bells in his brain.

Bullard closed the doors and moved the levers necessary to start their ride up to the *Today* floor. Garroway had subconsciously noticed that the operator was wearing a new medal on his jacket, and one that seemed vaguely familiar to him. The pendant ribbon was singular, bright red, and suspended from it was an emerald green laurel wreath and below that a striking Maltese Cross accented with more laurel branches and a circle circumscribing dual French flags.

It was dazzling, quite beautiful, really, and in the back of his mind Garroway thought he knew what he was looking at, but equating what he believed it might be with the modest man beside him working as an elevator operator didn't quite make sense.

Squinting, Garroway began, "Gene?"

"Yes, Mr. Garroway?"

"What's that you're wearing on your uniform?"

"Why, it's the Legion of Honor, Mr. Garroway. It's France's highest decoration. I was awarded the medal just a couple months back." Bullard beamed slyly, knowing he was creating the exact dumbfounded expression in Garroway he had hoped to inspire.

"How did you...?" Garroway caught himself. Where he was headed was, "How did you, a seemingly undistinguished black man zipping up and down in an elevator, probably earning not much above minimum wage, get such a decoration? Did you find it in a pawn shop?"

Fortunately, instead of being so condescending, Garroway

paused long enough that Bullard began to fill in the blank: "I was in the Great War, Mr. Garroway. And the second war, too. I fought at Verdun, among other places. Flew combat, too. Shot down a couple of Boche planes, I did."

"Wait. Stop," Garroway commanded.

"Here? Between floors?"

"No, no, I meant, stop pulling my leg. Who the hell are you? What are you doing driving an elevator?" The questions built up in Garroway's head and started tumbling out, too excited to stay tucked inside.

Bullard chuckled and replied, "Well, sir, it's a long story."

"I want to hear it. And I mean now. Can you come with us, to my office?"

"But who's going to take my shift, Mr. Garroway?"

"Never mind that. I'll ring the building supervisor. Soon as you hear from him and get someone to take your place, you come to my office, okay?"

Puzzled, Bullard could only say, "Sure, Mr. Garroway. Soon as I can."

An hour later, a relaxed and bemused Eugene Bullard was sipping coffee with Dave Garroway, the *Today* producer, and two assistants who frantically scribbled notes.

"So how many medals did you say you have, Gene?"

"Fifteen altogether now, Mr. Garroway, with this one," Bullard responded, pointing to the Légion d'Honneur pinned to his jacket.

"Can you bring them with you, on the show?"

"Yes, I can."

In the previous minutes, Bullard had agreed to make an appearance on *The Today Show*. Garroway was over the moon with the idea, fascinated that he had found a truly outstanding story right under his nose—in the company elevator, no less. It was bound to be a hit with his audience and the potential positives had helped lift his black mood.

The appearance was scheduled for the following week, on December 22, a sort of Christmas gift to his audience. That would give time for Garroway's staff to check out the elevator operator's tale—just in case. After Van Doren, you could never be too careful.

Bullard's claims did check out as facts, of course, and millions of faithful viewers soon discovered Bullard's incredible story. Finally, in his sixty-fifth year, Eugene James Bullard was to have the proverbial "fifteen minutes of fame" in his own country. It was almost exactly that amount of time as Bullard, in his Rockefeller Center elevator operator's uniform, sat and chatted, on live TV, with Dave Garroway. As requested, he did, indeed, bring along a plaque upon which were mounted all fifteen of the medals he had won fighting for France. Bullard and Garroway talked about his life as a young man in Georgia, then his adventures as a stowaway, entertainer, prize fighter, soldier, fighter pilot, and longtime Paris jazzman and nightclub impresario.[66]

The *Today* appearance fostered a number of other on-camera interviews, mostly for the New York market. Everyone wanted a piece of the humble elevator operator who, in reality, had been a highly decorated war hero, boxer, combat pilot, and friend to everyone who had been anyone in the antebellum club scene of Paris in the Jazz Age. Interestingly, the interviewers always wanted him in his elevator operator's uniform—not his swaggering pilot's outfit or his Foreign Legionnaire's garb. The story was "better," more "American," if the audience saw him attired as a humble everyman who had suddenly appeared in their midst as a full-blown hero.

---

66 Sadly, no recordings, video or audio, of the broadcast survive. There are several publicity photos, however, and a couple are included in this book.

Bullard was not compensated for any of these appearances, and he continued to subsist on his elevator operator's pay. The momentary fame did, however, inspire him to bring forward another idea that he had been secretly nurturing for many years: an autobiography. This idea was also being pushed by his old friend Ted Parsons, by then a retired US Navy rear admiral. Parsons had actually been egging him on for years to tell his story, but Bullard had always demurred.

Then, with his small dose of national exposure, it seemed a more plausible and perhaps even a necessary project. There was only one challenge: Bullard had overcome his lack of a formal education along the way through plain hard work and incredible experiences, but he could not write that well in English. His French was more than passable, but his English skills were lacking.

Good fortune intervened. A church friend introduced Bullard to Louise Fox Connell, a freelance writer and playwright who had written extensively for such publications as *Glamour*, *Parents Magazine*, *Vogue*, *Mademoiselle*, and the *Delineator*. Louise, a white woman, was also a staunch advocate for civil rights and racial equality and had joined the ACLU, NAACP, and the Congress of Racial Equality, known as CORE. Encouraging black writers and activists was part of her skill set.

Connell was fascinated by the Eugene Bullard story. Whether she knew or suspected that part of it was "fanciful" she never said, but she was convinced that most of it was real. She agreed to work with Bullard and help him organize his papers, notes, and other material. Over a series of sit-downs, he told her everything he remembered (and maybe even then some). Connell condensed it all into a thirteen-page typed outline. She gave the outline back to Bullard and encouraged him to tackle each bullet point one by one until, together, they could flesh out the entire story.

When Bullard asked her how much she would charge him for the project, she replied, "Nothing." It was more important to her, she insisted, to battle racism through stories like Bullard's than to receive compensation.

He labored for many months, handwriting in his large, florid script, on legal pads. Connell would polish up what she was given and send her work to a typist—a typist who she paid. Connell also pounded the pavement to find someone who would publish the book. In this she was far less successful than in the creation of the manuscript, but it was not for lack of trying.

Connell persuaded several publishers to take a look at the work in progress, but she was turned down everywhere. One publisher told her that the story "made the daydreams of Walter Mitty look pale by comparison." It was just too unbelievable. Another drawback, Connell was told, was that so much of the story took place in France, and the French had soured on their relationship with America during the early 1960s. Even after World War II, and even after the United States had assisted the French military with massive amounts of aid during their struggles with the Viet Minh and the disaster of Dien Bien Phu in 1954, de Gaulle's "France First" stance was turning off most Americans. Despite the continued popularity of the retired Jackie Robinson and the emergence of young black actors and entertainers like Sidney Poitier and Harry Belafonte, America at the dawn of the '60s was simply not interested in inspirational tales of courageous black men who had fought for another country.

Bullard was disappointed, but as usual, he was not about to give up. And one day in 1960, he received what he called "the greatest honor of his life." It began when an ornately handwritten envelope arrived at his apartment in early April. Curious, he carefully slit open the envelope and pulled out an invitation card that read: "General de Gaulle, President of the French Republic, and Madame de Gaulle, request Mssr. Eugene Jacques Bullard[67] to do them the honor of being present at the reception which they are giving at the Armory of the Seventh Infantry Regiment, 643 Park Avenue, at 4:45 p.m., Tuesday, April 26th."

Bullard's delight could hardly be measured. Proudly wearing all fifteen of his French decorations, including the newly awarded Légion d'Honneur, he arrived on time in his neatly pressed khaki dress uniform of the French Foreign Legion.

President de Gaulle had been in the United States to meet with President Dwight Eisenhower, during the latter's last year in office. De Gaulle wanted to strategize with his old World War II compatriot concerning an upcoming summit conference with Soviet Premier Nikita Khrushchev, scheduled to be held in Paris that spring. De Gaulle also wanted to revisit New York City, where he had been so warmly received when World War II was still raging and victory was not yet assured. Madame de Gaulle also had designs on visiting several swanky Fifth Avenue boutiques.

Over one million people lined the boulevards, cheering, as de Gaulle was swept through the city via motorcade. He gave speeches at City Hall and the Waldorf-Astoria Hotel. Shortly after 6:00 p.m. he entered the Seventh Regiment Armory where five thousand members of the French community erupted into applause and cheers. Three hundred children culled from local French schools offered a rousing rendition of "La Marseillaise," which ended with another round of thunderous applause.

After another brief speech, his doleful eyes scanned the

---

67   The de Gaulles used the French version of "James," as in "Jacques."

crowd. They settled on a table near the dais where a number of VIPS had been seated. De Gaulle stepped away and headed for a beaming, bespectacled black man with a wide row of dazzling medals on his chest.

The towering de Gaulle marched straight to Bullard and stood in front of him. The old soldier and pilot, wide-eyed and incredulous, leaped to his feet, snapped to rigid attention, and saluted. The general, as any proper French officer would do, saluted back, then stuck out his right hand.

"Sergeant Bullard, I believe?" President de Gaulle announced in his booming baritone.

"*Oui, mon General, je suis Bullard,*" Bullard replied, extending his hand to take the general's proffered grip.

De Gaulle grabbed the gnarled hand in a vice grip and used it to pull the startled old warrior into a bear hug, complete with a congratulatory pounding on the back.

"*Tout notre pays est dans votre dette*" (*All of our country is in your debt*), the president told Bullard, looking straight into his eyes. "*Merci, Sergeant.*"

Tears began to form in the corners of those eyes and Bullard could only whisper softly, "*Merci, mon general. Merci beaucoup.*"

The rest of the evening was a whirl of conversations and music and accolades for those who were considered without question to be heroes of France. The evening offered the opportunity for Bullard to be reunited with a friend from Paris days, a still-beautiful woman who had also been recognized for her service during the war. In its coverage of the event, the *New York Amsterdam News*, headquartered in Harlem, included a photograph of Bullard embracing and being kissed by Josephine Baker.

27

THE HERO GOES HOME

Not long after the marvelous experience of being honored by President de Gaulle, Bullard began experiencing pains in his abdomen. He lost his appetite and began losing weight—and by this point in his life, he did not have much weight to spare. He basically ignored the discomforts figuring, after a long life of stress and worry, he probably had ulcers. He began watching what he ate and he drank less wine. The pains subsided. Bullard did not think much more if it.

He continued his work schedule and responded, with gusto, to the many invitations he began receiving, because of his new-found notoriety, to address various civic and fraternal groups, mostly on behalf of the old Escadrille or the veterans of France Forever. Toward the end of 1960, Bullard received a very welcome surprise visitor: Major Roger Bader, who was by then retired Colonel Bader. The two old comrades, who had weathered the lead-filled storms of Verdun in World War I and then the shell-shocked days of Orléans in the next war, dined at Bullard's apartment in Harlem, took walks around Manhattan, and spent hours poring over Bullard's old maps of Fort Duaumont. It was a truly happy occasion.

In April 1961, Bullard was invited to take part in a Franco-American military memorial celebration at the Lafayette Statue on Union Square. He wore his uniform, of course—much easier to fit into because of the weight loss—and was honored to be chosen as a flag bearer for the ceremonies. According to one attendee, as he clasped the furled French tricolor "his huge black fist was an object of wide-eyed curiosity." There is a picture of Bullard at this memorial, all decked out in his khakis and medals, an image that turned out to be the very last photograph to be taken of Eugene Bullard.

The pains in his abdomen returned, this time with a vengeance, and they did not go away, no matter what he tried. His daughters finally convinced him to get checked out at Metropolitan Hospital in East Harlem (now Metropolitan Hospital Center) at 1st Avenue and 97th Street. He resisted for so long mainly out of concern for what the doctor might cost. He was still working at age sixty-five as he needed to pay the rent. He could have obtained some welfare and disability benefits, plus some food stamp assistance, but he would not even consider it. Bullard was a proud man and would not accept any compensation he had not earned.

He entered the hospital on August 18, 1961. After some tests and the elimination of several ordinary causes, his physician recommended an exploratory surgery. The results were very discouraging: Bullard had an advanced and aggressive form of intestinal cancer. It was determined that further surgeries would likely prove ineffective. There might be a bit of relief, perhaps some prolonging of life, with a series of new medications the doctor could recommend, but the prognosis was basically "attend to your affairs."

Bullard took the news with equanimity. He had escaped death so many times in his life that he truly felt lucky to have survived as long as he had. He professed no fear: "God is my friend," he told his daughters. "He has always been my friend. The sooner I die, the sooner the suffering will be over." Never one for much religion, these sentiments may seem curious; but, apparently, Bullard had found some way to make peace with his Maker and to embrace at least a modicum of solid Catholicism.

In many ways, Bullard was finally in a good place, at least mentally and psychologically, if not physically. Both Jacqueline and Lolita were married and he had grandchildren. He was a familiar and respected figure in his neighborhood. While most of his adventures and achievements were only then becoming known and appreciated in the United States, he had earned a measure of international recognition. Most enjoyable, of course, was to have been lauded, several times, as a hero of France. He had done his best to lead an honorable life as a father and a man and a black man who had resisted racism at every opportunity. He had friendships that had lasted for decades.

Bullard was being told that only a few grains of sand remained in the hourglass of his life. He had no complaints. His illness was only bringing him closer to the God he had finally come to accept. Yes, it was also the God who had taken his young son away, but maybe that same God could finally reunite them. At least, that was the hope he expressed to his living children.

Between the end of August and the beginning of October a steady stream of visitors and friends paraded in and out of Metropolitan Hospital. For the most part, Bullard rested comfortably, propped up in his bed, sporting a pair of yellow pajamas. There were always flowers and gifts of food (which he could not eat, for the most part), and the occasional smuggled glass of wine, as well as plenty of laughter. Sadness was not allowed in his room.

Louise Connell brought him a final draft of his typed autobiography which brightened his eyes and gave him enormous pleasure. He was still hopeful that he could live to see it published, but both knew that this was a rapidly diminishing possibility. Bullard urged Louise to contact his old friend Langston Hughes, suggesting that the former Le Grand Duc dishwasher, who had evolved into a famous poet, would find a way to get it published. (For whatever reasons, Hughes declined to get involved.)

By the early part of October, Bullard had slipped into the final sequence of his terminal illness. He managed a smile as he told one visitor, "Man, if I had as many needles sticking out of me as I've (had) stuck in me, I'd look like a porcupine."

He was able to celebrate his sixty-sixth birthday on October 9, but when Connell visited him on the twelfth, he was in and out of consciousness and the doctors told her he was at the end. She sat by his bed and cried quietly. He must have heard the sobbing. He awoke and stared at her. The staff had inserted a breathing tube to assist his respiration. He reached up and pulled out the tube so he could speak.

He smiled at Louise and uttered what would be his last words: "Don't fret, honey. It's easy." At 10:10 p.m., Bullard breathed his last.

In accordance with his final wishes, Eugene James Bullard was laid out in a freshly pressed French Legionnaire's uniform. His expensive brass coffin (paid for by his surviving pals in the Lafayette Escadrille) was covered with the French Tricolor. A funeral mass was held on October 17, 1961 at St.

Vincent de Paul Church. Hundreds of mourners attended, including members of France Forever, the Federation of French War Veterans, the Verdun Society and American Legion Post Number 1.

Bullard was interred in a simple plot in the Federation of French War Veterans Cemetery in Flushing, Queens. It is marked by a one-foot-square slab bearing his name and the years of his birth and death.

Ninety-nine years to the day after Bullard was born, then-Governor Zell Miller proclaimed October 9, 1994, to be "Eugene Bullard Day" in Georgia. The state from which he had fled as an adolescent, seeking a life free of racism, had progressed to when it could recognize a black native son and his many accomplishments.

As proud as he would have been of "Eugene Bullard Day," an event that had taken place three weeks earlier would have given him even greater satisfaction. He finally became an American military pilot and commissioned officer. On September 14, 1994, he was posthumously appointed a second lieutenant in the United States Air Force. The ceremony included a special guest who had accompanied his daughter, Jacqueline: Richard Reid, who had joined the US Air Force, served honorably and retired as a master sergeant. He was Bullard's grandson.

Today, a floor-to-ceiling glass case at the US Air Force Museum in Dayton, Ohio, proudly displays a life-size mannequin of Eugene Bullard decked out in a replica flying suit of the Lafayette Flying Corps. Also on display are all fifteen of his decorations from the government of France and a copy of his USAF 2nd Lieutenant's commission. The National Air and Space Museum at the Smithsonian in Washington, DC, has a bust of Bullard along with a recitation of his many accomplishments.

He had, indeed, come a long way since, as a youngster, with a dollar and a half in his pocket, he had raced down those dusty railroad tracks knowing that his father, Big Chief Ox, would soon be in hot pursuit. Eugene Bullard had become a hero of France…and, finally, America too.

★ ★ ★ ★ ★

AUTHOR NOTE

One would think that a man who during his sixty-six years became the first African American combat pilot, a well-known nightclub impresario in Paris, championship-caliber prizefighter, French Resistance spy, civil rights pioneer, and much-decorated hero in two wars would have a shelf of books written about him. There certainly should have been at least one screen version of his saga by now, "in a theater near you." This was not so with Eugene Bullard, however. The lack of published material on this multitalented man can be attributed to several possible causes, not the least of which were racism, his many years away from America as an expatriate, and Bullard's own modest nature. He was proud of his achievements, sure, but not devoted to trumpeting the many amazing acts of his life. He was, more than anything else, a plucky survivor who was just as surprised by his own accomplishments as anyone.

Eugene Bullard first came to our attention via research Phil was doing on another book project concerning America in World War I. Buried in a reference to the pioneering aviators of that war was a short paragraph on Bullard who was referenced as the "first Negro fighter pilot"—a phrase that Bullard would later use on his own business cards. Digging a little further, Tom found that Bullard's life story had been touched upon (albeit briefly) in the 2006 movie *Flyboys*. In that film, the actor Abdul Salis played the part of Eugene Skinner, an African American boxer who has been accepted as an athlete in France, and is motivated to "pay back" his adopted country. Both of us felt there had to be more to this intriguing character than just a historical footnote and a small role in a not-so-memorable movie.

To testify to Bullard's place in history, which he clearly understood, he had his mechanic boldly paint a red heart, pierced by a dagger, on the side of his SPAD. In addition, Bullard had him add, surrounding the bleeding heart, the phrase *"Tout Sang Que Coule Est Rouge"* or "All Blood That Flows is Red." This was a pointed reminder to all that no matter the color of Gene's skin, his blood would run red just like everyone else's. When Bullard began, very late in his life, to write his autobiography he chose the title "All Blood Runs Red," which is slightly different but certainly carries the same powerful message. Out of respect for Bullard's work, we have decided to keep the title as he last penned it.

The relatively few sources of information about Eugene Bullard's legendary life compelled us to excavate deeper to learn what we could and to give extra scrutiny to the material we found. For example, when he was supposed to be stowing away on a freighter to France at age eleven, as Bullard often told his listeners, Phil found him on the 1910 Census for Thomasville, in Thomas County, Georgia, when he would have been age fifteen. He was then living in a boardinghouse and working in the local sawmill. We were fortunate that even minimal information like this existed at all because only scant records of the names, dates, places, and movements regarding middle and lower-class peoples in the South, especially minorities and the less educated, were kept. Adding to our dilemma, the few mentions of Eugene Bullard's life when he was under the age of nineteen that have been published prior to this book are nearly all in conflict with one another.

As we researched the rest of his story we encountered more conflicting information. Bullard vividly describes his marriage to Marcelle Straumann, daughter of a French countess from a rich and aristocratic family. The surviving official records, many bombed, burned, purged or simply lost in the Nazi occupation of Paris, tell a different story. Marcelle's father was, indeed, prosperous but he was a self-made, middle-class grocer. Her mother was no countess, but an everyday housewife, and Marcelle herself was a seamstress. Bullard relates that Marcelle "passed away" some years after their marriage, by Gene's telling, sometime in the mid-1930s. The truth is that Marcelle outlived him. For reasons never expressed by either, they separated a few years after their second daughter, and last child, was born, which was in 1928. Marcelle was white, Eugene was black—was he ashamed that she left him, giving up the children to him? He never says, preferring the "noble" narrative of death over abandonment or divorce.

There are some anecdotes, even ones from Bullard's unpublished memoir, that we could not include here because they were uncorroborated or even disproven. That did not make this book any less enjoyable to research and write. We discovered that, warts and all, Eugene Bullard's verifiable story is more than worth the telling.

The best, by far, of the previous tomes on the very narrow Bullard bookshelf has been Craig Lloyd's *Eugene Bullard, Black*

Expatriate in Jazz-Age Paris. Although Professor Lloyd's work is rather slim at 150 pages, he has essentially bracketed the major events in Bullard's life and did a great deal of excellent research to gather his observations. Dr. Lloyd also had the advantage of spending most of his career in Bullard's hometown of Columbus, Georgia, and helped build the archive at Columbus State University that contains just about all the relevant materials available on Bullard's life.[68]

From there, the task was to dig up as many contemporary accounts as possible and find anecdotes about, or at least mentions of, Bullard in autobiographies and biographies of luminaries he counted as friends and patrons, from Ernest Hemingway to Cole Porter, Josephine Baker to Louis Armstrong. Still, we have to accept the reality that 100 percent reliability as to the finite details of Bullard's life was then and is now impossible. As narrators of his story, the best that can be accomplished, and the tactic taken herein, is to state with certainty only those details that can be triangulated. All major details and events related in these pages have, to the best of our abilities, been corroborated by at least two independent sources and, whenever possible, three.

Luckily, there are no doubts as to the major milestones in Eugene Bullard's tale, and there are, certainly, more than enough to form a complete and amazing picture of this man's incredible life and times.

Even today, with all the gadgetry, innovation, and the lightning speed of universal communication and travel, it would be hard to imagine one life, like Bullard's, so jam-packed with adventure, twists, turns, and changes. He was ever ready to

---

68   Dr. Craig Lloyd, a native New Yorker, served as Professor of History and Archivist at Columbus State University until his retirement in 2001. Lloyd, a graduate from Middlebury College in Vermont, initially arrived at CSU, then Columbus College, in August of 1971 after completing his PhD at the University of Iowa.

move on to the next phase, to grasp an opportunity, to turn adversity into opportunity. As he, himself, said at the very end of his life, "I guess I touched all the bases." Did he ever—and he hit many home runs along the way.

BIBLIOGRAPHY

Bergreen, Lawrence. *Louis Armstrong: An Extravagant Life*. New York: Broadway Books, 1998.

Bricktop, with James Haskins. *Bricktop*. New York: Welcome Rain, 2000.

Buckley, Gail. *American Patriots: The Story of Blacks in the Military from the Revolution to Desert Storm*. New York: Random House, 2001.

Bullard, Eugene J. *All Blood Runs Red: My Adventurous Life in Search of Freedom*. Unpublished manuscript, 1961.

Carisella, P. J., and James W. Ryan. *The Black Swallow of Death*. Boston: Marlborough House, 1972.

Cockfield, Jamie H. "Eugene Bullard, America's First Black Military Aviator; Flew For France During WW I." *Military History*, February, 1966.

Duberman, Martin B. *Paul Robeson*. New York: Knopf, 1988.

Editors of *Encyclopaedia Britannica*, 2013. "Cakewalk." *Encyclopaedia Britannica*. Last modified December 2, 2013. https://www.britannica.com/art/cakewalk.

Furst, Alan. *Mission to Paris*. New York: Random House, 2012.

Hall, James Norman and Charles Bernard Nordhoff. *The Lafayette Flying Corps, 2 vols*. Boston: Houghton-Mifflin, 1920.

Hanna, David. *Rendezvous with Death: The Americans Who Joined the Foreign Legion in 1914 to Fight for France and Civilization*. Washington, DC: Regnery History, 2016.

Haney, Lynn. *Naked at the Feast: A Biography of Josephine Baker*. Robson Books, Ltd., 1995.

Hansen, Arlen J. *Expatriate Paris: A Cultural and Literary Guide to Paris of the 1920s*. New York: Arcade, 1990.

Hemingway, Ernest. *A Moveable Feast*. New York: Scribner, 1964.

Hughes, Langston. *The Big Sea: An Autobiography*. New York: Hill & Wang, 1963.

Johnson, Jack. *In the Ring and Out*. London: Proteus, 1977.

Johnson, James Weldon. *Along This Way: The Autobiography of James Weldon Johnson*. New York: Viking, 1968.

Keith, Philip A. *America and the Great War*. Southampton, New York: Peconic Bay Publishing, 2016.

Kluver, Billy and Julie Martin. *Kiki's Paris: Artists and Lovers, 1900-1930*. New York: Abrams, 1989.

Koo, Madame Wellington with Isabella Taves. *No Feast Lasts Forever*. New York: Quadrangle, 1975.

Lloyd, Craig. *Eugene Bullard, Black Expatriate in Jazz-Age Paris*. University of Georgia Press, 2000.

Marshall, S.L.A., and the editors of *American Heritage. The American Heritage History of World War I*. New York: Simon & Schuster, 1964.

Mason, Herbert Malloy, Jr. *High Flew the Falcons, The French Aces of World War I*. Philadelphia: Lippincott, 1965.

McAuliffe, Mary. *When Paris Sizzled: The 1920s Paris of Hemingway, Chanel, Cocteau, Cole Porter, Josephine Baker, and Their Friends.* New York: Rowman & Littlefield, 2016.

McConnell, James R. *Flying for France: With the American Escadrille at Verdun.* Doubleday, New York: Doubleday, 1917.

McCullough, David. *The Greater Journey: Americans In Paris.* New York: Simon and Schuster, 2011.

Meltzer, Milton. *Langston Hughes: A Biography.* New York: T. Y. Crowell & Co., 1968.

Mizener, Arthur. *The Far Side of Paradise: A Biography of F. Scott Fitzgerald.* Boston: Houghton-Mifflin, 1949.

Moley, Raymond, Jr. *The American Legion Story.* New York: Meredith, 1966.

Panassié, Hugues. *Louis Armstrong.* New York: Scribners, 1971.

Parsons, Edwin C. *I Flew With the Lafayette Escadrille.* New York: Arno Press, 1972.

Penrose, Roland. *Picasso: His Life and Work.* 2nd ed., New York: Schocken, 1962.

Philonenko, Alexis. *Histoire de la Boxe.* Paris, France: Critérion, 1991.

Porch, Douglas. *La Légion Étrangère, 1831-1962.* Paris, France: Fayard, 1994.

Robeson, Susan. *The Whole World in His Hands: A Pictorial Biography of Paul Robeson.* Secaucus: Citadel Press, 1981.

Robinson, Edward G. with Leonard Spigeglass. *All My Yesterdays: An Autobiography.* New York: Hawthorn, 1973.

Rockwell, Paul Ayres. *American Fighters in the Foreign Legion, 1914-1918.* Boston: Houghton-Mifflin, 1930.

Roosevelt, Eleanor. "My Day, October 31, 1959." *The Eleanor Roosevelt*

Papers Digital Edition (2017). Accessed 8/8/2019. https://www2.gwu.edu/~erpapers/myday/displaydoc.cfm?_y=1959&_f=md004577.

Rose, Phyllis. *Jazz Cleopatra: Josephine Baker in Her Time.* New York: Doubleday, 1989.

Rumer, Thomas A. *The American Legion: An Official History, 1919-1989.* New York: Evans, 1990.

Schwartz, Charles. *Cole Porter: A Biography.* New York: Dial Press, 1977.

Seigel, Jerrold. *Bohemian Paris: Culture, Politics, and the Boundaries of Bourgeois Life, 1830-1930.* New York: Viking, 1986.

Smith, Mary. "The Incredible Life of Monsieur Bullard," *Ebony Magazine*, December 23, 1967, pp. 120-128.

Stoval, Tyler. *Paris Noir: African Americans in the City of Light.* New York: Houghton-Mifflin, 1996.

Strack, Joseph George. "R For Relaxation." *TIC Magazine*, September 1948, pp. 11–16.

Tucker, Sophie. *Some of These Days.* New York: Doubleday, 1945.

Wallace, Irving, David Wallechinsky, and Amy Wallace. "The Black Swallow," *Parade Magazine*, September 26, 1982, p. 19.

Wiser, William. *The Crazy Years: Paris in the Twenties.* New York: Athenaeum, 1983.

Yallop, David A. *The Day the Laughter Stopped: The True Story of Fatty Arbuckle.* New York: St. Martin's Press, 1976.

Collections:

Connell, Louise Fox. Papers. Schlesinger Library, Harvard University, Cambridge, Massachusetts.

Smith, Ada Louise "Bricktop." Papers, Archives, Schomberg Center for Research on Black Culture, New York, NY.

ACKNOWLEDGMENTS

The original idea to write about Eugene Bullard came to us via Joe Shaw, our editor and good friend at the Press Newspaper Group in Southampton, New York. His simple expression, "I'd sure like to read a book about this man," propelled us forward, so it is to Joe we render "first honors" for getting this ball rolling.

The sole archive for papers, photos data and background on Eugene Bullard exists at the Simon Schwob Memorial Library at Columbus State University, part of the University of Georgia system, in Columbus, Georgia. Assistant professor David Owings is the head of the CSU Archives and was Phil's affable and most helpful host when he spent time in Columbus plunging through the well-organized boxes of available information on Bullard, his family, and the area's history.

All successful books begin with a well-prepared proposal to a talented agent who can grasp the vision for the project. We were so very fortunate to have just such an agent in Scott

Gould at RLR Associates. Scott immediately saw the potential and worked with us diligently and expertly to bring this story to the right publisher. We could not have done it without Scott and we owe him a tremendous debt of gratitude.

We are very excited to be under the guidance and imprint of Hanover Square Press and our outstanding editors, Peter Joseph and John Glynn. Hanover Square has launched an exciting new line of important nonfiction works, and we are so very lucky to be part of this adventure. Our editors have kept a keen eye for what makes sense and how a story should flow and the guidance they provided was spot-on.

There are unfortunate wretches who toil alone over dimly lit keyboards and cold cups of coffee. Phil and Tom are not among those cave-dwelling types. "The Muse," as Phil likes to call his invaluable partner, Laura Lyons, was there as a constant "lamp in the darkness" guiding his keystrokes and keeping him focused. This book could not have been completed without Laura's love and constancy.

Also motivating Phil to move forward is his "best pal," his son, Pierce, who is about to write his own story; that is, going off to college and the career that will help him achieve his goals and dreams—whatever those may be. Excellent sales of this book, dear readers, will also help us pay for this "launch party!"

Tom thanks Leslie Reingold for her ongoing support, his friends for being friends (including members of the "Round-table"), and those who try in their everyday lives to shrink the racial divide that continues to trouble American society.

ABOUT THE AUTHORS

Phil Keith is the author of six books, including *Blackhorse Riders*, which won the 2012 USA Best Book Award for Military History, was a finalist for the 2013 Colby Award and earned a 2013 silver medal from the Military Writers Society of America. He holds a degree in history from Harvard and is a former navy aviator. During three tours in Vietnam, he served with distinction and was awarded, among other decorations, the Purple Heart, Air Medal, Presidential Unit Citation and the Navy Commendation Medal.

Tom Clavin is the author of eighteen nonfiction books and has worked as a newspaper and website editor, magazine writer, TV and radio commentator, and reporter for the *New York Times* covering entertainment, sports and the environment. Four of his books have been *New York Times* bestsellers: *Dodge* City; and with Bob Drury, *The Heart of Everything That Is, The Last Stand of Fox Company* and *Halsey's Typhoon*.

INDEX